Silent Films on Video

Silent Films on Video

*A Filmography of Over 700 Silent
Features Available on Videocassette,
with a Directory of Sources*

by ROBERT K. KLEPPER

McFarland & Company, Inc., Publishers
Jefferson, North Carolina, and London

British Library Cataloguing-in-Publication data are available

Library of Congress Cataloguing-in-Publication Data

Klepper, Robert K., 1966–
    Silent films on video : a filmography of over 700 silent features
available on videocassette, with a directory of sources / by Robert
K. Klepper.
      p.   cm.
    Includes bibliographical references and index.
    ISBN 0-7864-0157-5 (lib. bdg. : 50# alk. paper) ∞
    1. Silent films — Catalogs.   2. Video recordings — Catalogs.
I. Title.
PN1995.75.K58   1996
016.79143'75 — dc20   96-11757
                                                   CIP

Manufactured in the United States of America

McFarland & Company, Inc., Publishers
  Box 611, Jefferson, North Carolina 28640

To Norma Desmond
no truer words were ever said
about the silents
than the ones she spoke in
Sunset Boulevard

Acknowledgments

The author wishes to thank the following people:

For moral support, Teresa, John, and Sandy Hunt, Altha A. and Kenneth H. Klepper, Leeanna and Tommy Jeter, Jovonna Ivester, Dr. Martin Roberts, Ph.D., Jim Jorden, Joy Reuter, Mike Suchcicki, Kimberley Varner-Schweizer, and Jean Sperbeck.

For answering questions or providing information, William M. Drew, Kevin Brownlow, Danny Burk, Bill Eggert (Silent Film Society of Atlanta), Robert Giroux, James Card, Diana Serra Cary (a.k.a. "Baby Peggy"), the late, great Lillian Gish, John Cavallo, Jack Bona, James Billington of the Library of Congress, Michael P. Lentz, Jan-Christopher Horak (George Eastman House), Kaye McRae (George Eastman House), Richard Koszarski, Robert Marrero, and John Sherwood.

Contents

Introduction

One of the most fascinating periods of Hollywood history is the silent era. For many years after the original releases of most of the last silents in the late 1920s, it had been next to impossible for silent film enthusiasts to find opportunities to see silent films. Through the 1950s, the silent era films were all but forgotten, left to collect dust (and, in many cases, literally turn to dust, disintegrating) in studio vaults. As a result of years and years of neglect, more than 90 percent of all silent films produced no longer exist. The great majority of the silents produced by the William Fox Company were destroyed in a horrible warehouse fire in 1937. In 1947, Universal Studios destroyed all of its silent film negatives to retrieve the silver from them.

Since the 1950s, a resurgence in the history and appreciation of silent cinema has resulted in as many films from the silent era as possible being preserved, restored, and duplicated. The silent film enthusiast can be thankful that film archivists started a movement to collect and preserve these movies before all of the silent era films were lost forever. Even with the resurgence of interest in the silent era, it was not until the widespread use and distribution of VCRs and videocassettes that it became possible for many of us enthusiasts to have widespread access to silent films. Until then, only those who lived near a major film archive in New York, Los Angeles, or some of the bigger cities could see the beloved treasures from Hollywood's golden era. The rest of us (unless we could afford to purchase 16mm prints at $200 to $1000+ each) were limited to a few infrequent television screenings on PBS or cablevision, usually at odd hours. Those of us in smaller cities will find videos available for rental to be very, very limited as to the silent titles offered. Hence, that leaves us with the option of buying the classics we want to see on videocassette.

The purpose of this book is to provide information to the silent film enthusiast desiring to build a collection. Information concerning the video

1

versions of over 700 silent film features is included, along with sources from which to purchase them. When there is more than one source or more than one video version of the same title available, their significant differences are noted. For the reader's convenience, the prices for videos as of December 31, 1994, are listed. As prices and business policies are always subject to change, those listed here should be verified before placing your order.

All silent films dealers listed in this book include musical accompaniment on their silent film video copies. "Silent" films were never meant to be seen without some kind of musical accompaniment.

Many movies from the silent era were filmed on color tinted stock. These color tints were important in emphasizing atmospheric and mood changes. Some videocassette versions of these movies include original color tints, and some do not. Color tinted video copies are noted whenever such information is available. While the author personally prefers color tinted silent film copies, some enthusiasts prefer black and white prints.

This book is divided into several parts. The first contains full-length reviews of 29 selected features. These are arranged in chronological order detailing the significance of each in motion picture history, and providing facts about the players and circumstances surrounding the making of the picture. This part of the book provides a rough history of the evolution of the silent feature film in America from 1912 to 1929.

Part two is an alphabetical listing of most of the feature films from the silent era known to be currently available on videocassette in the United States, with pertinent information for each title. The descriptions vary in completeness in accordance to how much information was accessible. Interesting side facts appear throughout the descriptions.

Part three is a listing of some of the more important silent era short films available on video.

A fourth major part of the book lists all of the different video sources and how to contact them, as well as other important information such as business policies.

ROBERT K. KLEPPER
August 1995

One: Full Reviews
of 29 Selected Silents

Included in this part are in-depth reviews of 29 selected titles representing a wide scope of silent films — classics, blockbuster epics, westerns, comedies, etc. Other films selected for review are silent films which are in some way unique or obscure. Some of these include *The Viking* (1928), which was one of three silent features filmed entirely in Technicolor, and one about which little has been written; Alla Nazimova's reportedly all-gay 1923 production of *Salome,* the first known American film with an all-gay cast to receive a wide theatrical release; *A Fool There Was* (1914), which is the only one of Theda Bara's major films known to exist, and the first of her highly successful "vamp" movies; and *The Eyes of Julia Deep* (1918), which is the only one of Mary Miles Minter's six known existing movies available on videocassette.

Many readers may find it odd that no Charles Chaplin features were selected for review. The reasoning behind this was that there is already so much information available about Chaplin — moreso than possibly any other actor in history. His name alone speaks for itself.

Buster Keaton's *The Three Ages* (1923) was chosen over some of his more famous movies (i.e., *The General, College, The Navigator*) for three main reasons. Being a parody of *Intolerance* gives it a more significant place in motion picture history; it was Keaton's very first feature film; and less has been written about *The Three Ages* than Keaton's more widely renowned films.

As to westerns, some readers probably expected a William S. Hart film to be reviewed at length. As in the case with Chaplin's comedies, anybody who knows silent film history is aware that William S. Hart and Tom Mix were two of the preeminent male stars of silent westerns; the names speak for themselves and give the reader an idea of what to expect.

But, how many people would know to look for Helen Hayes, the 1932 Best Actress Oscar recipient (for *The Sin of Madelon Claudet*), in a rare silent western appearance? In how many other books on silent film history can one read about *Riders of the Range* in detail?

The reader can now see that there is a method to the reasoning behind why some movies that were omitted from the review section were passed over, and why some odd surprises are found instead.

Queen Elizabeth (1912)

Produced in Europe
Distributed in America by Adolph Zukor
Directed by Louis Mercanton
Cast: *Queen Elizabeth* Sarah Bernhardt; *Robert Devereaux, Earl of Essex* Lou Tellegen; *Countess of Nottingham* Mlle. Romain; *Earl of Nottingham* M. Maxudian

This is the photographed stage play that brought motion pictures into an era of respectability even among the social upper class who would never before have "lowered" themselves to watch a "flicker." The great attraction is the legendary stage actress Sarah Bernhardt. Originally filmed in Europe, the American distribution rights were acquired by Adolph Zukor. The film was such a phenomenal success that Zukor used the profits to form the "Famous Players in Famous Plays" corporation, a forerunner of Paramount Pictures.

Bernhardt, who was 68 at the time *Queen Elizabeth* was filmed, considered the movie medium as "my one chance at immortality." Although she had a wooden leg which made walking difficult and painful, Bernhardt played the part with incredible grace and dignity. In most of the scenes, she is pictured either sitting or standing. The majority of the scenes in which she walks are very brief, or with another actor or actress holding her hand. If one looks closely, one can actually catch a glimpse of her wooden leg in the scene during which she is lifted upon hearing of the defeat of the Spanish Armada, and taken by Essex to see *The Merry Wives of Windsor*.

Lou Tellegen played the Earl of Essex, the man with whom Queen Elizabeth falls in love. When a fortune-teller foresees death at the scaffold for Essex and an unhappy life for Elizabeth, Elizabeth is prompted to give Essex a ring. She promises that should he ever get into any trouble, the return of the ring to her would save him from the fate of the scaffold, no matter how great his fault.

Essex engages in an adulterous affair with Mary of Nottingham, which, upon discovery, makes a rather bad enemy of her husband, the Earl of Nottingham, who vows revenge. In league with Lord Bacon (another enemy of Essex), an anonymous letter accusing Essex of treason is written. Elizabeth dismisses the letter as rubbish — until she, too, discovers Essex's affair with Mary of Nottingham. She then reasons that if Essex is unfaithful to her, he must be capable of being unfaithful to his country, and signs his death warrant for treason.

Elizabeth sends Mary of Nottingham to Essex for the ring, with intentions of granting him clemency upon its return. The only problem is that Lord Bacon tells the Earl of Nottingham about the clemency plans, who in turn intercepts the ring and throws it into the Thames River, thereby sealing Essex's fate.

Elizabeth, upon looking at the corpse of Essex, discovers that the ring is missing, and finally finds out the awful truth that he had indeed not been too proud to ask for clemency. She lives a miserable life after the unjust death of her lover, thus proving the predictions of the fortune teller correct.

Some interesting things to observe while watching this movie are the techniques. Take note that there are no closeup shots whatsoever. Although such had been invented, the producers of the introductory features equated doing closeups to cutting off part of the performer's body. It was insisted that all shots be full-length. Also notice how the actors and actresses bow to the audience at the beginning of the film.

Lou Tellegen died a horrible death in 1935, 23 years after the filming of *Queen Elizabeth*. He apparently was distraught over the fact that his career had faded, and committed suicide.

Sarah Bernhardt's real life comment about the movies being her one chance at immortality has held up. Thanks to videotape and the fact that a good print of her film performance managed to survive the years, she can still be seen performing on stage in your living room — many decades after the performance and after her 1923 death at age 79.

Videocassette Sources

MC Film Festival $24.95
  Video Yesteryear's version which also includes *Salome* (1923) on the same tape.

Nostalgia Family Video . . . . #2071 $19.95

The Perils of Pauline (1914)
Selig Productions
Directed by Louis Gasnier
Cast: *Pauline Marvin* Pearl White; *Harry Marvin* Crane Wilbur; *Koerner, Secretary/Villain* Paul Panzer; *A Child Extra* Milton Berle

This early directorial effort by Louis Gasnier (the director who gave us the cult classic *Reefer Madness* in 1937) was the fourth serial made, and the most famous of them all. In addition, it is the oldest serial known to be available on videocassette. Originally filmed in 20 episodes, this nine-chapter collection is the most complete version known to be available.

If you expect cliffhanger endings with Pauline tied to the railroad tracks, the author warns you not to be disappointed when such does not materialize. *The Perils of Pauline* was produced before the cliffhanger format became commonplace in serials. If there was an episode in which Pauline was tied to the railroad tracks, it is not contained in this nine-episode collection. The perils of bombed ships, runaway hot-air balloons, being trapped in a burning house, and a rigged auto race are among those resolved within the respective episodes in which they occur.

To summarize the story, *The Perils of Pauline* is basically about a wealthy heiress orphaned by her parents' death and currently living with her guardian and his son. Pauline and Harry Marvin are urged by the family to marry. The son, Harry, is more than willing, but Pauline is not. She first wants to have at least one year of freedom to experience exotic adventures and write about them in a book of romantic adventures. Her guardian dies, and leaves the responsibility of managing Pauline's fortune (until her marriage) to his "trusted" secretary, Mr. Koerner. Little does the father know that Koerner is an escaped prisoner being blackmailed; he is desperate for money and is willing to do anything to get it.

Throughout Pauline's adventures, Koerner and his accomplice scheme to cause Pauline's death or "disappearance" in hope of getting their grubby hands on the fortune with which Koerner has been entrusted. Therefore, the attempts to cash in turn "the adventures of Pauline" into "the perils of Pauline."

Somehow, some way, Pauline always manages to escape her perils at the last minute, walking in the door right when Koerner and accomplice are positive that they have succeeded in getting rid of her.

In the last episode, Pauline decides that she has experienced all the adventures that she has set out to experience. Hence, she is ready to settle down and marry.

This is an important contribution to motion picture history, as it was the first serial to become a box office hit. It was also one of the more expensive undertakings up to the date of its release, costing $25,000 to produce. *The Perils of Pauline* established Pearl White as queen of the serials, and is the only one of White's serials known to be available on videocassette. Although the author was rather disappointed with the entertainment value of this serial, it is still one that every silent movie buff should see just for the sake of saying they have done so.

The Perils of Pauline was remade as a talkie in 1934 with Evalyn Knapp playing the role of Pauline. A 1947 Technicolor movie of the same title starred Betty Hutton as Pearl White, and was a highly fictionalized biography of Pearl White's life.

Videocassette Sources

Grapevine Video	#POP	$24.95
Discount Video Tapes		$29.95
Nostalgia Family Video	#1051	$29.95

A Fool There Was (1914)

William Fox Company
Directed by Frank Powell
Cast: *The Vamp* Theda Bara; *The Child* Runa Hodges; *The Wife (Mrs. Schuyler)* Mabel Frenyear; *The Husband (Mr. John Schuyler)* Edward Jose; *Wife's Sister* May Allison; *The Friend* Clifford Bruce; *One of the Victims* Victor Benoit; *The Doctor* Frank Powell; *Doctor's Fiancée* Minna Gale

This is a movie with significant historical importance in many ways. It was the first film produced by William Fox, the founder of the Fox Film Company. In addition, Theda Bara, the leading actress, was the first publicity-made star in this, the first of her many "vamp" movies. Bara was actually Theodosia Goodman, a pure and innocent girl from Ohio who was considered by many in Hollywood to be one of the nicest people in the movies, with a heart of gold. The real Theda Bara's private life was an extreme contrast to her public image, promoted with press conferences during which she dressed herself in black and portrayed herself as an evil woman born under the sphinx to an Arab princess and an Italian artist out of wedlock. Her screen name was an anagram for "A-R-A-B D-E-A-T-H."

This vamp movie is the only one of Theda Bara's major films known to have survived the years. The only other example of her work that survives is *The Unchastened Woman* (1925), which was basically a spoof on her earlier work. Unfortunately, the unique prints of her versions of *Salome* and *Cleopatra* were destroyed in a nitrate fire at the Museum of Modern Art. Since the one surviving example of Bara's work happened to be her first film, it is naturally not as polished as her later work was. While very advanced for 1914 standards, the techniques used were still relatively primitive even by silent film standards.

To give the reader an idea of what is meant by the term "vamp," take into consideration that "vamp" is an abbreviated form of vampire. It was on Rudyard Kipling's *The Vampire* that *A Fool There Was* is based. Theda Bara's classical vamp portrayal is typically an evil woman who stakes out her victims, corrupts their morals, uses them for what she can get out of them, and literally leaves them for dead once she has sucked them dry and is ready to move on to the next victim.

In this film, Bara plays a woman who reads about a wealthy man taking off for Europe, and stakes him out as her next victim. Once she boards the ship, her last victim follows her, furious that she is leaving after having ruined him. He pulls a gun on her, and she lightly taps the gun with a rose, and the title card bearing the words, "Kiss me, my fool!" appears on the screen. The victim then turns the gun on himself instead and commits suicide. It is ironic that while the last victim's body is being carried off the ship, the next victim is just arriving. The words, "Kiss me, my fool" were quoted for an entire generation after the release of *A Fool There Was*.

Another interesting side fact is that May Allison, who plays the role of the wife's sister, was in reality married to James R. Quirk, who was at one time the editor of *Photoplay* magazine.

Videocassette Sources

Discount Video Tapes		$19.95
Grapevine Video	#13-127	$16.95
Nostalgia Family Video	#1708B	$19.95
Video Yesteryear	#1870	$24.95

The Birth of a Nation (1915)

Epoch Producing Company
Directed by D.W. Griffith
Cast: *Elsie Stoneman* Lillian Gish; *Ben Cameron ("the little Colonel")* Henry
B. Walthall; *Flora Cameron* Mae Marsh; *Margaret Cameron* Miriam
Cooper; *Mrs. Cameron* Josephine Crowell; *Dr. Cameron* Spottis-
woode Aitken; *Austin Stoneman* Ralph Lewis; *Phil Stoneman* Elmer
Clifton; *Ted Stoneman* Robert Harron; *Silas Lynch* George Siegmann;
Gus, the Renegade Negro Walter Long; *White Arm Joe* Elmo Lincoln;
Jeff the Blacksmith Wallace Reid; *Abraham Lincoln* Joseph Henabery;
General Ulysses S. Grant Donald Crisp; *Robert E. Lee* Howard Gaye;
John Wilkes Booth Raoul Walsh; *Lydia, Stoneman's Mulatto House-
keeper* Mary Alden; *Wade Cameron* J.A. Beringer; *Mammy, the Faith-
ful Servant* Jennie Lee; *Senator Charles Sumner* Sam DeGrasse

This film is a landmark in motion picture history, and is another
with many "firsts" to its credit. It was the first feature length motion picture to run more than two hours. It was the first movie to charge a $2
admission fee. It was the first American movie to be screened at the White
House (Italy's 1914 *Cabiria* beat it by a few months). Most of all, it was
the first movie to generate controversy, owing to what was perceived by
many as racist overtones. When this movie was originally released, it
sparked near riots in many cities, thus causing D.W. Griffith to have to
fight a few legal battles to allow its screening. The NAACP protested
against it; the Ku Klux Klan was resurrected and used it as a propaganda
film.

The Birth of a Nation recreates the Civil War and reconstruction
focusing on the viewpoint of the Southern states. The story starts out at
the home of a Southern family (the Camerons) who are receiving friends
from the North (the Stonemans) at their Piedmont, South Carolina, residence. As the story progresses into the Civil War, one sees the same friends
facing each other on the battlefield. The battle scenes are very well done,
and were shot at what is today the site of Universal Studios in California.
The living conditions of the soldiers are portrayed with grim reality, most
notably in the scenes in which they are shown with their daily rations of
parched corn. The scene of dead soldiers on the battlefield preceded by
the title saying "War's peace" is especially arousing to the emotions.

As the film continues into the reconstruction period, the audience
is shown a portrayal of how the white South was crushed beneath the heels

of the black South. The blacks rig elections, forcibly denying the whites access to the ballot boxes. Black legislators are portrayed as unrefined, while passing laws which require whites to salute black officers, legalize interracial marriages, etc.

Gus, the renegade negro played by Walter Long with black makeup (the major black roles in this movie were played by made-up whites), takes advantage of the blacks' newfound power, and attempts to rape Flora Cameron. Forced on top of a cliff, Cameron jumps to her death, choosing to die rather than face the dishonor of rape. This incident proves to be "the straw that breaks the camel's back" and prompts Ben Cameron (also referred to as "the little Colonel") to form the Ku Klux Klan with the intent of rescuing whites from black terrorism. This portrayal of the KKK as heroes was what created the controversy and public outcry against this film. To this day, 80 years after its production, this movie remains one of the most controversial in existence.

While controversial and racist, *The Birth of a Nation* is, nonetheless, one of the most important films in all of cinematic history. One of the highlights of the film is the excellent portrayal of the Lincoln assassination. For this scene, Griffith built a replica of Ford's Theater using the original building plans. He went so far as to recreate the presentation of *Our American Cousin* exactly as it had been done on the night of the assassination. If one can put the racial overtones aside, this is quite probably the most accurate celluloid representation of Civil War times to exist. Note the fact that the year of release was only 50 years after the Civil War, when many people who had actually been through the war were still alive to give first-hand accounts.

The Birth of a Nation is widely available on video. Sometimes, copies can be found at record/video stores in your local malls. However, if buying from a store, beware of the cheap copies one often finds for under $10. Most of these are transferred from poor quality prints and contain no musical accompaniment whatsoever. Why settle for inferior copies when so many companies offer good quality copies at reasonable rates?

Videocassette Sources

Discount Video Tapes $19.95
    Color tinted, complete version.

Kino Video $39.95
    Complete, color tinted version with orchestral score. Includes a documentary called *The Making of Birth of a Nation*, with rare stills and outtake footage.

Nostalgia Family Video . . . . #1813 $19.95
  Color tinted, complete version with orchestral score. Includes the 1918
  black rebuttal film *Birth of a Race* directed by John Noble.
Republic Pictures Home Video . . . . #0308 $19.98
  Color tinted with music score, slightly edited.
Video Yesteryear . . . . #7 $39.95
  Complete version in black and white, with original organ score by Rosa
  Rio. Includes a rare D.W. Griffith interview from 1930.

Intolerance (1916)
Wark Producing Company
Directed by David Wark (D.W.) Griffith
Cast: *The Woman Who Rocks the Cradle* Lillian Gish. THE MODERN
  STORY: *The Dear One* Mae Marsh; *The Boy* Robert Harron; *The
  Dear One's Father* Fred Turner; *Jenkins* Sam DeGrasse; *Mary T. Jenk-
  ins* Vera Lewis; *The Friendless One* Miriam Cooper; *Musketeer of the
  Slums* Walter Long; *The Kindly Police Officer* Tom Wilson; *The Gov-
  ernor* Ralph Lewis; *The Judge* Lloyd Ingraham; *The Priest* Reverend
  A.W. McClure; *The Friendly Neighbor* Dore Davidson; *The Strike
  Leader* Monte Blue. THE JUDEAN STORY: *Jesus Christ* Howard
  Gaye; *Mary, Mother of Jesus* Lillian Langdon; *Mary Magdalene* Olga
  Grey; *Taller Pharisee* Gunther Von Ritzau; *Shorter Pharisee* Erich
  Von Stroheim; *Bride of Cana* Bessie Love; *Bridegroom* George Walsh.
  THE FRENCH STORY: *Brown Eyes* Margery Wilson; *Prosper Latour*
  Eugene Pallette; *Brown Eyes' Father* Spottiswoode Aitken; *Brown Eyes'
  Mother* Ruth Handford; *The Mercenary* A.D. Sears; *King Charles IX*
  Frank Bennett; *Duc d'Angou (effeminate heir)* Maxfield Stanley;
  Catherine de Medici Josephine Crowell; *Henry of Navarre* W.E.
  Lawrence; *Marguerite of Valois* Constance Talmadge; *Admiral Col-
  igny* Joseph Henabery. THE BABYLON STORY: *The Mountain Girl*
  Constance Talmadge; *The Rhapsode* Elmer Clifton; *Belshazzar* Alfred
  Paget; *Princess Beloved* Seena Owen; *Nabonidus* Carl Stockdale; *High
  Priest of Bel* Tully Marshall; *Cyrus the Persian* George Siegmann;
  Mighty Man of Valor Elmo Lincoln. NOTEWORTHY EXTRAS WHO
  APPEARED: Alma Rubens, Kate Bruce, Mildred Harris, Natalie Tal-
  madge, Pauline Starke, Donald Crisp, Wallace Reid, Douglas Fair-
  banks, Sr., Carol Dempster, Marguerite Marsh (Mae's sister),
  George Fawcett, Frank Campeau, Nigel DeBrulier, Mary Alden,

Carmel Myers, W.S. Van Dyke, Jewel Carmen, Tod Browning, Owen Moore, Winifred Kingston

Intolerance is D.W. Griffith's answer to those who were offended by and criticized *The Birth of a Nation*. It has been regarded by many respected film historians as one of the greatest American films of all time. The grandeur of this spectacle has never been topped, and it is unlikely that *Intolerance* will ever be topped. The cost of rebuilding the Babylon sets alone would make the cost of doing so prohibitive. Few films can come even close to being worthy of comparison.

Intolerance consists of four separate but parallel stories portraying intolerance throughout four different ages of human history spanning 2,500 years. The image of Lillian Gish rocking the cradle (in a blue tint in the color tinted versions) serves to link the stories. Although many film critics state that Griffith was unclear in defining the meaning of the interlinking image, William M. Drew lays these arguments to rest quite easily in his 1986 book *D.W. Griffith's Intolerance: Its Genesis and Vision.*

The four periods of history covered in *Intolerance* are the Babylonian (539 B.C.), the Judean (about A.D. 27), the Renaissance (1572 France), and the Modern (1914 America). The audience is shown how intolerance has reared its ugly head in such destructive, unthinkable events as the greatest treason in history which resulted in the fall of Babylon due to intolerance of a newly introduced religion, the crucifixion of Jesus Christ (referred to as the man of men — the greatest enemy of intolerance), and the massacre of St. Bartholomew. The Modern Story portrays an example of how intolerance directly and indirectly ruined the lives of Americans in the early part of this century. However, it also gives us hope with a portrayal of how perfect love can win out over intolerance — and in this particular instance saves an innocent man from the gallows.

Originally shot for a then-unheard-of $1,900,000 (or $2,100,000 — depending on which book one reads), *Intolerance* would probably cost upwards of $500,000,000 to re-shoot today, if shot using sets and costumes as lavish and extraordinary as those in this version. D.W. Griffith financed the film himself, after buying out his skeptical financial backers with long-term notes, and using his profits from *The Birth of a Nation*. At the box office, *Intolerance* lost a great deal of money, and the debts it incurred took years to pay off. Part of the reason for the financial failure was the timing of its release. In its initial few months, *Intolerance* was grossing more than *The Birth of a Nation* had in its first few months of release. Unfortunately, by mid–1917, America was ready to enter World War I, and the box office receipts for this pacifist film plummeted. While Griffith needed high box office receipts for a few years to recoup the costs of *Intolerance,* he only benefited from a few months of such.

The battle scenes and sets in the Babylon Story are the most elaborate and historically realistic ever to grace a screen. The instruments of war used are burning oil, bows and arrows, stones, and the large moving towers which were necessary for the offensive armies to climb up and over the 300 foot high walls of Babylon (of which replicas were constructed). These battle scenes are not for the weak at heart, as decapitations, stabbings, and the other horrors of ancient war are graphically portrayed and grimly realistic.

The backdrop sets for the Babylon banquet hall are still the largest in Hollywood history to date, only possibly equaled by the castle set in Douglas Fairbanks, Sr.'s 1922 production of *Robin Hood.* Neither set has been topped since. The size of the backdrop for the Feast of Belshazzar necessitated the invention of the modern-day crane shot. Another invention that is directly attributed to *Intolerance* is the first false eyelashes which were created for the part of Princess Beloved, portrayed by Seena Owen.

Many of the actors and actresses who appeared in *Intolerance* were to later become especially noteworthy names in the areas of acting and or directing. Bessie Love, who played the bride in the Judean Story, went on to play in *The Lost World* (1925), which was a box-office triumph as the first dinosaur movie. In addition, she is credited with introducing "the Charleston" to the screen that same year in Monta Bell's *The King on Main Street.* Erich Von Stroheim went on to direct *Greed* (1924), hailed by respected film critics as one of the great masterpieces of silent drama even in its butchered form. Other Stroheim directorial credits include *Foolish Wives* (1922) and *The Wedding March* (1928). In the talkies, he had a lucrative acting career in such movies as *The Great Gabbo* (1929), *Grand Illusion* (1937), and *Sunset Boulevard* (1950). Tully Marshall went on to play character roles in a number of great silents, including Lon Chaney, Sr.'s *The Hunchback of Notre Dame* (1923) and *The Cat and the Canary* (1927). Elmo Lincoln went on to play the first screen Tarzan in 1918. Margery Wilson, the lovely "Brown Eyes" from the French Story, went on to play leading heroine roles in a number of westerns. Mae Marsh, who gave one of the finest dramatic performances of the silent era, also went on to star in a number of noteworthy films, and could often be seen in cameos as recently as the 1960s. Walter Long played a number of villain roles in the silent era, notably as Plumitas with Rudolph Valentino in *Blood and Sand* (1922). Miriam Cooper would become the wife of director/actor Raoul Walsh. George Walsh, brother of Raoul, would go on to a reputation as a fabulous stuntman, and was originally the first choice for the lead in *Ben-Hur* (1927).

With the possible exception of *The Birth of a Nation*, *Intolerance* was the greatest single advance in the motion picture medium, being to Hollywood what the 1969 moon voyage was to NASA. Many of the techniques currently used in today's motion pictures are traceable either to *Intolerance* or to D.W. Griffith, the genius behind it all — who kept the "script" in his head during the entire time *Intolerance* was being produced.

There are many different versions of *Intolerance* available on videocassette. The original theatrical release print was approximately 3 1/2 hours in length. The versions available vary in completeness and color tint status. Kino's version is the most complete, containing two scenes not available in any other video version. Video Yesteryear's version has the longest running time, as it is transferred at a slower rate of speed than the other versions.

Videocassette Sources

Discount Video Tapes. $19.95
    No further information is in their catalogue.

Grapevine Video. . . . . #IDWG $24.95
    Runs 2 hours, 50 minutes.

Home Box Office Video. #90564 $59.99
    Features new color tints with an orchestral score composed and conducted by Carl Davis. Runs approximately 2 hours, 50 minutes.

Kino Video. $29.95
    Features the original 1916 color tints, with an organ score. Runs 2 hours, 57 minutes.

Republic Pictures Home Video . . . . #2002 $19.98
    Color tinted, edited version running 2 hours and 3 minutes. Piano score.

Video Yesteryear . . . . #464 $39.95
    Black and white, with original organ score by Rosa Rio. Runs 3 hours, 28 minutes.

The Eyes of Julia Deep (1918)

American Film Company
Directed by Lloyd Ingraham
Cast: *Julia Deep* Mary Miles Minter; *Terry Hartridge* Alan Forrest; *Lottie Driscoll* Alice Wilson; *Timothy Black* George Periolat; *Mrs. Turner* Ida Easthope; *Mrs. Sarah Lowe* Eugenie Besserer; *Sheriff Plummet* Carl Stockdale

For the first time in over 70 years, those of us who have read a segment on Mary Miles Minter in the majority of movie history books that exist can actually see one of her movies. As is well known, Minter's career was unjustly ruined by false media speculations concerning the mysterious death of her friend, William Desmond Taylor. Taylor was a Paramount director who had directed some of Minter's later films.

Although most books, when reflecting on Mary Miles Minter, paint her as a beautiful, but lousy actress (citing her work in *The Ghost of Rosy Taylor* and *A Cumberland Romance*), her good performance in *The Eyes of Julia Deep* demonstrates otherwise. This was one of her better movies with American before joining Paramount, and her essence and beauty — as well as her substance as a serious actress — comes through.

Minter gives a heartwarming, charming performance as Julia Deep, a shopgirl who stops an irresponsible playboy from killing himself after he has squandered the last of his inheritance. Minter as Deep is sympathetic, yet firm enough to let Hartridge (played by Alan Forrest) know that she cannot and will not be fooled. When Hartridge inquires of Deep what she would do with his life, a title card flashes on the screen with the response, "I'd put you to work and make you earn a profit!" Few actresses can pull off a part quite like Minter in portraying a young woman so innocent, sweet, and demure — yet strong and forceful with intellect and purpose.

Although Minter said herself that she did not particularly care for acting and was only in it for the money, this could be attributed to the fact that most of the roles assigned to her were shallow. The "Julia Deep" role demonstrates that when the role itself had any substance at all, Minter had the talent to play it to the hilt. Had her career lasted until she turned 21 and could assume control of her affairs — independent of her domineering, money-hungry mother — she may very well have demanded and received better roles. She might have grown to enjoy the acting profession and use her abilities to the fullest potential.

When comparing Mary Miles Minter and Mary Pickford, it is obvious that Minter was the better looking of the two actresses. Pickford was an astute businesswoman who ingeniously marketed herself as "little Mary." Unfortunately, when she tried to graduate to adult roles, she was not well-received, despite her fabulous performances. Whereas Minter had a classic beauty which would have eased her transition into more mature roles, Pickford was locked into playing little girls with long, blonde curls.

In appraising the acting talent of the two, let us compare Minter's "Julia Deep" role to Pickford's role in *My Best Girl* (1927), for which she received Danny Peary's "Alternate Oscar" for 1927-28. Both roles were portrayals of shop girls, and each was considered to be among the better performances of each respective actress. While Pickford's performance was excellent — especially toward the end in which she tries to pretend to be a scandalous floozy to turn off her boyfriend, Minter's competent performance as Julia Deep demonstrates that she certainly was not the lousy actress she has been painted. The author enjoyed the Minter movie just as well as the Pickford movie. It is this author's opinion that had Minter's career not been cut so short, and had she not gained so much weight in the late 1920s, that she had the potential to have at least equaled Pickford's stature in the silent era.

Contrary to the critics who have stated that Mary Miles Minter did not add much to the party in the films in which she appeared, she quite obviously is the party in *The Eyes of Julia Deep*; her performance carries the entire movie. Hopefully, her reputation as a beautiful, delightful, and talented actress can now be restored.

Videocassette Source
Grapevine Video . . . . #EOJD $16.95

The Mark of Zorro (1920)
United Artists
Directed by Fred Niblo
Cast: *Zorro* Douglas Fairbanks, Sr.; *Don Diego Vega* Douglas Fairbanks, Sr.; *Sgt. Pedro* Noah Beery, Sr.; *Don Carlos* Charles H. Mailes; *Wife of Carlos* Claire McDowell; *Lolita* Marguerite de la Motte; *Captain Ramon* Robert McKim; *Governor Alvarado* George Periolat; *Frey Felipe* Walt Whitman; *Don Alejandro* Sidney De Gray; *Child Extra* Noah Beery, Jr.; *Child Extra* Milton Berle

Douglas Fairbanks, Sr., who in 1916 had been an extra with D.W. Griffith, was, by 1919, one of his three partners in the United Artists Corporation. The other two partners in the company included Charlie Chaplin and Mary Pickford, who married Fairbanks in 1920. *The Mark of Zorro* was Fairbanks' first big feature film, as well as one of his earliest contributions to the newly formed partnership. It was also one of his very best films.

Based on *The Curse of Capistrano*, this original Zorro adaptation is a fast-paced action movie without a single dull moment. It seems that Fairbanks is always up to something in one of the two roles he plays. As Don Diego Vega, he is always trying to make up new card or handkerchief tricks, or trying to make himself look as uninterested, klutzy, or frail as possible to mask his second identity as Zorro. As Zorro, Fairbanks is either engaged in an exciting swashbuckling session (which he always wins) or performing other incredible stunts in his efforts to bring the tyrannical governor and corrupt henchmen to justice. In the time that is left, Fairbanks is busy romancing the heroine, Lolita, as either of his two roles, the Zorro role being the victorious.

There is an interesting side fact about Marguerite de la Motte, who plays heroine Lolita. In real life, she was married to actor John Bowers. It was on this couple's life that the movie *A Star Is Born* was allegedly based.

Many readaptations of Zorro have been made, some of them quite good. Included among the later adaptations have been serials, comedy parodies, and, of course, the famous 1940 talkie remake starring Tyrone Power, Jr. None of the remakes have quite managed to recapture the zest of this original silent adaptation.

Videocassette Sources

Discount Video Tapes. $19.95
Grapevine Video . . . . #22-239 $16.95
MC Film Festival $39.95
> Video Yesteryear's black and white version with an original organ score by Rosa Rio.

Republic Pictures Home Video . . . . #2686 $19.98
> Taken from a color tinted print restored by Paul Killiam in 1970, with a piano score.

Way Down East (1920)

Griffith–United Artists

Directed by D.W. Griffith

Cast: *Anna Moore* Lillian Gish; *David Bartlett* Richard Barthelmess; *Lennox Sanderson* Lowell Sherman; *Squire Bartlett* Burr McIntosh; *Mother Bartlett* Kate Bruce; *Kate, the Young Niece* Mary Hay; *Maria Poole* Emily Fitzroy; *Hi Holler* Edgar Nelson; *Seth Holcomb* Porter Strong; *A Dancing Girl (bit part)* Norma Shearer

Way Down East was adapted from an old stage play, and when D.W. Griffith paid $175,000 for the screen rights to it, many in Hollywood had doubts about his sanity. Quite obviously, even to the most casual of historic observers, Griffith knew what he was doing. *Way Down East* was the most commercially successful of Griffith's later films, second only to *The Birth of a Nation*.

The story starts out slowly, introducing and establishing the characters. The film gradually moves faster and faster, building up to an explosive climax. For pure entertainment value, *Way Down East* was one of the best melodramas to come out of the silent era.

This old stage drama is about a poor young girl named Anna Moore (magnificently played by Lillian Gish) who is tricked into a mock marriage by the wealthy Lennox Sanderson. When Moore tells Sanderson she is about to give birth to his child, he finally owns up to the truth of the fake ceremony, but leaves her to fend for herself. Following the death of her sympathetic mother, Moore hides away in nearby Belden under the name of "Mrs. Lennox" and gives birth to her baby. The baby later dies, and Marie Poole, Moore's puritanical, villainous landlady, orders her out of the house on account of the gossip concerning her non-existent "husband."

Moore finds work as a maid at the estate of Squire Bartlett, one of the richest farmers in the area. The estate just happens to be across the street from the posh country residence of none other than Lennox Sanderson, who makes threats to expose Moore's past if she does not leave. At the urging of David Bartlett, the handsome young son of Squire Bartlett, Moore stays on and becomes a beloved member of the family despite Sanderson's idle threats.

All is well until Moore's past is found out about by Martha Perkins, the town gossip (reminds one of the Gladys Kravitz character in the *Bewitched* television series that ran from 1964 to 1974), who considers it her "bounden duty" to inform the Squire. What follows after the disclosure is a great climactic ending, which starts out with Moore being thrown out of the house and into a snowstorm. Griffith keeps the audience on pins and needles waiting to find out if she will tell the dirt on Sanderson and if she will be rescued in time before she plummets over the waterfall.

It should be noted that the snowstorm sequence was the real thing. Griffith and his crew actually waited for winter time to film the winter sequences, and then waited for an actual snowstorm to film the blizzard scenes. The icicles forming on Lillian Gish's eyelashes were genuine and not the product of creative makeup artistry. In addition, D.W. Griffith ended up in the hospital as a result of this movie. Apparently, the dynamite blast used to break up the solid river ice went off sooner than expected, and caught Griffith before he had the chance to attain a safe distance.

In the author's opinion, Gish's role as Anna Moore ranks with her *Broken Blossoms* role as one of her two very best silent era performances.

Videocassette Sources

Discount Video Tapes. $19.95
   Amber toned w/orchestra score, sound effects.
Grapevine Video . . . . #WDEDWG $19.95
Kino Video. $24.95
   Color tinted.
Nostalgia Family Video. . . . . #1179 $19.95
Video Yesteryear. . . . . #881 $39.95
   Black and white with original organ score.

Orphans of the Storm (1921)

Griffith–United Artists
Directed by D.W. Griffith
Cast: *Louise Girard* Dorothy Gish; *Henriette Girard* Lillian Gish; *Chevalier de Vaudrey* Joseph Schildkraut; *Danton* Monte Blue; *Count de Linieres* Frank Losee; *Countess de Linieres* Catherine Emmett; *Marquis de Praille* Morgan Wallace; *Mother Frochard* Lucille LaVerne; *Jacques Frochard* Sheldon Lewis; *Pierre Frochard* Frank Puglia; *Picard* Creighton Hale; *Jacques Forget-Not* Leslie King; *Robespierre* Sidney Herbert; *King Louis XVI* Leo Kolmer; *The Doctor* Adolphe Lestina; *Sister Genevieve* Kate Bruce; *A Starving Peasant* Flora Finch

Orphans of the Storm, set during the French Revolution, was one of the last of D.W. Griffith's truly great masterpieces. Griffith put a great deal of research into this picture, using first-hand account biographies and historical references, as well as paintings from the time period. The result of this meticulous research is one of the most authentic and detailed portrayals of the French Revolution in the history of the movies.

Dorothy Gish, an extremely under-rated actress, steals the show as the blind sister Louise. Although her specialty was comedy (which she subtly demonstrates in a few scenes), her performance in this film is a fantastic dramatic achievement. If the Oscars had been awarded in 1922, Dorothy Gish would have deserved at least a nomination for Best Actress.

Lillian Gish, who plays the sister Henriette, as usual turns in another fine performance. The scene in which she pleads to the dreaded Committee of "Public Safety" for one hour with her sister before going off to the guillotine is especially heart-rending.

Among the outstanding supporting players are Lucille LaVerne and Monte Blue. LaVerne (who, incidentally, provided the voice of the wicked queen in Walt Disney's *Snow White and the Seven Dwarfs* in 1937) makes an excellent villain as Mother Frochard, the nasty hag who takes Louise after her sister's kidnapping and preys on her blindness and beauty, forcing her to beg in the streets to earn her keep. Monte Blue is fabulous as Danton, one of the leaders of the Revolution who risks his life to plead to the Tribunal for the lives of Henriette and de Vaudrey, the latter sentenced to the guillotine as an aristocrat; the former sentenced likewise for sheltering an aristocrat.

The climax of the movie is an excellent chase sequence in which Danton races against time in his effort to effect a last-minute rescue of Henriette from the blade of the guillotine.

Watch closely for Flora Finch, who plays a bit part near the beginning of the movie as a starving peasant to whom de Vaudrey gives a loaf of bread and some money. Finch was a significant actress in the early teens in a series of one-reelers in which she costarred with the famed comedian John Bunny until his death in 1915.

Videocassette Sources

Grapevine Video . . . . #OOSDWG $19.95
Nostalgia Family Video . . . . #1552 $19.95
    Black and white.
Republic Pictures Home Video . . . . #3078 $19.98
    Color tinted version with piano score.

The Three Ages (1923)

Joseph Schenk Productions
Directed by Buster Keaton, Eddie Cline
Cast: *The Faithful Admirer* Buster Keaton; *The Adventurer* Wallace Beery;
The Girl Margaret Leahy; *The Girl's Mother* Lillian Lawrence; *The Girl's Father* Joseph Roberts

Toward the beginning of the end of D.W. Griffith's directorial career in the early 1920s, the major comedians began to graduate from short films to features. In 1921, Charles Chaplin and Harold Lloyd respectively released their first features *The Kid* and *A Sailor-Made Man.* Buster Keaton followed two years later with *The Three Ages,* which is a unique contribution to motion picture history as a parody of D.W. Griffith's *Intolerance.*

The Three Ages opens in much the same manner as *Intolerance,* with the camera focused on a book entitled *Three Ages* opening up. The theme is slightly different; rather than dealing with intolerance throughout different ages of history, love is the chosen theme which is demonstrated not to have changed throughout the Stone Age, the Roman Age, or the Modern Age. Each interlinking story features Keaton and nemesis Wallace Beery (famous for his role as Magua, the evil Indian in Maurice Tourneur's *Last of the Mohicans* in 1920, and for his Oscar-winning performance in the 1931 version of *The Champ*) as rivals fighting for the affection of the same girl, Margaret Leahy. The girl's parents always seem to favor Beery over Keaton. After being put to the test in a variety of challenges, Keaton always emerges victorious in the end. Furthermore, "for those who do not believe that love has remained the same throughout all the ages," the finale of the movie shows the same outcome in all three ages — Keaton with his wife and several children tagging along.

This hilarious movie finds Keaton in a variety of misadventures. During the Stone Age, he is challenged to a duel with clubs. When it is discovered that he cheated by wedging a stone into his club, Keaton is sentenced to take a tour of the neighborhood tied to the tail of an elephant which drags him all the way.

The Roman Age finds Keaton challenged to a chariot race. Keaton shows up in a dog sled. When the dogs get sidetracked from the race while chasing a cat, Keaton solves the problem by tying the cat to a pole extending from the front of the sled — just out of reach of the dogs. He still loses the race by just a hair, and is thrown into the dungeon with a lion. Leave

contracts leprosy, and ends up begging Moses and God for forgiveness. After showing this example of how non-compliance with the Ten Commandments comes back to haunt people, the movie fades into the Modern Story.

The Modern Story brings us to the home of the McTavish family, circa 1923. Martha McTavish, a widow, is shown reading the story of the Ten Commandments to her two sons — John and Dan McTavish. John McTavish, played by Richard Dix, chooses to live his life in compliance with the principles of the Ten Commandments. Dan McTavish, played by Rod LaRocque, chooses to live his life in defiance of the Ten Commandments, instead directing his energy toward making money — breaking any law of God or man as he sees fit in order to do so. It all catches up with him when he decides to use a cheaper grade of concrete mix — increasing profits but not meeting safety regulations. Dan's punishment begins at once, starting with the south wall of the new church caving in and killing his mother. This is followed by a scandal sheet which is about to expose the fact that McTavish illegally smuggled in cheap concrete mix, subjecting Dan to a possible prison sentence. In the process of trying to scrape together enough money to buy out the scandal sheet, Sally Lung, Dan's adulterous mistress (played by Nita Naldi), informs him that she is the mysterious escapee on the loose from a leper colony, thus having caused Dan to contract leprosy as well. He ends up shooting Lung, and is killed in a motor boat accident while trying to flee the country and escape prosecution.

Meanwhile, John McTavish, the brother who has chosen to live in accordance with the Ten Commandments, lives a comfortable life, and, in the end, wins back Mary Leigh (played by Leatrice Joy), who at first abandoned him and the "old fashioned" Ten Commandments for John and "wealth." Leigh, having been married to the evil brother, is cleansed and cured of the leprosy contracted from her husband once she sees the light and resolves to mend her ways.

This is a classic story of the effects of karma in two different eras of history, demonstrating that the commandments are just as valid now as they were in the time of Moses. This particular epic is often referred to as Cecil B. DeMille's greatest masterpiece.

Videocassette Sources
Columbia House Video Club . . . . #0306605 $19.95
Movies Unlimited . . . . #06-1432 $19.99

Salome (1923)

Alla Nazimova–United Artists
Directed by Charles Bryant
Costumes and sets designed by Natacha Rambova
Cast: *Salome* Alla Nazimova; *King Herod* Mitchell Lewis; *Wife of Herod*
    Rose Dione; *John the Baptist (Jokanaan)* Nigel De Brulier; *Narraboth*
    Earl Schenk; *Namaan, the Executioner* Frederick Peters; *Narraboth's*
    Blonde Friend Arthur Jasmina

Salome was the last in a series of films independently produced and
financed by Alla Nazimova, who had notoriety as an openly lesbian actress.
This is a short, but interesting movie, as it is alleged by many sources to
feature an exclusively homosexual cast. Nazimova, as homage to Oscar
Wilde, reportedly hired an all-gay cast to star in this movie based on
Wilde's stage play. The exotic costumes and sets were based on sketches
by Aubrey Beardsley contained in the English translation manuscript
(Wilde's original text was written in French) of the play by Lord Alfred
Douglas, who was, during that time in 1895, Wilde's companion. All of
the costumes and sets were designed by Natacha Rambova, who was then
Mrs. Rudolph Valentino.

The plot is relatively simple, with Nazimova playing the lead role of
Salome, who is the daughter of the wife of King Herod. Herod, being an
incestuous pervert, falls in lust with stepdaughter Salome. He makes an
offer to give her anything she asks, in return for her performance of a
dance routine. She initially refuses.

The plot thickens when Salome visits the dungeon in which John
the Baptist, also referred to as Jokanaan, is held prisoner for having pub-
licly denounced Herod in his sermons. She becomes "enamored" with
him, whereas he wants nothing to do with her, refusing to let her touch
him in any way. While all of this is going on, it seems that Salome is
cursed, as everyone who crosses her path seems to die a horrible death.
For some strange reason, she finally consents to dance for her stepfather
on the condition that he gives her *anything* she may ask for. Then comes
the highlight of the movie — the dance of the seven veils. This sequence
features some exotic costume styles which were way ahead of their time.
The dress worn by Nazimova in this sequence looks like something that
would be worn in current times.

After completing the dance, Salome informs Herod of the price —
the head of John the Baptist on a silver platter. Her entire motivation was

that if she could not kiss Jokanaan while he was alive, she would kiss the mouth of his severed head. The end of the movie consists of a black shade being lowered over a title card which says, "And there was none in the world so black as the name of Salome."

There were two adaptations of *Salome* filmed during the silent era. The other one starred Theda Bara and was produced in 1918. This is the only adaptation known to survive.

Videocassette Sources
MC Film Festival $24.95
> Video Yesteryear's version, which includes *Queen Elizabeth* (1912) on the same tape.

Nostalgia Family Video . . . . #1465B $19.95

Safety Last (1923)
Hal Roach Productions
Directed by Sam Taylor
Cast: *The Boy* Harold Lloyd; *The Girl* Mildred Davis; *The Cop* Noah Young; *The Pal* Bill Strother; *The Kid* Mickey Daniels; *The Grandma* Anna Townsend

This one receives the author's nomination for best comedy of the silent era. The major attraction of this film is the stunt work that Harold Lloyd did in his "human fly" sequence. When one knows that this is the real thing, with minimal trick photography (the building was situated above a tunnel on one side, giving the illusion that Lloyd was slightly further from the ground than he really was), it is all the more impressive. What is really unbelievable is that Lloyd did these stunts with two fingers missing from his right hand. The fingers had been blown off during a 1920 photo session in which the allegedly fake bomb Lloyd was using turned out to be an actual explosive.

The story line is about a young man from a small town who is going to the big city to make good. The girl, played by Mildred Davis (Lloyd's real-life wife) promises to marry Lloyd once he has made good. To present such an image, Lloyd sells his phonograph to buy her a beautiful charm, and then spends his entire week's pay on a chain to go with the charm. Davis reasons that since Lloyd is doing so well and making so much money, it would be dangerous to leave him in the big city by himself any longer, and decides to pay him a surprise visit. Lloyd has to do some acting to pull off the false illusion that he is the general manager of the department store, as opposed to his actual job of counter clerk.

Overhearing the real general manager's conversation in which he pledges $1,000 to anybody who can come up with an idea to promote the store, Lloyd proposes that a "human fly" spectacle be staged at the department store building. The manager agrees to the proposal, and Lloyd calls his roomate, offering him $500 (half of the $1,000) to scale the building. The roommate readily agrees, but when he shows up, he encounters a police officer who has an ax to grind with him. Lloyd ends up having to perform the stunt himself— until the pal can "ditch the cop," which never happens.

This is an all-time comedy classic, and one of the best-known from the silent era.

Until very recently, it was next to impossible to find any of Lloyd's silent film features on videocassette. For a while, five of his silent features were available only as a complete set for $150. It is now possible to purchase *Safety Last* as well as Lloyd's other features on videocassette separately.

Videocassette Source
Movies Unlimited . . . . #44-1944 $19.99

Greed (1924)
MGM
Directed by Erich Von Stroheim
An MGM/UA Home Video Release
Cast: *McTeague* Gibson Gowland; *Trina* ZaSu Pitts; *Marcus Schouler* Jean Hersholt; *Mr. Sieppe* Chester Conklin; *Mrs. Sieppe* Sylvia Ashton; *Maria* Dale Fuller; *Selina* Joan Standing; *August Sieppe* Austin Jewell; *The Sieppe Twins* Oscar and Otto Gottell; *McTeague's mother* Tempe Piggott

Every great director has invariably had one particular movie that has stood out among the rest of their works as "their masterpiece." The most recent motion picture so recognized is *Schindler's List* (1993), the film that brought Steven Spielberg his first Best Director Academy Award. *Greed* is so recognized by film critics as Erich Von Stroheim's masterpiece.

Originally, *Greed* was intended to be a faithful screen version of Frank Norris' 1899 novel *McTeague,* and the original director's cut was approximately nine hours in length. Irving Thalberg and other MGM officials refused to allow its release at such an immense length. Stroheim sent it to his trusted friend director Rex Ingram, who cut it to 3 1/4 hours. Thalberg edited it still further to a little over two hours and renamed it.

Even in its edited form, *Greed* has stood the test of time as one of the greatest dramatic masterpieces in the history of cinema. If one watches the movie before having read the book, it is impossible to tell that parts of the story were left out. It is only upon reading the novel that one discovers that Maria, the housekeeper, was supposed to develop into a significant character, and that the characters Miss Baker, Old Grannis, and junk dealer Zerkow are completely lost. Nonetheless, what survives of this film is a chilling portrayal of how Trina McTeague's obsession with money led to the downfall of herself, her husband, and her cousin Marcus Schouler.

The actors, actresses, and entire crew worked under grueling conditions with infinite determination to complete this work of art. ZaSu Pitts, famed as a great comedienne of the silent and early talkie eras, turns in a fabulous dramatic performance as Trina. Jean Hersholt spent months in the hospital recovering from a painful rash that resulted from the blistering hot Death Valley sequences. One of the cooks in the movie crew died, and others were hospitalized. These movie players, along with Von Stroheim, were obviously dedicated to their art to work under such conditions.

More than 70 years after its initial release, this classic masterpiece still conveys a powerful message.

Videocassette Source
Movies Unlimited. . . . . #12-1136 $29.99

Riders of the Range (1924)
Clifford S. Efelt Company
Directed by Otis B. Thayer
Cast: *Martin Lethbridge* Edmund F. Cobb; *Inez Cortez* Helen Hayes; *Alice Randall* Dolly Dale; *Blunt Vanier* Frank Gallagher; *Gregg Randall* Clare Hatton; *Bob Randall* Roy Langdon

This is a rare surviving grade B western featuring an early appearance of Helen Hayes. Most people have a hard time believing it, and are open to the possibility that the Helen Hayes billed is not the Helen Hayes who won the 1932 Best Actress Oscar. Rest assured that it is her, and she is a wonderful and vibrant addition for the brief time that she is featured. Hayes' appearance in the film for which she received second billing was actually a very small walk-on cameo of about 90 seconds' duration. Leading heroine Alice Randall is played by Dolly Dale. Roy Langdon, the producer of the film, also plays a supporting role as the alcoholic wayward brother, Bob Randall. Edmund F. Cobb, a relatively well-known silent era western star, plays the lead as Martin Lethbridge, president of the local Cattle Rancher's Association.

There is little to this movie or the story. Sheepherders move into cattle herders' territory. Good guys on both sides are trying to keep peace. Bad guys on the cattle herders' side, led by villain Blunt Vanier, conspire to kill cattle and blame it on the sheepherders as an excuse to drive them out of the area. Martin Lethbridge, the leader of the cattle herders, falls in love with Alice Randall, the daughter of the leader of the sheepherders.

In the end, the bad guys are caught, and Lethbridge and Randall get married and live happily ever after.

The movie itself has all of the qualities of a truly horrendous, predictable western. The print is so faded in parts that it is sometimes difficult to read the title cards. Nonetheless, the very rare early footage of Helen Hayes makes *Riders of the Range* worth having a copy of.

Videocassette Source
Discount Video Tapes. $19.95

The Red Kimona (1925)
Mrs. Wallace Reid Productions
Screenplay adaptation by Dorothy Arzner
Story by Adela Rogers St. John
Directed by Walter Lang
Cast: *Narrator* Dorothy Davenport (Mrs. Wallace) Reid; *Gabrielle*
    Priscilla Bonner; *Clara* Nellie Bly Baker; *Howard Blaine* Carl Miller;
    The Jail Matron Mrs. Mary Carr; *Mrs. Fontaine* Virginia Pearson;
    Gabrielle's Father Tyrone Power, Sr.; *District Attorney* Sheldon Lewis
    Freddy, the Chauffer Theodore Von Sitz; *Mrs. Fontaine's Housekeeper*

Emily Fitzroy; *Dr. Mack* George Siegmann; *The Inquisitive One* Pat
Farley

This is a narrative based on real-life events, depicting a 1917 incident of a woman unjustly exploited. Priscilla Bonner gives a convincing
performance as Gabrielle, a woman who falls for an empty promise of
marriage by con artist Howard Blaine, in a desperate effort to escape her
tyrannical father. Instead of marrying Gabrielle as promised, Blaine puts
her to work in a New Orleans whorehouse. Having no place else to go,
and desperate for money, Gabrielle puts up with years of bondage in the
house of ill fame.

Upon learning that Blaine is traveling to Los Angeles to marry
another woman, Gabrielle follows him there, and, on impulse, shoots
him dead. A sympathetic jury acquits her. After the trial, she is taken in
by one Mrs. Fontaine, a "notoriety-seeking old biddy" who exploits her
for the publicity value to further her reputation as a philanthropist —
only to throw her back out in the streets to fend for herself after the publicity value is gone. Unable to find legitimate employment, Gabrielle goes
back to New Orleans with the intention of returning to prostitution. An
unexpected chain of events results in her employment in a hospital
instead, and she eventually marries and lives happily ever after.

At the end of the movie is a personal plea by Dorothy Davenport
Reid for society to give fallen women a chance to make good as opposed
to shunning and condemning them, and thereby forcing them back into
seedy lifestyles. Reid reiterates that although Gabrielle, the subject of the
story, found peace and happiness, there are countless others like her who
are not so fortunate.

The Red Kimona delivers a very powerful message, and was years
ahead of its time. It is the only known surviving movie of the series of
three produced by Dorothy Davenport Reid in the immediate aftermath
of the January 18, 1923, death of her husband, Wallace Reid, from drug
addiction. The other two in the series were *Human Wreckage,* the first in
the series which exposed drug trafficking, and *Broken Laws,* which
addressed juvenile delinquency.

Over the years, detractors have accused Dorothy Reid of making this
series of films to exploit her husband's tragic, untimely death. On the contrary, Reid appears to have been a good woman coping with the pain of
having lost the man she loved to drug addiction in the best way that she
could. History has demonstrated that she was completely faithful to him
even after his death, as she never remarried before her own death in 1977.

Her efforts seem to have been sincerely motivated by the desire to educate the public about some of society's dangers, hopefully saving a few people from going through pain similar to that she had experienced. In this author's opinion, Reid deserves far more credit than past cynical critics have given her.

It is ironic to note that this movie, with its message against judgment, condemnation, and exploitation was based on a story written by none other than the infamous Adela Rogers St. John. St. John happened to be the queen of exploitation during the 1920s, and was the predecessor of gossip columnists Louella Parsons and Hedda Hopper. It was the exaggeration and distortion of facts in St. John's gossip columns that helped to ruin the careers of leading female stars Mabel Normand and Mary Miles Minter in the wake of the scandal surrounding the mysterious, unsolved murder of Paramount director William Desmond Taylor in 1922.

The Red Kimona features a number of interesting actors and actresses. The most recognizable name is Tyrone Power, Sr., whose son was, of course, the legendary 1940s heartthrob Tyrone Power, Jr. In addition, husband-wife acting team Sheldon Lewis and Virginia Pearson are featured. If one watches closely, one might recognize Emily Fitzroy, who plays Mrs. Fontaine's haughty housekeeper. She played a similar role as Maria Poole, the puritanical landlady in Griffith's *Way Down East* five years earlier.

In a final note, the author points out that Reid must have had some talent of her own as a motion picture producer. After she allegedly became a "career widow" producing the three-movie series previously mentioned, she remained in the field of motion picture production into the 1950s, holding her own long after the death of her husband.

Videocassette Sources

Discount Video Tapes. $19.95
Nostalgia Family Video . . . . #2790 $19.95
Video Yesteryear . . . . #997 $24.95

The Phantom of the Opera (1925)

Universal Studios
Directed by Rupert Julian
Cast: *The Phantom of the Opera* Lon Chaney, Sr.; *Christine Daae* Mary Philbin; *Raoul de Chagney* Norman Kerry; *Simon Buquet* Gibson

Gowland; *Carlotta* Mary Fabian; *Carlotta's Mother* Virginia Pearson; *Philippe de Chagney* John Sainpolis; *Ledoux of the Secret Police* Arthur Edmund Carewe; *Joseph Buquet* Bernard Siegel

In the mid–1920s, horror films began to gain popularity in the United States, owing partly to the success of German directorial genius F.W. Murnau's *Nosferatu.* This original version of *The Phantom of the Opera,* billed as "Universal's million-dollar super jewel production," has frequently been regarded as one of the greatest American horror films of all time, and the best of the many adaptations of Gaston LeRoux's 1911 literary work. It should be, as Lon Chaney went through more physical pain and torture than any other actor in history to pull off his gruesome illusions, notably as the phantom. What other "phantom" actor endured the pain and agony of having fishhooks jabbed into his cheeks and metal discs shoved up his nostrils?

In addition to no pain being spared, no expense was spared, as is evident with the lavish reconstruction of the interior of the Paris Opera House. Furthermore, the Bal Masque sequence was presented in color, which was outrageously expensive at the time.

This is probably the most popular of all the drama/horror films of the silent era. Theatrical screenings of it are a yearly Halloween tradition in many larger cities to this day, 70 years after its original release.

In addition to Lon Chaney, *The Phantom of the Opera* featured other significant actors and actresses. Norman Kerry was a top romantic lead actor in many silents, most notably with Mae Murray in *Merry-Go-Round* (1925) and with Lillian Gish in *Annie Laurie* (1927). He was also a close friend of Rudolph Valentino, and helped him to get some of his first movie roles in the late teens. Virginia Pearson was one of the most prolific of Theda Bara's many imitators. Although there is little written about her, she had roles in three notable movies in 1925 alone. She also appeared as Lady Vishuss in Larry Semon's cornball version of *Wizard of Oz* and as Mrs. Fontaine in Dorothy Davenport Reid's *The Red Kimona.* Another point of interest is Pearson's billing in *The Phantom of the Opera.* At the beginning of the movie, she is billed correctly as Carlotta's mother, with Mary Fabian as Carlotta. However, when the cast list is repeated at the end of the movie, Pearson is billed as Carlotta, and Mary Fabian and Carlotta's mother are omitted from the list altogether.

There are as many different video versions of this one movie as there are different adaptations of the story. The versions best representative of the way the movie was meant to be seen are available from Nostalgia Family Video, Discount Video Tapes, Kino Video, and Video Yesteryear. All four feature traditional organ or orchestral scores. Nostalgia, DVT, and Kino present the Bal Masque sequence in the original color; Video Yesteryear's Bal Masque sequence is advertised as tinted. Kino Video has released a deluxe, 70-year anniversary video version that is color-tinted with the color Bal Masque sequence in tact and an orchestral score. The price is $24.95. In addition to these sources, one can find copies in discount stores for under $10 each. Beware of these cheap copies; most are black and white prints with no musical accompaniment. Before you purchase them, make sure that you have the right to return them if they do not meet your standards of quality.

An alternative, modernized (and, in the author's opinion, butchered) version is manufactured by Video Treasures, and is available through Critic's Choice Video and many local retail outlets. Although the visual quality of this video version is breathtaking (enhanced with color tinting and an introduction by Christopher Lee, with color Bal Masque sequence in tact), it features a modern contemporary rock music score by Rick Wakeman of the rock group Yes. Some of the non-vocal parts of the music track are fabulous, but the vocal parts and the electric guitar just do not go well with silent movies. The result is a significant detraction from the ability to enjoy this horror classic. It seems that every time one really starts to enjoy the non-vocal, organ scored parts of the picture, Wakeman's voice or a screeching guitar insists on interrupting the enjoyment. This version is worth seeing just to see why it is morally reprehensible to try to "modernize" the silents with contemporary rock scores. A "modernized" version of *Metropolis* was released in the early 1980s, and the modern music style had the same detrimental effects on that movie.

Videocassette Sources for Traditional Versions

Discount Video Tapes. $19.95
Kino Video. $29.95
Nostalgia Family Video . . . . #2213 $19.95
Video Yesteryear. . . . . #871 $24.95

Videocassette Source for "Modernized" Version
Critic's Choice Video . . . . #DQVCS009638 $9.99

The Lost World (1925)

First National Pictures

Directed by Harry Hoyt

Cast: *Professor Challenger* Wallace Beery; *Sir John Roxton* Lewis Stone; *Paula White* Bessie Love; *Edward Malone* Lloyd Hughes; *Professor Summerlee* Arthur Hoyt; *Gladys Hungerford* Alma Bennett; *Mrs. Challenger* Margaret McWade; *The Ape Man* Bull Montana; *Colin McArdle* George Bunny; *Major Hibbard* Charles Wellsley

This was the first of the big dinosaur/monster extravaganzas, and still holds up well, seven decades after its original release. The 1993 release of Steven Spielberg's *Jurassic Park* resulted in significantly renewed interest in *The Lost World*. Although Harry Hoyt is described in most movie history books as a "C" grade director at best, the great cast and the technical genius of Willis O'Brien make up for any shortcomings in direction. The early stop-motion photography and special effects must be seen to be believed. The color tinting effects (in color tinted versions) are magnificent, especially in the sunrise sequence in which the orange tint gradually becomes brighter and brighter as the sun rises over the jungles of the lost world. Any silent movie that can manage to keep the undivided attention of the author's 5-year-old nephew (who usually detests "old" movies made before 1980) certainly has accomplished a rare feat.

The original *King Kong* (1933), which also features special effects work by Willis O'Brien, borrowed much of its storyline from this, the "grand-daddy" of the monster movies. Wallace Beery plays Mr. Challenger, a professor who managed to survive a previous expedition to the lost world in which dinosaurs still existed. He and a crew of skeptics return to the lost world, and Challenger gets the opportunity to prove the truth of his allegations. The expedition crew manages to transport an injured brontosaurus back to London alive, only to have it escape and wander through the city, wreaking havoc. In the end, the dinosaur makes its way to the river, and, presumably, back to its natural habitat.

The dinosaur photography in this movie is so meticulous that the monsters even "had faces" like those referred to by Gloria Swanson as Norma Desmond in *Sunset Boulevard* (1950). When the brontosaurus is shown in a close-up feeding on leaves, its facial expressions make it look so charming and harmless that the audience members find themselves rooting for the leaf-eater when it is attacked by the meat-eating allosaurus. One feels sympathy when the brontosaurus is knocked over the cliff, and then a sigh of relief when it manages to survive.

Another significant factor in this movie's success was the top-notch cast it featured. Three of the leading players went on in later years to win Oscar nominations and awards. Wallace Beery, of course, tied with Fredric March for the 1932 Best Actor Oscar, as well as receiving other nominations over the years. Bessie Love, as previously mentioned in the *Intolerance* review, received a Best Actress nomination for her first talking role in *The Broadway Melody* (1929). Lewis Stone received a Best Actor nomination in the 1928-29 season as well for his role in *The Patriot,* which was one of the last films of the silent era to win Oscar nominations of any type.

This is an all-time classic that can be enjoyed by people of all ages — from the 5-year-olds of the current generation to the 95-year-olds who remember seeing *The Lost World* as young adults.

Videocassette Sources
Discount Video Tapes. $19.95
      An excellent, color tinted print.
Nostalgia Family Video . . . . #1490 $19.95
      Color tinted.
Video Yesteryear . . . . #30 $24.95

Wizard of Oz (1925)
Chadwick Pictures
Screenplay adaptation written by L. Frank Baum, Jr., Larry Semon, and
    Leon Lee
Directed by Larry Semon
Cast: Larry Semon, Dorothy Dwan, Virginia Pearson, Bryant Washburn,
    Josef Swickard, Charles Murray, Oliver N. Hardy, William Hauber,
    William Dinus, Frank Alexander, Otto Lederer, Frederick KoVert,
    Mrs. Mary Carr

This book would be incomplete without a review of one of the truly awful pictures of the silent era. This one is so bad, it is hilarious. Readers are advised not to expect anything like the 1939 extravaganza. This silent version of *Wizard of Oz* earns two nominations from the author: (1) as worst screen adaptation of a novel in Hollywood history, and (2) as one of the worst films of the entire silent era.

This adaptation was cowritten by Larry Semon, who quite obviously revamped the story to make himself the star of the show as the Scarecrow, no matter how badly he had to bastardize the original story to facilitate such. Dorothy is played by Semon's wife, Dorothy Dwan. She towers over the Aunt Em character played by Mrs. Mary Carr (1874–1973), a petite woman in her 50s who was known in the silent era for her portrayal of older women.

The film starts out with an older man reading *The Wizard of Oz* novel to his granddaughter while showing figurines of Dorothy, the Tin Man, and the Scarecrow on a table next to him. The audience is then taken to Oz, a kingdom in which the ruler-to-be has vanished without a trace. One Prime Minister Kruel is the self-proclaimed dictator, aided by Lady Vishuss (played by Virginia Pearson, who obviously did not take the role seriously) and Ambassador Wikked. When coronation day draws near, Prince Kynd (played by Bryant Washburn, who started in movies in the teens) leads the townspeople to revolt against Kruel and demand the return of the rightful ruler of Oz. Kruel, in a precarious situation, summons the Wizard (played by Charles Murray) to perform some amazing feat to distract the crowd. He does just that, by appearing to produce "the phantom of the basket" from an empty box. This phantom, played by Frederick KoVert, looks like a drag queen, and wears a headdress that must span three feet and weigh in excess of 20 pounds.

At this point, the granddaughter asks the grandfather to read to her about Dorothy, the Tin Man, and the Scarecrow. The movie takes us to the farm in Kansas. With Dorothy's 18th birthday fast approaching, Aunt Em decides to tell her all about how she arrived at the farm shortly after her birth, in a basket with a note telling about secret papers inside which cannot be opened until Dorothy turns 18. In the meantime, we are introduced to a farmhand played by Larry Semon, and the "prince charming" of the farm played by none other than "Oliver N. Hardy," who are both vying for Dorothy's affections. Also introduced is Snowball, a black character portrayed by a man billed as "G. Howe Black" in a stereotypical "Stepin Fetchit" fashion.

After some corny slapstick routines, the big day, Dorothy's 18th birthday, arrives, upon which she is to open the secret papers and find out that she is the ruler of the kingdom of Oz. Villains arrive by airplane in Kansas, having been sent by Prime Minister Kruel and Lady Vishuss to retrieve the papers and destroy them. During the fight for the papers, a cyclone strikes the farm, picking up the shack in which all our characters (except Aunt Em — what happened to her?) are whisked away to Oz, where Dorothy finally opens the papers which do indeed reveal her true identity as the new ruler.

The next scenes of consequence are those in which the Scarecrow (Larry Semon's character), the Tin Man (Oliver Hardy's character), and the Lion (the Snowball character) materialize. The rest is relatively easy to figure out.

This *Wizard of Oz* adaptation has many inconsistencies in the plot. Dorothy and Prince Kynd had to have been either (1) idiotic beyond belief, (2) sadomasochistically submissive, or (3) a combination of the two, to have fallen for some of lines from Kruel and associates as long as they did. This film is also typical of the characteristics of "bad silents" referred to in movie history books — loaded with stupid puns and corny plays on words — anything for a laugh. One example is in the introduction of Snowball, billed under the fictitious name of G. Howe Black, as "a bad case of meloncholic," while shown eating watermelons. This stereotypical portrayal of blacks (not unusual in the 1920s) as ignoramuses who lie around eating watermelon and who are too dumb to notice lightning striking their heads is especially appalling. The black characters in *The Birth of a Nation* were presented better than this. At least that film portrayed some of its blacks as intelligent enough to gain positions of authority, and the black servants who remained loyal to the Camerons were portrayed as intelligent and good enough to devise a method by which to save Dr. Cameron from the lynch mobs.

So, the reader may ask if this version of *Wizard of Oz* has any redeeming qualities. The answer is yes. There is some interesting early trick photography in the cyclone scene, and there are some interesting actors and actresses featured. Oliver Hardy is thinner than most people remember him as in this early solo appearance. Virginia Pearson, though her role is little more than a cameo, makes an excellent vampish Lady Vishuss. Mrs. Mary Carr was a perfect choice for Aunt Em.

As sorry as this film is, the very fact that it is an adaptation of *The Wizard of Oz,* with the original author's son having been a co-writer of the script, makes it worth watching just to satisfy one's curiosity. It is good for a few laughs when one has friends over — if for no other reason than to show them just how abysmal this movie is.

Videocassette Sources

Discount Video Tapes		$19.95
MC Film Festival		$24.95
Nostalgia Family Video	#1734	$19.95

Son of the Sheik (1926)
United Artists
Directed by George Fitzmaurice
Cast: *Ahmed, Son of the Sheik* Rudolph Valentino; *Ahmed Ben Hassan, the Sheik* Rudolph Valentino; *Yasmin* Vilma Banky; *Andre* George Fawcett; *Ghaba* Montague Love; *Ramadan* Karl Dane; *S'rir* William Donovan; *Diana, Wife of the Sheik* Agnes Ayres; *Albi* Bull Montana; *The Pincher* Bynunski Hyman

Rudolph Valentino had originally planned this tongue-in-cheek sequel to *The Sheik* (1921) as a much-needed Hollywood career boost. A combination of bad business decisions and bad press (largely unfounded and undeserved) had forced his popularity into a slump. Although *Son of the Sheik* was everything Valentino had hoped it would be, and probably would have revived his career and put him back on top, such was not to be. Instead it turned out to be his last movie, as Valentino died of peritonitis during a pre-release publicity tour promoting this film.

This last appearance was arguably his very best. It certainly brought out the very best in his acting talent. He demonstrated his athletic prowess and versatility in a challenging double role, playing both the sheik and his son. With the use of split-screen photography, he even played the roles side by side, appearing as both father and son simultaneously. Had the Oscars been around one year earlier, Valentino would have deserved a nomination for Best Actor of 1926-27.

Although many critics do not rate Valentino highly as an actor, his performance in *Son of the Sheik* demonstrates that when given decent material to work with, he indeed lived up to his image as the great lover of the screen. Some of his other good performances included *Eyes of Youth* (1919), in which he played a bit part as a villain; *Blood and Sand* (1922), which still remains the best screen portrayal of Juan Gallardo to date; the under-rated *Moran of the Lady Letty* (1921); and *The Four Horsemen of the Apocalypse* (1921), the film credited with transforming Valentino overnight from bit-part villain to romantic leading man.

With all the necessary ingredients for an exciting, action-packed movie — fast-paced swashbuckling scenes, last-minute rescues, excellent stuntwork, etc. — and its important contribution to cinematic history as the last and possibly best performance from one of the greatest male legends ever known to Hollywood — *Son of the Sheik* is essential to your silent film repertoire.

Videocassette Sources

Republic Pictures Home Video . . . . #3809 $19.98
      Color tinted.
Nostalgia Family Video . . . . #1847 $19.95
Discount Video Tapes. $19.95

Don Juan (1926)
Warner Bros.
Directed by Alan Crosland
An MGM/UA Home Video Release
Cast: *Don Jose de Marana* John Barrymore; *Don Juan de Marana (adult)*
      John Barrymore; *Don Juan (age 10)* Philippe De Lacy; *Don Juan (age
      5)* Yvonne Day; *Adriana della Varnese* Mary Astor; *Cesare Borgia*
      Warner Oland; *Lucrezia Borgia* Estelle Taylor; *Count Giano Donati*
      Montague Love; *Mai, Lady in Waiting* Myrna Loy; *Trusia* June Mar-
      lowe; *Donna Isobel* Jane Winton; *Leandro* John Roche; *Duke della
      Varnese* Joseph Swickard; *Pedrillo* Willard Lewis; *Marchis Rinaldo*
      Nigel de Brulier; *Marchise Rinaldo* Hedda Hopper; *Hunchback* John
      George; *A Murderess* Helene Costello; *Duke Margoni* Lionel Bra-
      ham; *Imperia* Phyllis Haver

This was the very first feature length movie to feature a "built-in"
sound effect/orchestra score, in perfect synchronization, using the then-
revolutionary sound-on-disc system from the Vitaphone Company. The
1926 audiences were amazed to hear the score and sound effects coming
from "behind the screen" rather than from an organist or orchestra on the
stage. It is also one of the legendary John Barrymore's better-known movie
performances.

Barrymore is excellent in this film, playing a double role as Don
Jose, father of Don Juan in the prologue, as well as the adult role of Don
Juan. In the title role, Barrymore certainly makes use of not only his athletic ability, but his extraordinary acting talent. He even manages to throw
in a "Jekyll-Hyde" sequence toward the end of the picture, contorting his
face into an evil grin to resemble Neri, the torture and poison expert
employed by the contemptible Borgias. Barrymore convincingly alters his
appearance without the use of makeup.

Don Juan is a light-hearted, combative adventure-romance without
an idle moment. In addition to the lavish production, it features two of

the most outstanding swashbuckling sequences from the silent era. It is difficult to choose between the one-on-one, double-sworded dual between Don Juan and villain Count Donati, or the sequence in which Barrymore's character takes on a dozen men — on horseback.

In addition to Barrymore, *Don Juan* features an all-star supporting cast. Mary Astor, the leading lady, was one of the preeminent female character actresses from the 1920s through the 1960s. Warner Oland spoke one word in *The Jazz Singer*—"STOP!"—and gained fame in the Charlie Chan movie series of the 1930s. Estelle Taylor, previously mentioned in *The Ten Commandments* (1923) was fairly well known. Myrna Loy, who played bit roles in *Ben-Hur* (1927) and *The Jazz Singer* (1927), also starred opposite William Powell in *The Thin Man* movie series and became one of the most popular actresses of all time. June Marlowe was the female heroine in some of the early Rin-Tin-Tin silents; she is perhaps best remembered as Miss Crabtree, the platinum blonde schoolteacher, in some of the early *Our Gang/Little Rascals* talkies. Montague Love and Joseph Swickard were fairly well-known character actors of the 1920s. Hedda Hopper, a minor actress in the 1920s-1950s time period, became infamous as one of the most powerful Hollywood gossip columnists over. Her name has always been connected with that of another notorious gossip columnist, Louella Parsons.

Considering all that *Don Juan* has going for it — technical innovation, superior cast, and excellent Bess Meredyth screenplay based on one of the most infamous characters of all time — there was no way it could miss.

Videocassette Sources

Columbia House . . . . #0917203 $9.95
Movies Unlimited . . . . #12-2144 $29.99

Ben-Hur: A Tale of the Christ (1927)
MGM
Directed by Fred Niblo
An MGM/UA Home Video Release
Cast: *Judah, Ben-Hur* Ramon Novarro; *Messala* Francis X. Bushman, Sr.; *Esther* May McAvoy; *Princess of Hur (Ben-Hur's mother)* Claire McDowell; *Mary, Mother of Jesus* Betty Bronson; *Tirzah* Kathleen Key; *Simonides* Nigel De Brulier; *Sheik Ilderim* Mitchell Lewis;

Sanballat Leo White; *Arrius* Frank Currier; *Balthasar the Egyptian* Charles Belcher; *Joseph* Winter Hall; *Iras the Egyptian* Carmel Myers

The most elaborate of the several 1920s biblical epics produced to purify Hollywood's tarnished image, this, the original version of *Ben-Hur*, is by far superior to the 1959 remake. One can even go so far as to say that the remake is quite boring and drawn-out, and cannot even compare to the excellence and grandeur of this original action-packed silent version. Many others who have seen both versions agree.

This is not to say that the 1959 version was a bad film. It obviously had something going for it to have won 11 of its 12 Academy Award nominations, including Best Picture of 1959. However, it is very difficult to improve on an original that was so splendidly and magnificently filmed. William Wyler tried by expanding and adding a few minor details not contained in the original, but the process of making the movie more detailed and historically accurate left the film with some very boring sequences.

The 1927 *Ben-Hur* was the most expensive film to date at the time it was produced, costing more than $4,000,000. The producers, directors, and staff overcame many obstacles to complete the film. For starters, production was begun on location by Samuel Goldwyn's company in Italy. Some of the Italian crew were making so much more money than they were used to that they did not want production, and, ultimately, their jobs, to end. Therefore, they did everything in their power to slow down production progress. Some of their shenanigans included burning down dressing rooms, sabotaging the sets, and even threatening to kidnap May McAvoy. After overcoming these setbacks and returning to Hollywood (where Goldwyn's company merged with Metro and Louis B. Mayer to form MGM), it became apparent that the distractions had marred the Italian location footage to the extent that it was unfit to use, and the whole picture was re-shot at MGM studios.

This video version of *Ben-Hur* is taken from a beautifully restored print, with the original tinting and Technicolor sequences intact. The Technicolor footage is the best quality of all of the color silent film footage that exists.

Among the highlights of this film are the pirate attack sequence, the sequence in the betting ring during which Messala and Ben-Hur come face to face for the first time in years, and, of course, the ever-unforgettable chariot race.

The sea battle against the pirates was directed by B. Reeves Eason, who was renowned as an excellent director of action scenes in westerns. Grotesquely realistic, it is one of the better battle scenes in movie history, giving even the great battle scenes in *Intolerance* stiff competition.

The betting ring sequence is a prime example of this version's superiority over the remake. In this version, one sees Sanballat teasing and chiding the Romans into betting against Ben-Hur, racing as "the unknown Jew." Sanballat urges Messala to bet 10,000 pieces of gold, with 6 to 1 odds — "the difference between a Roman and a Jew." Messala practically strangles Sanballat, calling him a braying fool and asking who has 10,000 pieces of gold to wager. At this point, the tension comes to a climax as Ben-Hur pushes his way through the crowd, pulls Messala off of Sanballat, and informs him that he, the unknown Jew, has that amount and more to wager, challenging Messala to wager 50,000 pieces of gold — with no odds. A somewhat hesitant Messala meets the wager after being sarcastically reminded by Ben-Hur that he is, after all, a Roman, while Ben-Hur is "only a Jew." This all takes place within the span of two minutes of footage, and is an exhilarating part of this movie. On the contrary, the betting sequence in the remake is dragged out into a nearly 10-minute uneventful session of dialogue, without any of the zeal of the original.

The chariot race is filmed using 42 cameras in a setting of over 100 acres. Extras were hired by the thousands for the crowd scenes. This chariot sequence holds up just as well as the race in the remake. The only major difference is that the spiked wheels on Messala's chariot which were in the remake did not exist in this original.

Another big plus for this silent *Ben-Hur* is the creative way in which color tinting and Technicolor sequences were used to define atmospheric and mood changes. This movie makes more effective use of these techniques than perhaps any other film from the silent era.

This classic MGM masterpiece ranks among the few pictures in history that can come close to being worthy of comparison to *Intolerance*.

Videocassette Sources

Columbia House Video Club. . . . . #0273607 $19.95
Movies Unlimited. . . . . #12-1831 $29.99

Napoleon (1927)

Produced in France
Directed, written, and produced by Abel Gance
An MCA/Universal Home Video Release
Cast: *Napoleon* Albert Dieudonne; *Robespierre* Edmund Van Daele; *Danton* Alexander Koubitsky; *Marat* Antonin Artaud; *St. Just* Abel Gance; *Charlotte Corday* Marguerite Gance; *Violine Fleuri* Annabella

This French bio-epic by Abel Gance was, for many years, believed to have been lost. Respected cinema scholar Kevin Brownlow took on the 30-plus years task of painstakingly acquiring bits and pieces of the original film from around the world. With the cooperation of Gance himself, he presented a restored version for theatrical re-release in 1981. To this day, bits and pieces of the film continue to surface, and the complete restoration of the original production remains an on-going process. The current (1996) status of the complete reconstruction stands at 5 hours, 13 minutes. This video version was edited from Brownlow's reconstruction into a 4-hour format by Francis Ford Coppola, under the authority of Robert A. Harris and Zoetrope Studios, featuring an orchestral score composed and conducted by Carmine Coppola (Francis Ford's father).

Napoleon is a unique example of extraordinarily advanced technical cinematographic innovation, placing it in a category of its own, incomparable to any other film in history. Some examples of cinematography innovation featured are rapid cutting, cross-cutting between images of a rough sea and the crowds of the first guillotine executions, and Polyvision, the three-screen process invented by Gance.

The biography starts in 1781 with one of Napoleon's first battles — a snowball fight at Brienne College. The movie also depicts how Napoleon was laughed at and ridiculed in his early years, and how he gradually gained respect and worked himself into a position of power. Also detailed are the rise and demise of revolution leaders St. Just and Robespierre, as well as Napoleon's courtship of and marriage to Josephine. The last scene covers Bonaparte's invasion of Italy as newly-appointed general-in-command, and is presented in Polyvision. The tricolor finale — presented in blue, white, and red — representative of France's tricolor flag — must be seen to be believed.

Although this version of *Napoleon* is a vast improvement over MGM's joke of a domestic release in 1928, it is a travesty that Kevin Brownlow's complete reconstructed version is not available on video in the United States or anywhere else. The 4-hour version is missing over an hour of available footage, and was transferred at 24 frames per second, as opposed to the correct speed of 20 frames per second. In addition, this version contains only a glimpse of the footage featuring Annabella (who currently resides in France), perhaps the most famous actress to have appeared in *Napoleon*. Nonetheless, until the complete reconstructed version is available to us, we can be thankful for the footage that we have in the Coppola video version.

A must for all movie enthusiasts!

Videocassette Sources
Columbia House Video Club . . . . #0212704 $29.95
Movies Unlimited . . . . #07-1428 $29.99

The Viking (1928)
Filmed in Technicolor
MGM
Directed by Roy William Neill
Produced by Herbert T. Kalmus
Color art direction by Natalie Kalmus
Cast: *Helga Nilsson* Pauline Starke; *Alwin* Leroy Mason; *Leif Ericsson* Donald Crisp; *Eric the Red* Anders Randolph; *Sigurd* Richard Alexander; *Egil* Harry Lewis Woods; *Kark* Albert McQuarrie; *King Olaf* Roy Stewart; *Lady Editha* Claire McDowell

This was the last of the three feature films from the silent era filmed entirely in Technicolor, and one which has been largely forgotten. The color art director for this feature was Natalie Kalmus (wife of Herbert T. Kalmus, one of the pioneers of the two-color Technicolor process), who later went on to take charge of the color art direction of the 1939 version of *The Wizard of Oz*. Originally, MGM had meant for this R. William Neill movie to be a Technicolor version of *Napoleon*. Those plans were scrapped when the studio received word of Abel Gance's *Napoleon* production then underway in France. Therefore, *The Viking* was born. Due to the rarity of Technicolor silent features, *The Viking* is a movie of significant historical importance. Yet, in 16 years of research, only a few of 600-plus books on motion picture history make so much as a scant mention of it.

Although not a film of epic or masterpiece status, this is an interesting movie based on a novel detailing the lives of Eric the Red and his crew of Viking voyagers. Typical of many films in the era of the Hayes office, this one dabbles in religion — portraying the conversion from paganism to Christianity of Eric the Red, much to the distaste of his father, Leif Ericsson. It also portrays how the Vikings invaded territories and took people captive, and the fear that the mere mention of the name "Viking" instilled into the people. In the final sequence, the arrival of the Vikings in Newport, Rhode Island, is portrayed, and a watchtower built by them which still stands is shown.

Although Donald Crisp is given top billing in the introductory title, his role as Leif Ericsson is relatively small. The leading actress, Pauline Starke, gives a good performance as Helga Nilsson. It is interesting to note that Starke, like the movie, was a significant part of early movie history. Yet, she is scarcely mentioned in movie history books. She was a prolific actress, having made several movies in the silent and the early talkie eras. Starke, who had been a protégée of D.W. Griffith, appeared as an extra in *Intolerance*. *Eyes of Youth* (1919) featured her as a supporting actress in the role of Clara Kimball Young's younger sister, and is also available on video.

Take note also of Claire McDowell, who plays a brief part as Alwin's mother at the very beginning of the movie. McDowell was a veteran actress who started in some early shorts under D.W. Griffith. She also appeared in *Ben-Hur* (1927), *The Big Parade* (1924), and *The Mark of Zorro* (1920), among others.

Considering that only three silent features were filmed in Technicolor (the other two are *Toll of the Sea* [1922] with Anna May Wong and *The Black Pirate* [1926], both listed elsewhere in this book), *The Viking* as well as the other two Technicolor silents are an asset to any silent film collection.

Videocassette Source
Discount Video Tapes $19.95

The Wind (1928)
MGM
Directed by Victor Seastrom
An MGM/UA Home Video Release

Cast: *Letty* Lillian Gish; *Lige* Lars Hanson; *Roddy* Montague Love; *Cora* Dorothy Cummings; *Beverly* Edward Earle; *Sourdough* William Orlamond

One of the last silent era films to rate masterpiece status, this is a drama in which Lillian Gish as Letty Mason comes from her quaint, comfortable home in Virginia to live at a ranch in the Mojave Desert in California, and is tormented by the constant winds and primitive living conditions. A classic of silent cinema, this was one of those silents which demonstrated how well the art of silent cinema had progressed and been perfected just in time to be wiped out by the talkies.

This MGM video version contains a 1988 prologue by Gish herself, in which she refers to it as a "motion" film, and recalls the horrendous filming conditions during which the temperature was rarely below 120°F. In order to do the wind effects, eight airplane propellers were used, which blew burning cinders all over the set. Gish refers to *The Wind* as her most uncomfortable movie making experience ever. To endure what she did obviously took a lot of guts, determination, and sheer grit. By this time, Gish was an actress of such stature that MGM gave her the right to choose her own stories, directors, scriptwriters, and fellow actors — she could have opted out of this one if she so chose.

In Danny Peary's book, *Alternate Oscars,* he gave the 1928-29 Best Picture and Best Actress "Alternate Oscars" to *The Wind* and Gish's magnificent performance in it. Louis B. Mayer, head of MGM, who at that time wielded a great deal of clout with the Academy Awards committee, sabotaged this film's Oscar consideration so that MGM's first musical, *The Broadway Melody,* could win Best Picture. Mary Pickford mounted a campaign for her talkie debut in *Coquette,* and, as one of the founders of the Academy, wielded enough influence to steer the coveted second Best Actress Oscar her way. Although Pickford's performance in *Coquette* was, in this author's opinion, Oscar-worthy, Gish's performance in *The Wind* is still the more Oscar-worthy of the two.

In comparison to Gish's other silent era performances, this performance as Letty Mason ranks a close third behind her performances in *Broken Blossoms* and *Way Down East.* Quite easily Gish's most outstanding post–Griffith performance, this is one that all Lillian Gish fans should have a copy of.

Videocassette Sources
Columbia House Video Club . . . . #0296004 $19.95
Movies Unlimited . . . . #12-1138 $29.99

The Crowd (1928)

MGM
Directed by King Vidor
An MGM/UA Home Video Release
Cast: *John Sims* James Murray; *Mary* Eleanor Boardman; *Bert* Bert Roach;
  Jim Daniel G. Tomlinson; *Mother* Lucy Beaumont; *Dick* Dell Hen-
  derson; *Junior* Freddie Burke Frederick; *Daughter* Alice Mildred Puter

In the first year of the Academy Awards, *The Crowd* won a nomination for Best Artistic Quality of Production, losing to F.W. Murnau's
Sunrise, a production of Fox Studios. Though not a masterpiece on an
epic or colossal scale like *Ben-Hur, Intolerance,* or *Napoleon,* it is a masterpiece in the sense of artistic imagery.

The Crowd is a film which is difficult to describe. Joe Franklin, author
of the 1959 book *Classics of the Silent Screen,* probably gave the best possible description, an excerpt of which is reproduced under the guidelines
of the book's copyright statement as follows:

> Without containing a single situation of "classic drama," [*The Crowd*]
> is one of the single most dramatic films of all time. Without a single
> torrid romantic exchange, it is the most poignant and moving love
> story I have ever seen.
>
>   Its plot is simply a cross-section of many human plots — the story
> of the meeting of two pleasant but ordinary people, their marriage, their
> hopes, their brief triumphs and more lasting disappointments, birth,
> and death. To go into more detail would be to make a great film sound
> trite, simply because human existence is often trite and I don't pro-
> pose, even indirectly, to minimize the power and honesty of this won-
> derful movie. [Copyright 1959 by Joe Franklin. Reprinted with the
> permission of Citadel Press/Carol Publishing Group]

King W. Vidor, another one of the great directorial geniuses of Hollywood, took unknown actor James Murray and moderately recognized
star Eleanor Boardman and cast them into roles which would prove to
be among the more memorable dramatic performances of the silent era.
That in itself was an amazing feat.

The artistic imagery referred to can be seen in the scenes in which
the camera focuses on a huge crowd of people which appears to be just
a bunch of unknown faces, and then zeroes in on the main characters of
the story. The audience is introduced to the characters, and the important events and tragic circumstances in their lives. Vidor makes the point

that despite how important many of us feel our lives are to us, we are, in reality, just faces in the crowd — small fish in a big sea.

Joe Franklin made another interesting point in his review of *The Crowd* in the previously mentioned book. James Murray, who played the lead role of John Sims, led a life which in many ways paralleled that of the character he played. Murray was an alcoholic, who, like Sims, lost all motivation to further his career. Unlike Sims, Murray did not have an outside force to turn his life around. It has been alleged that although King Vidor, around 1932, saw Murray panhandling on the streets for money to buy liquor, he tried but could not convince Murray to stay sober long enough to play the lead in *Our Daily Bread* (1933), the talkie sequel to *The Crowd*. Not long afterward, Murray's body was found floating in a river. It is not clear whether his death was the result of accident, murder or suicide.

Videocassette Sources
Columbia House Video Club . . . . #0296202 $29.95
Movies Unlimited . . . . #12-1134 $29.99

The Last Command (1928)
Paramount Pictures
Directed by Josef Von Sternberg
1927-28 Best Picture Nominee
1927-28 Best Actor Winner
A Paramount Home Video Release
Cast: *Grand Duke Sergius Alexander* Emil Jannings; *The Director (Leo Andreyev)* William Powell; *Natalie* Evelyn Brent; *The Assistant* Jack Raymond; *The Adjutant* Nicholas Soussanin; *The Bodyguard* Michael Visaroff; *Revolutionist* Fritz Field

This is an excellent movie directed by Josef Von Sternberg, also famous for *Docks of New York* (1928). He is best remembered as the director of two of Marlene Dietrich's most successful motion pictures — *The Blue Angel* (1930) and *Morocco* (1931).

Emil Jannings, the German actor who won the very first Best Actor Oscar for his performance as the Grand Duke Sergius Alexander, was magnificent in this role. In the first segment of the film, he portrays a very nervous, humble, frightened man whose head shakes uncontrollably as the result of some past trauma. He is a nobody — one of thousands of extras in the costume lines, glad to put up with the pushing and shoving to make that $7.50 per day he so desperately needs. However, when the movie cuts from 1928 Hollywood to 1917 Russia, Jannings' portrayal of Grand Duke Alexander, powerful Army general and cousin to the Czar, contrasts sharply.

This movie is a haunting portrayal of just how far and how quickly the high and mighty can fall. It is a classic tale of karma — "what goes around comes around." William Powell (who gained fame in the "Thin Man" movie series in the 1930s) plays the director on the Hollywood movie set at which the former Grand Duke Alexander applies for work. When Director Andreyev spots Alexander's photo in the pile of applicants, he remembers him as the general who whipped him and had him arrested as a revolutionist in Russia eleven years before. He hires Alexander, and is now in the position of having the upper hand.

With the use of cross-cutting, the movie goes back and forth between the two time periods, starting in present-day (1928) Hollywood, then back to 1917 Russia in which we see how the two main characters arrived in their present-day positions, and then back to 1928 Hollywood, where Director Andreyev and former-general-turned-Hollywood-extra Alexander meet for the first time since the former Grand Duke barely escaped from Russia alive as a result of the revolution.

As in the case of James Murray, star of *The Crowd,* it is ironic to see the similarities between Jannings' character in this movie and his actual life. Shortly after receiving his Oscar, Jannings went back to his native Germany. Under Hitler's regime, he produced propaganda films for the Nazis. Of course, Jannings and his fellow Nazis were defeated. When Jannings died in the 1950s, he was scarcely missed by the group of people who had once given him their highest honor.

Videocassette Sources
Columbia House Video Club. . . . . #0306506 $9.95
Movies Unlimited . . . . #06-1435 $29.95

Queen Kelly (1929)
Gloria Swanson Pictures–United Artists
Produced by Joseph P. Kennedy
Directed by Erich Von Stroheim

Cast: *Patricia Kelly* Gloria Swanson; *Prince Wolfram* Walter Byron; *Queen Regina V* Seena Owen

This film has notoriety as "the unfinished masterpiece." Having lost patience with Director Erich Von Stroheim's extravagant and excessive spending, Gloria Swanson fired him before the movie was completed. She then cut Stroheim's 11 completed reels to 8, slapped on an abrupt ending, and released this version in Europe. By "completion" time, the talkies had already overtaken the American market, thus prompting Swanson's decision against a theatrical release in the United States.

The photography in what is left of *Queen Kelly* is first class. The interior settings and decorum in the palace sets are especially lavish.

In this film, Gloria Swanson portrays an orphan by the name of Patricia Kelly. Raised in a convent, Kelly happens, on an outing, to cross paths with Prince Wolfram, the fiancé of Queen Regina V — a selfish, vicious, tyrannical woman (played to the hilt by Seena Owen, who certainly would have deserved a Best Supporting Actress Oscar or nomination if such had been given out in 1929).

Although Wolfram is scheduled to marry Regina (actually, it is the other way around) the next day, he is infatuated with Kelly, and determines to see her that night at all costs. He takes extraordinary measures, going so far as to create a fake fire in the convent to set off the alarm, allowing him to take Kelly under the guise of rescuing her. Wolfram gets Kelly to the palace, and they have a wonderful time — until Regina comes onto the scene and discovers them together.

Having been chased out of the palace with a whip by Regina, Kelly leaves with nothing but her nightgown and jumps into the river. Wolfram, who truly loves Kelly, goes to the convent to find her. At this point, the movie shortly comes to an abrupt end.

There is now a restored version which allows us to see what this movie would have been like if it had been completed as originally intended, incorporating previously unreleased footage in which the character of Kelly goes on to inherit the estate of her enormously wealthy aunt. When she goes to claim the inheritance, she discovers that the aunt had been the owner of a chain of brothels.

For the first time since its 1929 European release, videotape has finally made this unfinished masterpiece widely available for viewing in the United States. We can see both Swanson's European release version as well as the new, restored version.

Videocassette Sources for European Release

Discount Video Tapes. $19.95
> Pink toned print.

Nostalgia Family Video . . . . #2155 $19.95
Video Yesteryear. . . . . #1243 $24.95

Videocassette Sources for Restored Version

Kino Video. $29.95
Movies Unlimited . . . . #53-7651 $39.99

The Jazz Singer (1927)

Warner Bros.
Directed by Alan Crosland
An MGM/UA Home Video Release
Cast: *Jakie Rabinowitz (Jack Robin)* Al Jolson; *Mary Dale* May McAvoy; *The Cantor* Warner Oland; *Sara Rabinowitz* Eugenie Besserer; *Moisha Yadelsen* Otto Lederer; *Jakie Rabinowitz (age 13)* Bobby Gordon; *Harry Lee* Richard Tucker; *Concert Recital Cantor* Cantor Joseff Rosenblatt

It is appropriate to close the review section with a review of *The Jazz Singer,* as it was the silent that brought to a close the magnificent silent era with a few lines of spoken dialogue and some songs. Although it is widely credited as "the first talkie," that honor, according to *The Guinness Book of World Records,* actually belongs to *Lights of New York* (1928) — the first *all talking* motion picture.

The Jazz Singer was cleverly produced, and was probably the most appropriate type of story to open the talkie era with. When one hears Al Jolson sing, it is quite obvious that he indeed lived up to his reputation as "the world's greatest entertainer" at the time of production.

It is odd that May McAvoy, the leading actress in the film, was not chosen as one of the three characters to speak. Although rumor had it that McAvoy spoke with a pronounced lisp, such is unsubstantiated. To the contrary, McAvoy was very well received in *The Terror* (1928), England's debut talkie. Shortly after this film was made, McAvoy married Maurice Cleary, then-treasurer of United Artists. She did not get along with Darryl F. Zanuck at Warner Bros., so she made the decision to forget

Hollywood, and instead devote her time to her family. She later worked for MGM in bit parts in the 1940s and 1950s.

One may recognize Eugenie Besserer, who portrays Al Jolson's mother. Besserer is another prolific character actress whom movie history books tend to ignore. A couple of her other silent era credits include *The Eyes of Julia Deep* (1918) with Mary Miles Minter and the original 1923 version of *Anna Christie,* featuring costars Blanche Sweet and William Russell.

Although *The Jazz Singer* is a rather mediocre film compared to the many silent era masterpieces, it remains the best version of the three filmed (1927, 1953, and 1980). Its place as one of the five most important films in all of movie history makes it a must for any historically representative video collection.

Videocassette Sources

Columbia House Video Club . . . . #0361006 $19.95
Movies Unlimited . . . . #12-2238 $29.99

Two: Silent Features on Video

This section lists in alphabetical order nearly 700 silent film features on videocassette. Information included with the title are year of release, major cast members and, when available, the name of the director and studio and a brief description. Also included are the names of sources which offer the title and the prices as of December 31, 1994. If there are significant differences in multiple video versions, these are noted as well.

Across the Plains (1928)
Cast includes: Pawnee Bill, Jr. (a.k.a. Ted Wells), Ione Reed
Category: Western
Video Yesteryear (#1405 / $12.95)

The Adorable Cheat (1928)
Chesterfield Pictures
Directed by Burton King
Cast includes: Lila Lee, Burr McIntosh, Cornelius Reefe
Category: Romantic drama in which the boyfriend of Lee's character is accused of robbing her father during a weekend outing.
Grapevine Video (#ACLL / $16.95)
Video Yesteryear (#1447 / $12.95)

The Adventures of Prince Achmed (1927)
Produced in Germany
Directed by Lotte Reiniger

Grapevine Video (#AOPA / $16.95)
Color tinted

The Adventures of Tarzan (1921)
Featurized Serial
Directed by Robert F. Hill
Cast includes: Elmo Lincoln, Louise Lorraine
Category: Featurized version of the long-lost complete serial, with impressive stunt work by Elmo Lincoln.
Nostalgia Family Video (#2323 / $19.95)
Video Yesteryear (#466 / $39.95)

Aelita: Queen of Mars (1924)
Produced in Russia
Directed by Yakov Protazonov
Cast includes: Yulia Zheliabovsky, Emil Schoenemann

Category: Russian science fiction-fantasy film about a man who travels to Mars after shooting his wife.
Kino Video ($29.95)

After a Million (1924)

Cast includes: Kenneth McDonald, Ruth Dwyer
Category: Drama laced with anti–Bolshevik sentiment.
Video Yesteryear (#1722 / $12.95)

American Aristocracy (1917)

Triangle Films
Directed by Lloyd Ingraham
Cast includes: Douglas Fairbanks, Sr., Jewel Carmen, Albert Parker
Category: Comedy in which Fairbanks goes to an island resort of the "upper class" and wreaks havoc.
Grapevine Video (#19-194-1 / $16.95)
Nostalgia Family Video (#2331 / $19.95)

American Pluck (1923)

Chadwick Pictures
Cast includes: George Walsh, Wanda Hawley
Category: Romantic comedy-adventure
Video Yesteryear (#1518 / $12.95)

The Americano (1917)

Triangle Film Corporation
Directed by John Emerson
Cast includes: Douglas Fairbanks, Sr., Alma Rubens, Alan Hale, Thomas Jefferson, Spottiswoode Aitken, Carl Stockdale
Category: Comedy-adventure set in South America.
Grapevine Video (#22-238-2 / $16.95)
Nostalgia Family Video (#3361 / $19.95)

Anna Christie (1923)

Produced by Thomas H. Ince

First National Pictures
Directed by John Griffith Wray
Cast includes: Blanche Sweet, William Russell, George Marion, Eugenie Besserer, George Siegmann
Category: The original silent version of Eugene O'Neill's play, and also the only one of Blanche Sweet's post–Griffith features on video.
Grapevine Video (#ACBS / $19.95)

April Fool (1926)

Directed by Nat Ross
Cast includes: Alexander Carr, Mary Alden, Snitz Edwards, and "Baby Peggy" Montgomery
Category: Story about a poor man who strikes it rich and gives up everything so that his daughter can marry a man falsely accused of stealing $30,000 from his employer. Baby Peggy plays the daughter as a child in the first half of the film. She has written two books under her new name of Diana Serra Cary, and is living in California at the age of 78 at this writing. Her third book, *Whatever Happened to Baby Peggy?*, is scheduled for release Fall 1996.
Discount Video Tapes ($19.95)
Grapevine Video (#AFAC / $14.95)

Are Parents People? (1925)

Paramount Pictures
Directed by Malcolm St. Clair
Cast includes: Betty Bronson, Florence Vidor, Lawrence Gray, Andre de Berenger, Adolphe Menjou
Category: Comedy in which the character of Betty Bronson's parents are contemplating a divorce.
Grapevine Video (#5-39-2 / $16.95)
Nostalgia Family Video (#2356 / $19.95)

Arsenal (1929)

Produced in Russia

Directed by Alexander Dovzhenko

Category: Russian propaganda film dramatizing World War I events from the Russian viewpoint.

Discount Video Tapes ($29.95)

Nostalgia Family Video (#1824 / $19.95)

The Avenging Conscience (1914)

Mutual Pictures

Directed by D.W. Griffith

Cast includes: Henry B. Walthall, Blanche Sweet, Ralph Lewis, Spottiswoode Aitken, Mae Marsh, Robert Harron, George Siegmann

Category: Psychological drama based on Edgar Allan Poe's The Telltale Heart.

Grapevine Video (#ACDWG / $19.95)

Video Yesteryear (#463 / $24.95)

The Average Woman (1924)

Cast includes: Harrison Ford, Pauline Garon

Category: Romantic comedy

Nostalgia Family Video (#2318 / $19.95)

Babes in the Woods (1917)

Directed by Charles and Sidney Franklin

Cast includes: Virginia Lee Corbin and an all-child cast

Category: Children's fairy tale movie, an adaptation of Hansel and Gretel.

Discount Video Tapes ($19.95)

Nostalgia Family Video (#1839 / $19.95)

The Babylon Story from Intolerance (1919)

Directed by D.W. Griffith

Cast includes: Constance Talmadge, Alfred Paget, Seena Owen, Tully Marshall, Elmo Lincoln

Category: In an effort to boost box office receipts from Intolerance and cut losses, Griffith released, the Babylon story separately in 1919.

Video Yesteryear (#646 / $12.95)

Color tinted

Backstairs (1921)

Produced in Germany

Directed by Paul Leni and Leopold Jessner

Cast includes: Henry Porten, Fritz Kortner

Category: German expressionist romantic drama about a maid anxiously awaiting word from her missing lover.

Discount Video Tapes ($29.95)

Nostalgia Family Video (#2353 / $19.95)

Barbara Frietchie (1924)

Produced by Thomas H. Ince

Hodkinson Pictures

Directed by Lambert Hillyer

Cast includes: Florence Vidor, Edmund Lowe, Gertrude Short

Category: Based on a Civil War stage play.

Foothill Video ($7.95)

The Barbarian (1920)

Directed by Donald Crisp

Cast includes: Alan Hale, Jane Novak, Monroe Salisbury

Category: Drama of greed and racial prejudice.

Video Yesteryear (#1659 / $12.95)

Bare Knees (1928)

Gotham Pictures

Directed by Erie C. Kenton

Cast includes: Virginia Lee Corbin, Donald Keith, Jane Winton, Maude Fulton, Johnnie Walker

Category: Flapper movie

Grapevine Video (#BKVLC / $17.95)

The Bargain (1914)

Directed by Reginald Barker

Cast includes: William S. Hart, Clara Williams

Category: Hart's first feature-length western.

Discount Video Tapes ($19.95)

Grapevine Video (#14-134-2 / $19.95)

Nostalgia Family Video (#2350 / $19.95)

The Bat (1926)
United Artists
Directed by Roland West
Cast includes: Jack Pickford, Louise Fazenda, Andre de Berenger, Charles Herzinger, Emily Fitzroy, Jewel Carmen (wife of director West), Tullio Carminati
Category: Horror classic — the original silent version of the '59 Vincent Price classic which was for many years believed to be lost.
Discount Video Tapes ($19.95)
Nostalgia Family Video (#2304 / $19.95)

Battleship Potemkin (1925)
Produced in Russia
Directed by Sergei Eisenstein
Category: All-time classic directed by one of Russia's greatest directors. Cited by many established critics as one of the greatest films of all time. Portrayal of the early days of the Russian Revolution, concentrating on the deplorable conditions on the Navy ships which helped lead to the revolt. Contains the famous "Odessa steps" sequence.
Critic's Choice (#EARPC000225 / $19.98)
    Republic Pictures Home Video color tinted version
Nostalgia Family Video (#1402 / $19.95)
Video Yesteryear (#6 / $24.95)

Battling Bunyan (1925)
Crown Productions
Directed by Paul Hurst
Cast includes: Chester Conklin, Wesley Barry, Molly Malone, Frank Campeau, Harry Mann, and 1924 Olympic Champion Jackie Fields
Category: Comedy-drama about a boxer and his promoter.

Grapevine Video (#7-59-2 / $16.95)
Video Yesteryear (#224 / $12.95)

The Battling Fool (1924)
Directed by W.S. Van Dyke
Cast includes: William Fairbanks, Eva Novak, Edgar Kennedy
Category: Drama directed by W.S. Van Dyke, who had worked as an assistant director on *Intolerance,* and who gained fame for his masterpiece *White Shadows in the South Seas* in 1928.
Discount Video Tapes ($19.95)

Battling Orioles (1924)
Hal Roach Studios
Directed by Ted Wilde, Fred Guiol
Cast includes: Glenn Tryon, Blanche Mehaffey
Category: Baseball comedy about reincarnated members of the Baltimore Orioles baseball team.
Discount Video Tapes ($19.95)
Grapevine Video (#BOGT / $16.95)
Nostalgia Family Video (#2074 / $19.95)

Beau Brummel (1924)
Warner Bros.
Directed by Harry Beaumont
Cast includes: John Barrymore, Mary Astor, Irene Rich, Willard Lewis, Carmel Myers, Andre de Berenger, Richard Tucker, Alec B. Francis, William Humphrey
Category: Romantic drama directed by Harry Beaumont, whose *The Broadway Melody* won Best Picture for 1928-29. Very entertaining, with a magnificent performance by the legendary Barrymore, along with a star-studded cast.
Discount Video Tapes ($29.95)
Grapevine Video (#26-286 / $19.95)

Nostalgia Family Video (#1435 / $24.95)

Video Yesteryear (#1226 / $24.95)

Beau Geste (1927)

Paramount Pictures

Directed by Herbert Brenon

Cast includes: Ronald Colman, Neil Hamilton, Alice Joyce, Ralph Forbes, Mary Brian, William Powell, Noah Beery, Sr., Philippe De Lacy

Category: Romantic Foreign Legion adventure, with a touch of mystery. Original version of the 1939 Gary Cooper classic. Features an excellent, all-star cast.

Discount Video Tapes ($19.95)

Bed and Sofa (1927)

Produced in Russia

Directed by Abram Room

Category: Drama-comedy about a woman determined to do as she pleases, not as society dictates. Examines the social problems of abortion and inadequate housing.

Movies Unlimited (#53-7020 / $29.99)

Beggars of Life (1928)

Paramount Pictures

Directed by William Wellman

Cast includes: Louise Brooks, Richard Arlen, Wallace Beery

Category: A rare and bizarre classic, in which Brooks' character murders her foster father in self-defense and then tries to escape.

Grapevine Video (#BOLLB / $19.95)

Behind the Front (1926)

Paramount Pictures

Directed by Edward Sutherland

Cast includes: Wallace Beery, Raymond Hatton, Mary Brian, Richard Arlen, Chester Conklin, Tom Kennedy

Category: War comedy which was one of the highest grossing films of 1926. The director, Edward Sutherland, was married to Louise Brooks for a couple of years in the late 1920s.

Grapevine Video (#BFB&H / $16.95)

Nostalgia Family Video (#2302 / $19.95)

The Bells (1926)

Chadwick Pictures

Directed by James Young

Cast includes: Boris Karloff, Lionel Barrymore, Fred Warren, Lola Todd

Category: Drama of greed and mystery which borrows from the story line of Edgar Allan Poe's *Tell-Tale Heart* and Griffith's *The Avenging Conscience.*

Grapevine Video (#15-149-1 / $16.95)

Nostalgia Family Video (#2374 / $19.95)

Video Yesteryear (#964 / $24.95)

The Beloved Rogue (1927)

Warner Bros.

Directed by Alan Crosland

Cast includes: John Barrymore, Conrad Veidt, Mack Swain, Slim Summerville, Marceline Day, Nigel DeBrulier, Victor Henry; Dickie Moore (famous member of the *Our Gang* series) appears as a baby

Category: Action-filled swashbuckler set during 15th century France, with a top-notch cast.

Discount Video Tapes ($19.95)

Nostalgia Family Video (#2303 / $19.95)

Video Yesteryear (#1745 / $39.95)

Below the Deadline (1929)

Directed by J.P. McGowan

Cast includes: Frank Leigh, Barbara Worth

Category: Drama with elements of crime, mystery, and revenge.
Video Yesteryear (#1512 / $12.95)

Ben-Hur: A Tale of the Christ (1927)

See complete review on pages 40–42

Berlin: Symphony of a Great City (1927)

Produced in Germany
Directed by Walter Ruttman
Category: German expressionistic film about life in Berlin, Germany.
International Historic Films (#007 / $24.95)

Betsy Ross (1917)

World Film Company
Directed by Travers Vale, George Cowl
Cast includes: Alice Brady, John Bowers, Robert Cummings, Nellie Fillmore
Category: Bio-drama depicting the life of the woman credited with designing the first American flag. In the title role is Alice Brady, who went on to win a Best Actress Nomination for *My Man Godfrey* (1937), and won the Best Supporting Actress Oscar for *In Old Chicago* (1938).
Discount Video Tapes ($19.95)
Grapevine Video (#BRAB / $16.95)

Beyond the Border (1925)

Ragstram Productions
Directed by Scott R. Dunlap
Cast includes: Harry Carey, Mildred Harris, Tom Santschi
Category: Western
Grapevine Video (#3-29-1 / $16.95)

The Big Parade (1924)

MGM
Directed by King Vidor
An MGM/UA Home Video Release

Cast includes: John Gilbert, Renée Adorée, Claire McDowell, Hobart Bosworth, Karl Dane
Category: Classic war film, hailed as one of the great war films of the silent era. Also one of the top grossing films of the silent era, second only to *The Birth of a Nation*.
Movies Unlimited (#12-1832 / $29.99)

Big Stakes (1922)

Cast includes: J.B. Warner, Elinor Faire
Category: Western
Nostalgia Family Video (#2366 / $19.95)

The Birth of a Nation (1915)

See complete review on pages 9–10

The Black Pirate (1926)

Filmed in two-strip Technicolor
United Artists
Directed by Albert Parker
Cast includes: Douglas Fairbanks, Sr., Billie Dove, Donald Crisp, Anders Randolph, Mary Pickford (uncredited)
Category: Early two-strip technicolor classic about a man whose family is killed by pirates and seeks revenge. Features some good swashbuckling scenes, and a stunt in which Fairbanks slides down a ship's sail on a knife, while splitting the sail in half. In the scene in which Fairbanks kisses the princess, Mary Pickford donned Billie Dove's wig and posed for the scene herself, as she refused to let another woman kiss her husband.
Technicolor Video Version Sources
Grapevine Video (#BPDF / $24.95)
Nostalgia Family Video (#1118 / $19.95)
Black and White Video Version Sources
Discount Video Tapes ($19.95)
Video Yesteryear (#780 / $39.95)

The Blackbird (1926)

MGM
Directed by Tod Browning
Cast includes: Lon Chaney, Sr., Renée Adorée, Doris Lloyd, Owen Moore
Category: Horror thriller in which Chaney portrays a thief who masquerades as a crippled preacher. He plays the game one time too many, and ends up actually becoming crippled.
Foothill Video ($7.95)

The Blasphemer (1921)

Produced by the Religious Film Association
Category: Religious exploitation film
Video Yesteryear (#226 / $12.95)

Blind Husbands (1919)

Universal Studios
Directed by Erich Von Stroheim
Cast includes: Erich Von Stroheim, Francelia Billington, Sam DeGrasse, Gibson Gowland, Jack Perrin, Fay Wray (?)
Category: Romantic drama about a man having an adulterous affair. The film challenged the then-current attitudes about sex in America. This was Erich Von Stroheim's directorial debut. *Note:* One source states that Fay Wray made her film debut as a bit player in this film; the author has been unable to confirm Wray's participation.
Nostalgia Family Video (#2359 / $19.95)
Video Yesteryear (#467 / $24.95)

The Block Signal (1921)

Cast includes: Alan Hale, Sidney Franklin
Foothill Video ($7.95)

Blonde for a Night (1928)

Producer's Distribution Company

Directed by E. Mason Hopper
Cast includes: Marie Prevost, Franklin Pangborne, Harrison Ford
Category: Light, romantic comedy in which Prevost disguises herself as a blonde to see if her husband will cheat on her.
Discount Video Tapes ($19.95)
Nostalgia Family Video (#2394 / $19.95)

Blood and Sand (1922)

Paramount Pictures
Directed by Fred Niblo
Cast includes: Rudolph Valentino, Nita Naldi, Lila Lee, Walter Long, Charles Belcher, Leo White, Rose Rosanova
Category: The classic Valentino romantic drama featuring an all-star cast under the direction of Fred Niblo of *Ben-Hur* fame. This version has some interesting sub-plots not contained in subsequent remakes, and effectively gets across the message concerning the inhumanity and brutality of bull fighting. This was one of the first films edited by Dorothy Arzner.
Grapevine Video (#13-128 / $19.95)
Nostalgia Family Video (#1312 / $19.95)
Republic Pictures Home Video (#0341 / $19.98)
Color tinted
Video Yesteryear (#521 / $24.95)

Blood and Steel (1925)

Directed by J.P. McGowan
Cast includes: Helen Holmes, William Desmond, Robert Edeson
Category: Railroad drama of revenge and retribution.
Nostalgia Family Video (#2393 / $19.95)

The Blot (1921)

Directed by Lois Weber

Cast includes: Claire Windsor, Louis Calhern, Marie Walcamp

Category: Sensitive portrayal of the plight of the family of an under-paid college professor, directed by the preeminent female director of the silent era. Highly recommended.

Discount Video Tapes ($19.95)

Grapevine Video (#2-20 / $19.95)

Nostalgia Family Video (#2391 / $19.95)

Video Yesteryear (#1442 / $12.95)

Blue Blazes Rawden (1918)

Directed by William S. Hart

Cast includes: William S. Hart, Jack Hoxie, Ann Little, Lloyd Bacon, Frank Whitson, Andrew Robson, Maude George

Category: Western

Discount Video Tapes ($19.95)

Grapevine Video (#14-140-2 / $16.95)

Nostalgia Family Video (#2390 / $19.95)

The Blue Light (1931)

Produced in Germany

Leni Riefenstahl Studio–Film Company

Directed by Leni Riefenstahl

Cast includes: Leni Riefenstahl, Mathias Waimann

Category: German drama in which a girl who is scorned by her neighbors leads a visitor to precious jewels that emit a strange blue light. The directorial debut of Leni Riefenstahl, who also cowrote, produced, and starred. Riefenstahl is best remembered for directing *Triumph of the Will* (1934), which remains the most powerful propaganda documentary ever produced.

Grapevine Video (#BLLR / $19.95)

Video Yesteryear (#1525 / $19.95)

Body and Soul (1926)

Directed by Oscar Micheaux

Cast includes: Paul Robeson

Category: All-black drama, starring award-winning actor Paul Robeson in his film debut. A very rare find.

Discount Video Tapes ($29.95)

La Bohème (1925)

MGM

Directed by King Vidor

Cast includes: Lillian Gish, John Gilbert, Renée Adorée, Karl Dane, Roy D'Arcy, Edward Everett Horton

Category: The classic tearjerker romance which was Lillian Gish's first film for MGM. Gish's death scene is especially impressive.

Foothill Video ($7.95)

Borderland Rangers (192?)

Cast includes: Jack Fairbanks

Category: Western

Nostalgia Family Video (#2383 / $19.95)

Brass (1923)

Warner Bros.

Directed by Sidney Franklin

Cast includes: Marie Prevost, Monte Blue, Patricia "Miss" DuPont, Helen Ferguson, Irene Rich, Pat O'Malley, Harry Myers

Category: Romantic comedy

Foothill Video ($7.95)

Braveheart (1925)

Producer's Distribution Company

Directed by Alan Hale

Cast includes: Rod LaRocque, Lillian Rich, Tyrone Power, Sr., Jean Acker, Sally Rand, Robert Edeson

Category: Romantic drama in which an Indian (played by LaRocque) falls in love with a white woman. Also the only movie appearance of Jean Acker (Rudolph Valentino's first wife) on video.

Discount Video Tapes ($19.95)
Nostalgia Family Video (#1723 / $19.95)
Video Yesteryear (#1846 / $24.95)

The Broadway Drifter (1927)
Cast includes: George Walsh, Dorothy Hall
Category: Jazz Age film with flappers, playboys, and gamblers.
Video Yesteryear (#1149 / $12.95)

Broken Blossoms (1919)
Directed by D.W. Griffith
Cast includes: Lillian Gish, Richard Barthelmess, Donald Crisp
Category: Classic dramatic tearjerker. This is one of the greatest performances by Lillian Gish, who plays a battered, teenage victim of child abuse. A relatively young Donald Crisp turns in one of his finest acting performances as well, playing the drunken Battling Burrows. The closet scene is rated by many as one of the greatest dramatic performances of all time.
Discount Video Tapes ($19.95)
Kino Video ($24.95)
    Color tinted
Nostalgia Family Video (#2067 / $19.95)
Republic Pictures Home Video (#0444 / $19.98)
    Color tinted
Video Yesteryear (#1045 / $24.95)

Broken Hearts of Broadway (1923)
Irving Cummings Productions–Select
Directed by Irving Cummings
Cast includes: Colleen Moore, Alice Lake, Tully Marshall, Creighton Hale, Johnny Walker
Category: Drama with Colleen Moore in one of her earlier big roles.
Discount Video Tapes ($19.95)

Grapevine Video (#4-38 / $18.95)
Nostalgia Family Video (#2408 / $19.95)

The Broken Law (1924)
Cast includes: Jack Meehan, Alma Rayford
Category: Western
Video Yesteryear (#1538 / $12.95)

The Buckaroo Kid (1926)
Universal Studios
Directed by Lynn Reynolds
Cast includes: Hoot Gibson, Ethel Shannon, Burr McIntosh
Category: Western
Grapevine Video (#35-1 / $16.95)

A Burlesque of Carmen (1915)
Written and directed by Charlie Chaplin
Cast includes: Charlie Chaplin, Ben Turpin, Edna Purviance, Leo White
Category: Comedy spoof of the famed opera *Carmen*.
Discount Video Tapes ($19.95)
Nostalgia Family Video (#2405 / $19.95)
Video Yesteryear (#1110 / $19.95)

The Busher (1919)
Charles Ray Features
Directed by James Storm
Cast includes: Charles Ray, Colleen Moore, John Gilbert, Junior Coghlan, Margaret Livingston
Category: Baseball film about a country boy who gets a shot at the big leagues.
Grapevine Video (#12-109-2 / $16.95)
Nostalgia Family Video (#2404 / $19.95)

By the Law (1926)
Produced in Russia
Directed by Lev Kuleshov
Cast includes: Sergei Komarov, Vladimir Fogel

Category: Classic Russian drama about two murder victims in Alaska whose companions have the opportunity to administer the punishment to their captured murderer.
Movies Unlimited (#53-7096 / $29.99)

By the Sun's Rays (1914)
Cast includes Lon Chaney, Sr.
One of Chaney's two earliest known performances available on video.
Foothill Video ($7.95)

The Cabinet of Dr. Caligari (1919)
Produced in Germany
Directed by Robert Weine
Cast includes: Conrad Veidt, Werner Krauss
Category: Classic German horror film, known for its impressive sets. This expressionist film portrays a man's gradual descent into insanity. Boring, incoherent, and disappointing.
Discount Video Tapes ($29.95)
Grapevine Video (#3-30-2 / $16.95)
International Historic Films (#002 / $24.95)
Kino Video ($29.95)
Nostalgia Family Video (#1431 / $19.95)
Republic Pictures Home Video (#0480 / $19.98)
    Color tinted
Video Yesteryear (#773 / $24.95)

Cabiria (1914)
Produced in Italy
Directed by Giovanni Pastroni
Cast includes: Lydia Quaranta, Umberto Mozzato
Category: One of the few surviving Italian features from the era in which Italy had a lucrative motion picture industry. The story is about a young girl named Cabiria who is first rescued from a volcanic erup-

tion disaster, and then saved from being offered as a religious sacrifice by the government. This movie features very impressive sets for the time, and was said to have been the inspiration for the Babylon story in D.W. Griffith's *Intolerance*. This one should be seen for the historic value.
Kino Video ($29.95)

California in '49 (1925)
Featurized Serial
Cast includes: Neva Gerber, Edmund F. Cobb
Category: Featurized version of an early western serial.
Foothill Video ($7.95)

California Straight Ahead (1925)
Universal Studios
Directed by Harry Pollard
Cast includes: Reginald Denny, Gertrude Olmstead, Tom Wilson
Category: Comedy about a trip to California.
Grapevine Video (#23-248 / $19.95)

Call of the Klondike (1926)
Cast includes: Gaston Glass, Earl Metcalfe
Foothill Video ($7.95)

The Call of the Wilderness (1926)
Cast includes: Sandow the dog
Category: Early canine drama, in which man's best friend comes to the rescue of his owner.
Video Yesteryear (#1555 / $19.95)

The Cameraman (1928)
MGM
Directed by Edward Sedgwick
An MGM/UA Home Video Release

Cast includes: Buster Keaton, Marceline Day, Vernon Dent, Edward Brophy

Category: Classic comedy featuring Keaton in his first MGM movie; one of his greatest box office hits.

Movies Unlimited (#12-2143 / $29.99)

Campus Knights (1929)

Chesterfield Pictures

Directed by Albert Kelly

Cast includes: Raymond McKee, Shirley Palmer, Jean Laverty

Category: Comedy

Grapevine Video (#18-187 / $16.95)

Captain Swagger (1928)

Pathé Pictures

Directed by Edward H. Griffith

Cast includes: Rod LaRocque, Sue Carol (Mrs. Alan Ladd), Richard Tucker

Category: Swashbuckler adventure film about a thief reforming his ways.

Discount Video Tapes ($19.95)

Grapevine Video ($16.95)

The Cat and the Canary (1927)

Universal Studios

Directed by Paul Leni

Cast includes: Laura LaPlante, Creighton Hale, Martha Mattox, Tully Marshall, George Siegmann, Gertrude Astor, Flora Finch, Arthur Edmund Carewe, Lucien Littlefield

Category: Classic horror comedy from Universal Studios, this was one of the first of the "old house" films, and among the best of its type.

Discount Video Tapes ($19.95)

Grapevine Video (#C&CLLP / $16.95)

Nostalgia Family Video (#1776 / $19.95)

Video Yesteryear (#767 / $24.95)

Champagne (1928)

Produced in Great Britain

Directed by Alfred Hitchcock

Cast includes: Betty Balfour, Gordon Harker

Category: Drama in which a spoiled brat daughter is taught how the other half lives.

Nostalgia Family Video (#1141 / $19.95)

Chang (1927)

Paramount Pictures

Produced by Merian C. Cooper, Ernest B. Schoedsack

1927-28 Academy Award Nominee for Best Artistic Quality of Production

Category: Documentary of the hardships of life in the Asian jungles, shot on location in Siam. Produced and directed by the movie producing duo of the 1933 King Kong.

Movies Unlimited (#80-5005 / $39.99)

A Chapter in Her Life (1923)

Directed by Lois Weber

Cast includes: Fred Thomson

Category: Drama about a woman who brings happiness to an unhappy family.

Nostalgia Family Video (#2422 / $19.95)

The Charlatan (1929)

Universal Studios

Directed by George Melford

Cast includes: Holmes Herbert, Margaret Livingston, Rockliffe Fellowes

Category: Murder mystery surrounding a magic show.

Grapevine Video (#Chh / $16.95)

Charley's Aunt (1925)

Christie Films

Directed by Scott Sidney

Cast includes: Sydney Chaplin, Ethel

Shannon, Lucien Littlefield, Phillip Smalley (husband of Lois Weber), Alec B. Francis
Category: Comedy in which Sydney Chaplin dresses in drag.
Grapevine Video (#CSAC / $19.95)
Nostalgia Family Video (#2281 / $19.95)

The Chaser (1927)
Cast includes: Harry Langdon
Category: Comedy
Foothill Video ($7.95)

The Cheat (1914)
Jesse Lasky Productions
Directed by Cecil B. DeMille
Cast includes: Sessue Hayakawa, Fanny Ward, Jeannie McPherson
Category: Early DeMille effort about a woman who gets into financial trouble as a result of her overspending, and has to borrow money from an unscrupulous Oriental man.
Grapevine Video (#CCBD / $14.95)
Video Yesteryear (#1658 / $24.95)

The Cheerful Fraud (1927)
Universal Studios
Directed by William Seiter
Cast includes: Reginald Denny, Gertrude Olmstead, Emily Fitzroy, Gertrude Astor
Category: Comedy
Grapevine Video (#12-112-2 / $16.95)

Child of the Prairie (1918)
Cast includes: Tom Mix
Category: Western
Video Yesteryear (#1214 / $24.95)

The Christus (1917)
Produced in Italy
Category: Early Italian silent documentary on the life of Jesus Christ.
Foothill Video ($14.95)

The Cigarette Girl of Mosselprom (1924)
Produced in Russia
Directed by Yuri Zhelyabuzhsky
Cast includes: Yulia Solnetseva, Igor Ilinsky
Category: Classic Russian social comedy, and one of the few early Russian comedies known to exist.
Kino Video ($29.95)

The Circus (1928)
Chaplin–United Artists
Written, directed, and produced by Charlie Chaplin
Winner of 1927-28 Special Academy Award
Cast includes: Charlie Chaplin, Merna Kennedy
Category: Classic comedy in which Chaplin goes to the circus. Chaplin received a special Academy Award for ingenuity in writing, directing, producing, and starring in this feature. Acclaimed by established critics as one of Chaplin's best.
Movies Unlimited (#04-3043 / $19.99)

City Girl (1930)
Fox Film Company
Directed by F.W. Murnau
Cast includes: Charles Farrell, Mary Duncan
Category: Romantic drama, which was Murnau's second-to-last film before his untimely death in 1931.
Grapevine Video (#CG20-208 / $19.95)
Nostalgia Family Video (#2412 / $19.95)

City Lights (1931)
Chaplin–United Artists
Produced and directed by Charlie Chaplin
Cast includes: Charlie Chaplin, Virginia Cherrill, Harry Myers

Category: Classic comedy-drama, in which Chaplin plays his "little tramp" character who sacrifices everything to restore sight to a blind flower girl. Considered by many of the established critics as Chaplin's masterpiece.

Columbia House Video Club (#0066902 / $19.95)

Movies Unlimited (#04-3044 / $19.99)

Civilization (1916)

Produced by Thomas H. Ince

Directed by Raymond West, Reginald Barker, and Ince

Cast includes: Enid Markey, Howard Hickman, Lola May, George Fisher, Charles K. French

Category: Classic pacifist epic, which so moved the 1916 audiences that it was partly credited for helping Woodrow Wilson to win the 1916 presidential election, touting a pacifist platform. Enid Markey (who, incidentally, became the first actress to play "Jane" in the original *Tarzan* movie of 1918) portrays an interesting role as a woman who leads the women's movement to stop giving birth to babies who will, in their view, be sent off to war to die.

Discount Video Tapes ($19.95)

Grapevine Video (#CTI / $19.95)

Nostalgia Family Video (#1823 / $19.95)

Video Yesteryear (#1070 / $24.95)

Clash of the Wolves (1925)

Warner Bros.

Cast includes: Rin-Tin-Tin, Charles Farrell, June Marlowe

Category: Early canine drama, featuring the famous Rin-Tin-Tin. This one is interesting to watch, as it was one of June Marlowe's earliest roles. It is interesting to note that before Warner Bros. ushered in the talkie era with the Vitaphone system, Rin-Tin-Tin was their biggest box-office attraction.

Nostalgia Family Video (#2411 / $19.95)

The Claw (1927)

Universal Studios

Directed by Sidney Olcott

Cast includes: Claire Windsor, Norman Kerry, Arthur Edmund Carewe

Category: Romantic drama about a man who tries to prove his virility to a woman who has jilted him.

Nostalgia Family Video (#2431 / $19.95)

The Clodhopper (1917)

Triangle Film Corporation

Directed by Victor Schertzinger

Cast includes: Charles Ray, Margery Wilson

Category: Drama about a poor boy who makes it in the big city. One of the few surviving examples of Margery Wilson's post–*Intolerance* work.

Discount Video Tapes ($19.95)

Grapevine Video (#12-113-1 / $16.95)

Video Yesteryear (#1236 / $12.95)

The Coast Patrol (1925)

Bud Barsky Corporation

Directed by Bud Barsky

Cast includes: Kenneth McDonald, Fay Wray

Category: Sea drama featuring an exhilarating, last-minute rescue sequence. One of Fay Wray's earlier big roles.

Discount Video Tapes ($19.95)

Grapevine Video (#CPFW7-61-2 / $14.95)

Video Yesteryear (#1554 / $12.95)

Cobra (1925)

Paramount Pictures

Directed by Joseph Henabery

Cast includes: Rudolph Valentino, Nita Naldi, Lillian Langdon, Eileen Percy, Gertrude Olmstead

Category: Valentino romance vehicle, in which Valentino's character is torn between a nice girl he works with or a gold-digging, vivacious vamp.

Discount Video Tapes ($19.95)

Grapevine Video (#20-215 / $19.95)

Nostalgia Family Video (#1119 / $19.95)

Video Yesteryear (#1814 / $24.95)

College (1927)

United Artists

Directed by James W. Horne

Cast includes: Buster Keaton, Florence Turner, Ann Cornwall, Snitz Edwards, Grant Withers

Category: Romantic comedy in which Keaton becomes an athlete to impress his female admirer, wreaking havoc on the baseball field. Keaton also experiences some hilarious misadventures while working his way through college. A fine Keaton performance.

Discount Video Tapes ($19.95)

Grapevine Video (#8-89-1 / $16.95)

Nostalgia Family Video (#2068 / $19.95)

Color tinted

Video Yesteryear (#225 / $24.95)

The Comeback (1924)

Produced in Germany

Cast includes: Max Schmeling

Category: German boxing drama

Nostalgia Family Video (#2446 / $19.95)

The Coming of Amos (1925)

Producer's Distributing Company

Directed by Paul Sloane

Cast includes: Rod LaRocque, Jetta Goudal

Category: Romantic drama

Nostalgia Family Video (#2444 / $19.95)

Conductor 1492 (1924)

Warner Bros.

Directed by Frank Griffin and Charles Hines

Cast includes: Johnny Hines, Doris May, Dan Mason, Ruth Renick

Category: Light romantic drama about a streetcar conductor with a heart of gold.

Grapevine Video (#16-168 / $16.95)

Nostalgia Family Video (#2440 / $19.95)

The Confession (1920)

Directed by Bertram Bracken

Cast includes: Henry B. Walthall, Francis McDonald, William Clifford, Margaret Landis

Category: Drama in which Walthall plays a priest whose brother is being convicted of a murder committed by another man, who has confessed to the crime in confidentiality.

Grapevine Video (#CHBW / $16.95)

Conrad in Quest of His Youth (1920)

Paramount Pictures

Directed by William C. DeMille

Cast includes: Thomas Meighan, Kathlyn Williams

Category: Drama about a man who returns from World War I and tries to re-establish ties with his siblings, old romantic interest, and old friends.

Nostalgia Family Video (#2308 / $19.95)

The Count of Monte Cristo (1912)

Famous Players in Famous Plays

Cast includes: James O'Neill (father of

playwright Eugene O'Neill), Herbert Rawlinson

Category: Classic drama, this was one of the first films released through "Famous Players in Famous Plays," the forerunner to Paramount Pictures. This is, in essence, a photographed stage play, using the crude production techniques which were prevalent during that time — no closeups, only full length shots, and some obviously fake "outdoor" scenes. Nonetheless, it is an important film for cinema history students, and very interesting to watch for O'Neill's performance. Incidentally, James O'Neill was also grandfather of Oona O'Neill Chaplin, who, of course, was Charlie Chaplin's last wife. This would make James O'Neill the great-grandfather of Geraldine Chaplin.

Discount Video Tapes ($19.95)

Nostalgia Family Video (#1577 / $19.95)

Video Yesteryear (#400 / $24.95)

The Country Kid (1923)

Directed by William Beaudine

Cast includes: Wesley Barry, Spec O'Donnell

Category: Drama about an evil uncle out to steal his nephews' inheritance.

Nostalgia Family Video (#1708 / $19.95)

County Fair (1920)

First National Pictures

Directed by Maurice Tourneur, Edward J. Mortimer

Cast includes: Helen Jerome Eddy, David Butler

Discount Video Tapes ($19.95)

The Covered Wagon (1923)

Paramount Pictures

Directed by James Cruze

A Paramount Home Video Release

Cast includes: Lois Wilson, Alan Hale, J. Warren Kerrigan, Ethel Wales, Tully Marshall

Category: The first western to be filmed on a colossal scale with a big budget. Cruze employed thousands of extras, and used authentic covered wagons, clothing, and other sets and decor which were from the actual 1840s time period portrayed. According to Robert Giroux's 1990 book *A Deed of Death,* Mary Miles Minter had been the first choice for the role played by Lois Wilson. It is unfortunate that Minter's mother, Charlotte Shelby, refused to let her star in it. Had Minter played the role, it might have saved her film career. The role made Lois Wilson a star.

Movies Unlimited (#06-1719 / $19.99)

The Coward (1915)

Produced by Thomas H. Ince

Directed by Reginald Barker

Cast includes: Charles Ray, Frank Keenan.

Category: Classic Civil War drama

Grapevine Video (#6-60-1 / $16.95)

Video Yesteryear (#1042 / $24.95)

The Crackerjack (1925)

East Coast Pictures

Directed by Charles Hines

Cast includes: Johnny Hines

Category: Comedy

Video Yesteryear (#1188 / $12.95)

The Cradle of Courage (1920)

Directed by Lambert Hillyer

Cast includes: William S. Hart, Tom Santschi

Category: Western about a World War I veteran who decides to

amend his wicked ways upon his return.
Nostalgia Family Video (#1099 / $19.95)

The Crazy Ray (1923)
Produced in France
Directed by René Clair
Cast includes: Henri Rollan, Albert Prejean
Category: French science fiction movie about a mad scientist who attempts to hypnotize all of Paris.
Nostalgia Family Video (#1822 / $19.95)

The Cricket on the Hearth (1923)
Cast includes: Paul Gerson
Category: Classic fantasy story of a magic cricket, based on the Charles Dickens' Christmas story.
Discount Video Tapes ($19.95)

The Crowd (1928)
See complete review on pages 47–48

Custer's Last Fight (1912)
Produced by Thomas H. Ince
Category: Early pioneer western feature pitting cowboys against Indians. A historically important film for cinema scholars.
Discount Video Tapes ($19.95)
Nostalgia Family Video (#2089 / $19.95)

The Cyclone Cavalier (1925)
Cast includes: Reed Howes, Carmelita Geraghty
Category: Western-adventure set in Central America.
Nostalgia Family Video (#2470 / $19.95)

Daddies (1924)
Warner Bros.

Directed by William Seiter
Cast includes: Mae Marsh, Claire Adams, Harry Myers, Willard Louis
Category: Light comedy about four orphans raised by four bachelors. One of Marsh's rare existing non–Griffith films.
Grapevine Video (#DMM / $14.95)

Dames Ahoy (1930)
Universal Studios
Directed by William James Craft
Cast includes: Glenn Tryon, Helen Wright, Otis Harlan, Gertrude Astor
Category: Rare, original silent version about three sailors trying to track down an attractive blonde thief while on shore leave. Otis Harlan was the uncle of Kenneth Harlan, and also was featured in Disney's *Snow White and the Seven Dwarfs* (1937) as the voice of "Happy."
Grapevine Video ($14.95)

The Dancer's Peril (1917)
Cast includes: Alice Brady, Montague Love
Category: Romantic drama featuring family problems which result when a Russian aristocrat falls in love with a commoner.
Nostalgia Family Video (#2467 / $19.95)

Dancing Mothers (1926)
Paramount Pictures
Directed by Herbert Brenon
Cast includes: Clara Bow, Alice Joyce, Donald Keith, Conway Tearle
Category: Jazz Age movie in which Clara Bow plays a supporting role as a flapper whose mother disapproves of her relationship with a wealthy playboy.
Discount Video Tapes ($19.95)
Grapevine Video (#DM10-6-1 / $16.95)
Nostalgia Family Video (#2107 / $19.95)

Dangerous Hours (1919)
Produced by Thomas H. Ince
Directed by Fred Niblo
Cast includes: Lloyd Hughes, Barbara Basleton, Claire DuBrey, Walt Whitman
Category: Anti-communist propaganda film, produced during the post–World War I "Red" hysteria.
Video Yesteryear (#1490 / $12.95)

Dangerous Traffic (1926)
Cast includes: Francis X. Bushman, Jr., Mildred Harris, Jack Perrin
Category: Gangster movie featuring many good chase sequences and gun duels.
Video Yesteryear (#1705 / $24.95)

Daniel Boone Through the Wilderness (1926)
Cast includes: Roy Stewart, Robert Bradbury, Jr.
Category: Historical western
Foothill Video ($7.95)

The Darkening Trail (1915)
Directed by William S. Hart
Cast includes: William S. Hart, Enid Markey, George Fisher, Louise Glaum
Category: Western
Grapevine Video (#DTWSH / $14.95)

D'Artagnan (1916)
See listing under *The Three Musketeers* (1916)

Daughters of Eve (1928)
Produced in Germany
Cast includes: Anny Ondra
Category: German "vamp" movie
Nostalgia Family Video (#1129 / $19.95)

David Copperfield (1913)
Produced in England
Cast includes: Alma Taylor
Category: England's first feature-length film, and the earliest known surviving adaptation of the Dickens classic on video.
Nostalgia Family Video (#2474 / $19.95)
Color tinted

The Deerslayer (1923)
Mingo Pictures
Cast includes: Bela Lugosi
Category: "Poverty row" drama based on the literary classic by James Fenimore Cooper. Many sources state that Bela Lugosi appears in this film. This author has not been able to spot him, as is the case with many other distinguished cinema scholars.
Nostalgia Family Video (#2018 / $19.95)

Desert of the Lost (1927)
Action Pictures
Directed by Richard Thorpe
Cast includes: Wally Wales, William J. Dyer, Peggy Montgomery
Category: Western. Several sources erroneously include this title in "Baby Peggy" Montgomery's filmography. "Baby Peggy" Montgomery and Peggy Montgomery were two different people. The Peggy Montgomery featured in this film was an actress in her 20s who retired shortly after the talkie era began. No relation to "Baby Peggy."
Discount Video Tapes ($19.95)
Grapevine Video (#DOLWW / $16.95)

Desert Rider (1923)
Directed by Robert N. Bradbury
Cast includes: Jack Hoxie, Evelyn Nelson

Category: Western, rated as one of Jack Hoxie's better films.

Grapevine Video (#DRJH / $16.95)

The Desert Secret (1924)

Directed by Fred Reel, Jr.

Cast includes: Bill Patton, Pauline Curley

Category: Western in which Bill Patton plays a lucky gold prospector of the "Old West," and Pauline Curley comes to his aid when the other townspeople learn of his find and try to jump his claim. This is the only Pauline Curley title currently available on video. Ms. Curley is currently in her early 90s and living in California.

Grapevine Video (#DSBP / $14.95)

Desert Valley (1926)

Fox Film Corporation

Directed by Scott R. Dunlap

Cast includes: Buck Jones, Virginia Brown Fair, Eugene Pallette

Category: Very rare early Buck Jones western.

Grapevine Video (#DVBJ / $18.95)

Destiny (1921)

Produced in Germany

Directed by Fritz Lang

Cast includes: Lil Dagover, Rudolf Klein-Rogge

Category: Germany fantasy romantic melodrama, in which a woman has to perform a formidable task to save her lover from the angel of death. One of Lang's earlier efforts.

Discount Video Tapes ($29.95)

Grapevine Video (#DFL / $19.95)

Nostalgia Family Video (#1231 / $19.95)

Video Yesteryear (#1283 / $24.95)

The Devil Horse (1926)

Hal Roach Productions

Directed by Fred Jackman

Cast includes: Yakima Canutt, Rex (the devil horse), The Killer (horse), Lady (horse), Gladys Morrow

Category: Western, acclaimed as one of the best of Canutt's early films.

Grapevine Video (#DHYC12-114-1 / $14.95)

Devil's Island (1926)

Cast includes: Pauline Frederick, Marion Nixon, George Lewis, Richard Tucker, John Miljan

Category: Prison romantic drama about a woman whose husband is exiled to Devil's Island. She chooses to join him there, and later determines to help her son escape. Pauline Frederick was one of the few stage legends who actually enjoyed a successful film career when recruited by Hollywood.

Nostalgia Family Video (#2453 / $19.95)

Video Yesteryear (#1829 / $24.95)

Diary of a Lost Girl (1929)

Produced in Germany

Directed by G.W. Pabst

Cast includes: Louise Brooks

Category: German classic about the difficulties faced in a woman's life when she explores her sexuality. Very controversial and daring for its time, this was the Pabst-Brooks collaboration follow-up to Pandora's Box.

Discount Video Tapes ($29.95)

Grapevine Video (#DOLG / $19.95)

Kino Video ($29.95)
    Restored version

Dick Turpin (1925)

Fox Film Company

Directed by John Blystone

Cast includes: Tom Mix, Alan Hale, Fred Kohler

Category: Western
Nostalgia Family Video (#1647 / $19.95)

The Disciple (1915)

Directed by William S. Hart
Cast includes: William S. Hart, Dorothy Dalton, Robert McKim, Jean Hersholt
Category: Western
Video Yesteryear (#1430 / $24.95)

The Docks of New York (1928)

Paramount Pictures
Directed by Josef Von Sternberg
A Paramount Home Video Release
Cast includes: Betty Compson, George Bancroft, Olga Baclanova, Gustav von Seyffertitz
Category: Grim drama about life on the ship docks of New York City, with first-class performances by Compson, Bancroft, and Baclanova.
Columbia House (#0306407 / $19.95)

Don Juan (1926)

See complete review on pages 39–40

Don Q., Son of Zorro (1925)

United Artists
Directed by Donald Crisp
Cast includes: Douglas Fairbanks, Sr., Donald Crisp, Mary Astor, Jean Hersholt, Warner Oland
Category: Classic adventure which was Fairbanks' sequel to *The Mark of Zorro*. This features the swash-buckling athlete at the height of his career. In addition to Fairbanks, the film features an all-star cast. Recommended.
Discount Video Tapes ($19.95)
Grapevine Video (#13-122 / $19.95)
Nostalgia Family video (#1436 / $19.95)
Video Yesteryear (#971 / $39.95)

Doomsday (1928)

Paramount Pictures
Directed by Rowland Lee
Cast includes: Gary Cooper, Florence Vidor
Category: Romantic drama about a woman who breaks up with the man she truly loves to marry a wealthy man, and soon realizes that happiness cannot be bought. One of Gary Cooper's most significant early roles.
Grapevine Video ($19.95)

Down to Earth (1917)

Paramount Artcraft
Directed by John Emerson
Cast includes: Douglas Fairbanks, Sr., Eileen Percy, Gustav Von Seyffertitz
Category: Satirical romantic comedy
Grapevine Video (#13-127-2 / $16.95)
Nostalgia Family Video (#2482 / $19.95)

Down to the Sea in Ships (1922)

Whaling Film Corporation
Directed by Elmer Clifton
Cast includes: Clara Bow, Raymond McKee, Anita Fremault (a.k.a. Anita Louise)
Category: Interesting sea drama, which was also Clara Bow's film debut in a supporting role.
Discount Video Tapes ($19.95)
Grapevine Video (#3-32 / $19.95)

The Drake Case (1929)

Cast includes: Robert Frasier, Doris Lloyd
Foothill Video ($7.95)

Dream Street (1921)

Directed by D.W. Griffith
Cast includes: Carol Dempster, Tyrone Power, Sr., Ralph Graves

Category: Interesting, rare Griffith drama portraying good vs. evil.
Video Yesteryear (#811 / $39.95)

Dr. Jack (1922)

Directed by Fred Newmeyer
Cast includes: Harold Lloyd, Anna Townsend, Mickey Daniels, Mildred Davis
Category: One of Lloyd's earlier feature films, which finds him in a haunted house.
Foothill Video ($7.95)

Dr. Jekyll and Mr. Hyde
(1911)

Cast includes: James Cruze
Category: Very rare, early one-reel adaptation of Stevenson's novel starring James Cruze, who would later become a prominent director at Paramount Pictures. Runs 11 minutes.
Grapevine Video (#DJ&MHDF / $14.95)
Includes the 1920 Sheldon Lewis version on the same tape.
Nostalgia Family video (#1581 / $19.95)

Dr. Jekyll and Mr. Hyde
(1913)

Universal Studios
Cast includes: King Baggot, James Gail
Category: The very first Universal Studios horror film, which runs 30 minutes, featuring King Baggot in the lead role before he, too, became a well-known director.
Discount Video Tapes ($19.95)
Nostalgia Family Video (#2480 / $19.95)

Dr. Jekyll and Mr. Hyde
(1920)

Paramount Pictures

Directed by John S. Robertson
Cast includes: John Barrymore, Martha Mansfield, Nita Naldi, Louis Wolheim, Brandon Hurst
Category: Most famous silent version of the Stevenson horror classic, in which John Barrymore delivers what is considered by many to be among the greatest performances of the entire silent era. The lead actress is Martha Mansfield, in her only film performance available on video. In 1923, while she was filming *The Warrens of Virginia* (released 1924), Mansfield's dress was accidentally set on fire, resulting in her horrible, tragic death at age 23 from the severe burns she suffered. Very highly recommended for Barrymore's performance, as well as for the rare chance to see the beautiful and talented Martha Mansfield.
Discount Video Tapes ($19.95)
Grapevine Video (#DJ&MHJB / $16.95)
Kino Video ($29.95)
Color tinted, contains clips from two other silent versions.
Nostalgia Family Video (#1581B / $19.95)
Republic Pictures Home Video (#1068 / $19.98)
Color tinted
Video Yesteryear (#1218 / $24.95)

Dr. Jekyll and Mr. Hyde
(1920)

Directed by Charles J. Hayden
Cast includes: Sheldon Lewis
Category: The little seen "other" 1920 version of the Stevenson story, which holds up just as well as more highly acclaimed versions, with a surprise twist at the end.
Nostalgia Family Video (#2479 / $19.95)
Video Yesteryear (#1504 / $24.95)

Dr. Mabuse, the Gambler, Part 1 (1922)

Produced in Germany
Directed by Fritz Lang
Cast includes: Rudolf Klein-Rogge, Audegede Nissen, Alfred Abel
Category: Part one of a thrilling, two-part crime suspense movie serial.
Discount Video Tapes ($29.95)
Nostalgia Family video (#1226 / $19.95)

Dr. Mabuse, the Gambler, Part 2 (1922)

Produced in Germany
Directed by Fritz Lang
Cast includes: Rudolf Klein-Rogge, Audegede Nissen, Alfred Abel
Category: Part 2 and conclusion of Lang's German classic.
Discount Video Tapes ($29.95)
Nostalgia Family Video (#1227 / $19.95)

The Drop Kick (1927)

Inspiration–United Artists
Directed by Millard Webb
Cast includes: Richard Barthelmess, Barbara Kent, Dorothy Revier, John Wayne (film debut in a cameo)
Category: Football murder mystery
Grapevine Video (#DKRB / $16.95)
Nostalgia Family Video (#1326 / $19.95)

Dynamite Dan (1924)

Cast includes: Boris Karloff, Kenneth McDonald
Category: Boxing drama
Nostalgia Family Video (#3239 / $19.95)

The Eagle (1925)

United Artists
Directed by Clarence Brown
Cast includes: Rudolph Valentino, Vilma Banky, Louise Dresser, Spottiswoode Aitken, Gustav Von Seyffertitz
Category: Intriguing story of murder and revenge. Valentino's next-to-last film.
Discount Video Tapes ($19.95)
Grapevine Video (#ERV / $16.95)
Nostalgia Family Video (#1313 / $19.95)
Video Yesteryear (#884 / $24.95)

Eagle of the Sea (1926)

Paramount Pictures
Directed by Frank Lloyd
Cast includes: Florence Vidor, Ricardo Cortez, Sam DeGrasse, Boris Karloff, George Irving
Category: Historical drama about buccaneer Jean LaFitte.
Foothill Video ($7.95)

Earth (1930)

Produced in Russia
Directed by Alexander Dovzhenko
Category: Hailed as one of the great masterpieces of Russian (and world) cinema, this is a drama about a pro–Communist agitator terrorizing a farm village.
Kino Video ($29.95)
Video Yesteryear (#1088 / $24.95)

Easy Virtue (1927)

Produced in Great Britain
Directed by Alfred Hitchcock
Cast includes: Franklin Dyall, Isabel Jean (at one time married to Claude Rains), Eric Bransby Williams, Benita Hume, Ian Hunter
Category: Early British Hitchcock drama about alcoholism and adultery.
Discount Video Tapes ($19.95)
Grapevine Video (#EVAH / $16.95)

Nostalgia Family Video (#2023 / $19.95)

Video Yesteryear (#1080 / $24.95)

Ella Cinders (1926)
First National Pictures
Directed by Alfred E. Green
Cast includes: Colleen Moore, Lloyd Hughes, Vera Lewis, Harry Langdon (cameo)
Category: Colleen Moore plays an ordinary girl who wins a trip to Hollywood and lands a major movie contract.
Discount Video Tapes ($19.95)
Grapevine Video (#ECCM / $16.95)
Nostalgia Family Video (#2502 / $19.95)

The End of St. Petersburg (1927)
Produced in Russia
Directed by V.I. Pudovkin
Cast includes: Ivan Chuvelev, A.P. Chistiakov
Category: Classic Russian strike drama, reminiscent of the times leading up to the Russian Revolution.
Discount Video Tapes ($29.95)
Kino Video ($29.95)
Nostalgia Family Video (#1825 / $19.95)

Eve's Leaves (1926)
DeMille Pictures–Producer's Distributing Corporation
Directed by Paul Sloane
Cast includes: Leatrice Joy, William Boyd, Walter Long, Arthur Hoyt, Robert Edeson
Category: Romantic comedy-adventure
Grapevine Video (#1-5 / $19.95)

Evolution (1923)
Produced by Max Fleischer
Animation by Willis O'Brien

Category: Rare, animated classic on the theory of evolution, very controversial for its day. Also includes a segment on Einstein's theory of relativity.
Nostalgia Family Video (#1203 / $19.95)

The Extra Girl (1923)
Produced by Mack Sennett
Directed by F. Richard Jones
Cast includes: Mabel Normand, George Nichols, Ralph Graves, William Desmond, Billy Bevan
Category: Normand's last feature-length comedy, in which she plays a country girl set on Hollywood stardom. Includes the famous sequence in which Normand leads a lion around the studio lot.
Grapevine Video (#7-75 / $19.95)
Nostalgia Family Video (#2496 / $19.95)
Video Yesteryear (#1171 / $24.95)

The Extraordinary Adventures of Mr. West in the Land of the Bolsheviks (1924)
Produced in Russia
Directed by Lev Kuleshov
Cast includes: Boris Barnet
Category: Russian comedy satire on American culture.
Kino Video ($29.95)

Eyes of Youth (1919)
Garson Studios
Directed by Albert Parker
Cast includes: Clara Kimball Young, Pauline Starke, Ralph Lewis, Milton Sills, Edmund Lowe, Rudolph Valentino
Category: Fantasy drama film starring Clara Kimball Young, one of the most popular of the Vitagraph

actresses in the early teens. Young plays a woman torn between ambition, family, wealth, and true love. Through a Hindu visiting America in hopes of spreading his message of purity of heart, she gets the opportunity to look into a crystal ball to see which way each path would lead five years down the road.
Grapevine Video (#4-42-1 / $16.95)
Nostalgia Family Video (#1315 / $19.95)
Video Yesteryear (#1433 / $24.95)

Eyes Right (1926)
Cast includes: Francis X. Bushman, Jr.
Category: Romantic drama about life in the military.
Discount Video Tapes ($19.95)
Nostalgia Family Video (#2494 / $19.95)
Video Yesteryear (#465 / $12.95)

Fall of the House of Usher (1928)
Cast includes: Melville Weber, Marguerite Gance
Category: Advertised in Nostalgia's catalogue as "two versions of Poe's classic horror story." English subtitles.
Nostalgia Family Video (#2291 / $19.95)

The Fall of the Romanov Dynasty (1928)
Produced in Russia
Directed by Esther Shub
Category: Russian silent documentary depicting the fall of the Czar and the rise of communism during the Russian Revolution.
Kino Video ($29.95)

False Faces (1919)
Universal Studios

Cast includes: Lon Chaney, Sr., Henry B. Walthall
Category: Very rare early spy drama from Universal Studios, featuring Chaney as a German spy. Advertised as having fair picture quality.
Nostalgia Family Video (#1574 / $19.95)

Fangs of Fate (1925)
Cast includes: Bill Patton, Dorothy Donald
Category: Western
Video Yesteryear (#1501 / $12.95)

The Farmer's Wife (1928)
Produced in Great Britain
Directed by Alfred Hitchcock
Cast includes: Jameson Thomas, Lillian Hall-Davies, Gordon Harker
Category: Rare British comedy directed by Hitchcock, about a farmer seeking a new wife after his first dies. One of Hitchcock's very few non-horror/mystery films.
Discount Video Tapes ($19.95)
Nostalgia Family Video (#2024 / $19.95)

The Fatal Passions of Dr. Mabuse (1922)
Produced in Germany
Directed by Fritz Lang
Featurized version of Lang's two-part movie serial, Dr. Mabuse, the Gambler. See pages 72 and 73.
Discount Video Tapes ($29.95)
Nostalgia Family Video (#2491 / $19.95)

Father Sergius (1917)
Produced in Russia
Directed by Yakov Protozanov
Cast includes: Ivan Mozhukhin
Category: Exceedingly rare example of Russian feature-length dramatic

cinema from the Czarist monarchy era. Based on Leo Tolstoy's story.
Video Yesteryear (#272 / $24.95)

Faust (1926)
Produced in Germany
Directed by F.W. Murnau
Cast includes: Emil Jannings, Camilla Horn, William Dieterle
Category: F.W. Murnau's last German movie before his emigration to America.
Grapevine Video (#13-129 / $19.95)
Nostalgia Family Video ($2489 / $19.95)
Video Yesteryear (#1467 / $24.95)

Feel My Pulse (1928)
Paramount Pictures
Directed by Gregory LaCava
Cast includes: Bebe Daniels, Richard Arlen, William Powell
Category: Delightful romantic comedy in which Bebe Daniels plays an heiress who runs into a lot of unexpected surprises when she retreats to her recently acquired island sanitarium for "peace and quiet."
Nostalgia Family Video (#2699 / $19.95)
Video Yesteryear (#518 / $24.95)

Fifty-Thousand Dollar Reward (1924)
Clifford S. Efelt Productions
Directed by Clifford S. Efelt
Cast includes: Ken Maynard, Esther Ralston, Lillian Leighton
Category: Ken Maynard's debut western.
Discount Video Tapes ($19.95)
Grapevine Video (#22-234-1 / $14.95)

Fighters of the Saddle (1929)
Cast includes: Art Acord
Category: Western
Nostalgia Family Video (#2522 / $19.95)

The Fighting American (1924)
Universal Studios
Directed by Tom Forman
Cast includes: Mary Astor, Pat O'Malley, Warner Oland, Raymond Hatton
Category: Romantic comedy
Grapevine Video ($16.95)

The Fighting Coward (1923)
Paramount Pictures
Directed by James Cruze
Cast includes: Mary Astor, Cullen Landis, Phyllis Haver, Ernest Torrence, Noah Beery, Sr., Van Mattimore (a.k.a. Richard Arlen)
Category: Romantic drama of a man trying to be something he is not to impress his girlfriend.
Grapevine Video (#FCCL / $16.95)
Nostalgia Family Video (#2308B / $19.95)

The Fighting Eagle (1927)
Warner Bros.
Directed by Donald Crisp
Cast includes: Rod LaRocque, Phyllis Haver
Category: Drama in which an Army officer during Napoleon's reign prevents an act of treason from occurring.
Nostalgia Family Video (#2521 / $19.95)

Fighting Jack (1926)
Goodwill Productions
Directed by Louis Chauder
Cast includes: Bill Bailey, Hazel Deane
Category: Western
Grapevine Video (#FJBB / $14.95)

The Fighting Legion (1930)
Universal Studios
Directed by Harry J. Brown
Cast includes: Ken Maynard, Dorothy Dwan, Frank Rice, Charles Whittaker

Category: Western which was filmed in both silent and sound versions; this is the silent version.
Grapevine Video (#FLKM / $16.95)

The Fighting Stallion (1926)
Goodwill Productions
Directed by Ben Wilson
Cast includes: Yakima Canutt, Neva Gerber
Category: Western
Discount Video Tapes ($19.95)
Grapevine Video (#FSYC / $16.95)
Video Yesteryear (#1220 / $24.95)

The Final Extra (1927)
Directed by James P. Hogan
Cast includes: Marguerite de la Motte, Grant Withers
Category: Drama containing touches of career and romantic rivalry, theater dancing, and mystery.
Discount Video Tapes ($19.95)
Video Yesteryear (#1145 / $12.95)

Flesh and Blood (1922)
Directed by Irving Cummings
Cast includes: Lon Chaney, Sr., Edith Roberts, Noah Beery, Sr., Ralph Lewis
Category: Drama of betrayal and revenge, in which Chaney plays a lawyer out to get revenge on the man who framed him and had him unjustly imprisoned for fifteen years. In order to carry out the revenge plan, Chaney's character disguises himself as a helpless cripple. A chilling, suspense-filled movie.
Discount Video Tapes ($19.95)
Nostalgia Family Video (#2517 / $19.95)
Video Yesteryear (#1182 / $24.95)

Flesh and the Devil (1927)
MGM
Directed by Clarence Brown

An MGM/UA Home Video Release
Cast includes: Greta Garbo, John Gilbert, Lars Hanson, Eugenie Besserer, Barbara Kent, George Fawcett
Category: Romantic melodrama in which two life-long army buddies fall in love with the same woman, creating a sticky love triangle. This was the very first film to feature the legendary teaming of Greta Garbo and John Gilbert.
Columbia House Video Club (#0296301 / $19.95)
MC Film Festival ($29.95)

Flirting with Fate (1916)
Triangle Film Corporation
Directed by William Christy Cabanne
Cast includes: Douglas Fairbanks, Sr., Andre de Berenger
Category: Comedy-drama in which Fairbanks plays a man who hires someone to kill him, and then changes his mind and decides he wants to live after all.
Discount Video Tapes ($19.95)
Nostalgia Family Video (#2698 / $19.95)

The Flying Scotsman (1929)
(Part-talkie)
Cast includes: Ray Milland
Category: Early adventure film starring Ray Milland, 16 years before he won the 1945 Best Actor Oscar for *The Lost Weekend*.
Discount Video Tapes ($19.95)

A Fool There Was (1914)
See complete review on pages 7–8

Foolish Wives (1922)
Universal Studios
Directed by Erich Von Stroheim
Cast includes: Erich Von Stroheim, Mae Bush, Maude George, Dale Fuller, Patricia "Miss" DuPont, Harrison Ford

Category: Romantic drama in which a man poses as an aristocrat to blackmail wealthy women.
Discount Video Tapes ($19.95)
Grapevine Video (#25-269 / $19.95)
Nostalgia Family Video (#1776 / $19.95)

For Heaven's Sake (1926)
Harold Lloyd Corportion–Paramount
Directed by Sam Taylor
Cast includes: Harold Lloyd, Jobyna Ralston
Category: Comedy in which Lloyd plays a wealthy aristocrat, who donates a large sum of money to the local homeless shelter operated by Jobyna Ralston and her father.
Foothill Video ($7.95)

The Forbidden City (1918)
Select Motion Pictures
Directed by Sidney Franklin
Cast includes: Norma Talmadge, Thomas Meighan
Category: Romantic drama with a plot similar to that of *Madama Butterfly*.
MC Film Festival ($24.95)

Fortune's Fool (1917)
Produced in Germany
Directed by Reinhold Schunsel
Cast includes: Emil Jannings
Category: German drama featuring Emil Jannings in one of his earlier performances.
Discount Video Tapes ($29.95)
Video Yesteryear (#17 / $24.95)

Forty-Nine Seventeen (1917)
Universal Studios
Directed by Ruth Ann Baldwin
Cast includes: Jean Hersholt, Joseph Girard
Category: Western directed by Ruth Ann Baldwin, one of the first female directors in Hollywood.
Grapevine Video (#FS-17 / $16.95)

The Four Horsemen of the Apocalypse (1921)
Metro Pictures
Directed by Rex Ingram
Cast includes: Rudolph Valentino, Alice Terry (wife of Rex Ingram), Alan Hale, Jean Hersholt, Nigel DeBrulier, Stuart Holmes, Wallace Beery, Noble Johnson
Category: Anti-war film portraying the life of an aristocratic family torn apart by World War I. Valentino's first big romantic male lead role, credited as bringing his status up from bit part villain to leading man.
Discount Video Tapes ($19.95)

Free to Love (1925)
Paramount Pictures
Directed by Frank O'Connor
Cast includes: Clara Bow, Raymond McKee
Category: Melodrama in which Bow plays an ex-convict taken in by a wealthy philanthropist. Complications arise when the philanthropist is found murdered and Bow's character becomes the first suspect.
Discount Video Tapes ($19.95)
Grapevine Video (#FTLCB / $16.95)
Nostalgia Family Video (#1438 / $19.95)

The Freshman (1925)
Harold Lloyd Corporation
Directed by Fred Newmeyer and Sam Taylor
Cast includes: Harold Lloyd, Jobyna Ralston, Charles Farrell, Grady Sutton (bit part)
Category: Comedy classic in which Lloyd ends up in a hilarious football game to impress his friends. One of Lloyd's more renowned features.
Foothill Video ($7.95)

From the Manger to the Cross (1912)

Kalem Pictures
Directed by Sidney Olcott
Cast includes: Percy Dyer, Robert Henderson-Bland, Gene Gauntier, Alice Hollister, Robert Vignola, Jack J. Clark, J.P. McGowan
Category: Lavishly produced, early biopic of the life of Christ, with scenes filmed on location in Jerusalem. One of the first six-reel films, and the only feature length film produced by Kalem.
Kino Video ($29.95)
Color tinted.

The Fugitive (1915)

Produced by Thomas H. Ince
Directed by Reginald Barker
Cast includes: William S. Hart, Enid Markey
Category: Classic western, and one of Hart's better early films. This one helped to establish the genre of westerns to follow.
Video Yesteryear (#962 / $19.95)

Galloping On (1926)

Directed by Richard Thorpe
Cast includes: Wally Wales
Category: Western
Grapevine Video (#GOWW / $16.95)

The Garden of Eden (1928)

United Artists
Directed by Lewis Milestone
Cast includes: Corinne Griffith, Louise Dresser, Lowell Sherman, Maude George, Charles Ray, Hank Mann
Category: Well-made romantic comedy featuring Corinne Griffith as a girl whose ambition is to become an opera star. She ends up in a nightclub, and quits when one of the requirements is to dress pro-

vocatively. Louise Dresser's character takes her to a fancy hotel for vacation, where she meets a wealthy musician and is able to finally realize her dream. The only Corinne Griffith feature on video.
Nostalgia Family Video (#1380 / $19.95)
Video Yesteryear (#1478 / $24.95)

The Gaucho (1927)

United Artists
Directed by F. Richard Jones
Cast includes: Douglas Fairbanks, Sr., Lupe Velez, Gustav Von Seyffertitz
Category: Romantic adventure, which was one of Fairbanks' better, yet more serious, films. Also features Lupe Velez in one of her earliest featured roles.
Discount Video Tapes ($19.95)
Grapevine Video ($19.95)

The General (1927)

United Artists
Directed by Buster Keaton, Clyde Bruckman
Cast includes: Buster Keaton, Marion Mack
Category: Classic comedy hailed by many established critics as one of the top ten greatest comedies of all time. Loosely based on an actual Civil War incident, Keaton plays a railroad engineer turned down for military service in the Confederacy due to the importance of his civilian position. Unwittingly, he ends up becoming a spy through a series of hilarious misadventures in his efforts to rescue the prized train of which he is so proud.
Critic's Choice Video (#DQRPC0001476 / $19.98)
    Republic Pictures' color tinted version
Discount Video Tapes ($19.95)

Nostalgia Family Video (#1704 / $19.95)

Video Yesteryear (#527 / $24.95)

The General Line (1929)

Produced in Russia

Directed by Sergei Eisenstein

Category: Russian drama classic about a woman in an economically disadvantaged village who convinces her neighbors to unite and form a co-op. Eisenstein's last silent.

Discount Video Tapes ($29.95)

Nostalgia Family Video (#1230 / $19.95)

Getting Gertie's Garter (1927)

Producer's Distribution Company

Cast includes: Marie Prevost, Charles Ray, Franklin Pangborne, Sally Rand, Harry Myers, Del Henderson

Category: Light romantic comedy, portraying a funny situation in which Gertie's ex-fiancé tries to retrieve her garter without her knowledge.

Discount Video Tapes ($19.95)

Nostalgia Family Video (#2551 / $19.95)

Color tinted

A Girl in Every Port (1928)

Paramount Pictures

Directed by Howard Hawks

Cast includes: Victor McLaglen, Robert Armstrong, Louise Brooks, Natalie Kingston, Sally Rand, William Demarest, Francis McDonald, Leila Hyams

Category: One of Howard Hawks' earliest directorial efforts, as well as one sporting an all-star cast. The film in which G.W. Pabst discovered Louise Brooks and starred her in her two most famous roles.

Discount Video Tapes ($19.95)

The Girl in the Pullman (1927)

Producer's Distribution Company

Directed by Erie C. Kenton

Cast includes: Marie Prevost, Harrison Ford

Category: Light romantic comedy which finds Prevost having second thoughts about divorcing her husband, and then proceeds to chase him on his honeymoon. The director of this film would go on to direct the highly acclaimed *Island of Lost Souls* (1932) with Charles Laughton.

Discount Video Tapes ($19.95)

Nostalgia Family Video (#2542 / $19.95)

The Girl of Gold (1925)

Cast includes: Florence Vidor

Category: Romantic film featuring Vidor as a flapper.

Nostalgia Family Video (#2540 / $19.95)

Girl Shy (1924)

Pathé Pictures

Directed by Fred Newmeyer and Sam Taylor

Cast includes: Harold Lloyd, Jobyna Ralston

Category: Comedy feature in which Lloyd writes a book on the secret of attracting women. Great chase sequence at the end.

Movies Unlimited (#44-1945 / $19.99)

The Girl with the Hat Box (1927)

Produced in Russia

Directed by Boris Barnet

Cast includes: Anna Sten, Ivan Koval-Samborsky

Category: Russian slapstick comedy, with a wild chase sequence over a winning lottery ticket.

Kino Video ($29.95)

A Girl's Folly (1917)
World Film Corporation
Directed by Maurice Tourneur
Cast includes: Robert Warwick, Johnny Hines, Doris Kenyon, June Elvidge, Leatrice Joy
Category: Comedy-drama about a farm girl who goes to Hollywood to break into pictures. She bombs, leaving her in a compromising situation.
Video Yesteryear (#1460 / $24.95)

Going Straight (1916)
Directed by Chester and Sidney Franklin
Cast includes: Norma Talmadge, Ralph Lewis, Eugene Pallette
Category: Drama of betrayal and blackmail, in which a reformed husband-wife criminal team try to start a new life under different identities, only to be blackmailed by a former partner in crime.
Nostalgia Family Video (#2573 / $19.95)
    Color tinted
Video Yesteryear (#1822 / $24.95)

The Gold Rush (1925)
United Artists
Produced, directed by Charlie Chaplin
Cast includes: Charlie Chaplin, Georgia Hale, Mack Swain
Category: Chaplin's comedy classic about gold prospecting in the mountains. Includes the famous sequence in which Chaplin eats his shoe. Established critics split their votes three ways on which film, in their opinion, is Chaplin's masterpiece, between *The Gold Rush, City Lights,* and *Modern Times.*
Columbia House (#0055608 / $19.95)
Discount Video Tapes ($19.95)
Nostalgia Family Video (#1439 / $19.95)

Republic Pictures Home Video (#7110 / $19.98)
    Color tinted
Video Yesteryear (#609 / $24.95)

Golden Stallion (1928)
Cast includes: Maurice "Lefty" Flynn
Category: Western
Foothill Video ($7.95)

The Golem (1920)
Produced in Germany
Directed by Paul Wegener, Henrik Galeen
Cast includes: Paul Wegener, Ernst Deutsch, Lyda Samonava
Category: Classic German film about a clay monster brought to life to save the Jews from being vanished from a Medieval-era village. Impressive special effects photography for the time.
Discount Video Tapes ($29.95)
Grapevine Video (#G-20 / $19.95)
International Historic Films (#006 / $24.95)
Nostalgia Family Video (#1928 / $19.95)
Video Yesteryear (#810 / $24.95)

Gosta Berling's Saga (1924)
Produced in Sweden
Directed by Mauritz Stiller
Cast includes: Greta Garbo, Lars Hanson, Ellen Cederstrom
Category: Swedish romantic drama, which was Garbo's second film, and the one that helped to establish her persona.
Grapevine Video (#22-237 / $18.95)
Video Yesteryear (#1258 / $24.95)

The Grand Duchess and the Waiter (1926)
Paramount Pictures
Directed by Malcolm St. Claire

Cast includes: Florence Vidor, Brandon Hurst, Adolphe Menjou

Category: Romantic film in which a millionaire disguises himself as a waiter to get in to see and attract the eye of a member of royalty whom he admires. Elsie Ferguson, star of the stage adaptation and known as "the aristocrat of the screen," was first choice for Vidor's part, but rejected the role at the last minute.

Nostalgia Family Video (#2699B / $19.95)

Grandma's Boy (1922)

Directed by Fred Newmeyer

Cast includes: Harold Lloyd, Anna Townsend, Mildred Davis

Category: One of Lloyd's most successful films at the box office, this is one in which he plays a double role as a boy in modern society and as his grandfather during Civil War times.

Foothill Video ($7.95)

Grass (1925)

Produced by Merian C. Cooper and Ernest B. Schoedsack

Category: Documentary about the harsh living conditions of the Bakhtiari people of then–Northern Persia (Iran), filmed under hazardous conditions. From the producing team of *Chang* (1927) and *King Kong* (1933). Known for its brilliant photography.

Movies Unlimited (#80-5001 / $39.99)

The Great K & A Train Robbery (1926)

Fox Film Company

Directed by Lewis Seiler

Cast includes: Tom Mix, Dorothy Dwan, William Walling, Tony (the horse)

Category: Western

Grapevine Video (#20-209-1 / $19.95)

Nostalgia Family Video (#1853 / $19.95)

The Great White Trail (1917)

Cast includes: Doris Kenyon

Category: Intriguing melodrama about a woman falsely accused by her husband of adultery.

Video Yesteryear (#1608 / $12.95)

The Greatest Question (1919)

Directed by D.W. Griffith

Cast includes: Lillian Gish, Josephine Crowell, George Nichols, Robert Harron, Eugenie Besserer, George Fawcett, Ralph Graves

Category: Rare Griffith classic in which Gish plays a servant to a farm couple that she knows are murderers.

Grapevine Video (#GQDWG / $18.95)

Gypsy Blood (1918)

Produced in Germany

Directed by Ernst Lubitsch

Cast includes: Pola Negri

Category: Rare, early German adaptation of *Carmen,* which was one of Pola Negri's earlier film performances.

Foothill Video ($14.95)

Hands Up (1926)

Paramount Pictures

Directed by Clarence Badger

Cast includes: Raymond Griffith, Marion Nixon, Virginia Lee Corbin, Mack Swain, Noble Johnson

Category: Civil War drama about a Confederate spy trying to stop Yankees from mining gold.

Grapevine Video (#HURG / $17.95)

Nostalgia Family Video (#2252 / $19.95)

Happiness (1934)

Produced in Russia

Directed by Alexander Medvedkin
Category: Controversial Russian slapstick comedy, which was banned for over 40 years in Russia. This is a hilarious satire of life in Russia under the Bolsheviks.
Kino Video ($29.95)

The Haunted Castle (1921)
Produced in Germany
Directed by F.W. Murnau
Cast includes: Werner Krauss
Category: German horror-suspense movie, in which visitors to the home of Count Oestsch mysteriously keep disappearing.
Discount Video Tapes ($29.95)
Nostalgia Family Video (#1204 / $19.95)
Video Yesteryear (#772 / $24.95)

Hawk of the Hills (1929)
Featurized Serial
Directed by Spencer Gordon Bennett
Cast includes: Allene Ray, Walter Miller, Paul Panzer
Category: Featurized adventure serial about prospectors in the west being terrorized by a half-breed leader of a tribe of Indians and renegade whites. One of only two examples of Paul Panzer's work on video.
Grapevine Video (#HOHAR / $14.95)

Hawthorne of the U.S.A. (1919)
Paramount Pictures
Directed by James Cruze
Cast includes: Wallace Reid, Lila Lee, Harrison Ford, Theodore Roberts
Category: One of the few surviving films featuring Wallace Reid.
Grapevine Video (#HOUSA / $17.95)
Color tinted

The Hazards of Helen, Episodes From (1914)

Four Episodes from the Serial
Kalem Productions
Directed by J.P. McGowan
Cast includes: Helen Holmes in the first three episodes; Helen Gibson in the final episode
Category: Railroad serial
Grapevine Video (#EFHOH / $14.95)

He Who Gets Slapped (1924)
MGM
Directed by Victor Seastrom
Cast includes: Lon Chaney, Sr., Norma Shearer, John Gilbert, Ford Sterling, Tully Marshall, Brandon Hurst, Clyde Cook
Category: Fascinating movie of betrayal and revenge occurring in a circus setting. This was MGM's very first release.
Foothill Video ($7.95)

Head Winds (1926)
Universal Studios
Directed by Herbert Blaché
Cast includes: House Peters, Patsy Ruth Miller, Arthur Hoyt
Category: Romantic story in which a man kidnaps a woman to keep her from marrying the wrong person.
Grapevine Video (#HHP / $16.95)

Heading Home (1920)
Directed by Lawrence Windom
Cast includes: Babe Ruth
Category: Babe Ruth's only film in which he played the leading role available on video.
Grapevine Video (#HHBR / $16.95)

The Headless Horseman (1922)
Cast includes: Will Rogers, Lois Meredith
Category: Comedy spoof of Washington Irving's famous tale, and one of the few Will Rogers silents available on video.

Discount Video Tapes ($19.95)
Nostalgia Family Video (#1601 / $19.95)
Video Yesteryear (#1706 / $24.95)

Heart of a Hero (1916)

Cast includes: Robert Warwick
Category: Bio-pic based on the life of Nathan Hale in the time of the American Revolution.
Nostalgia Family Video (#2589 / $19.95)

The Heart of Humanity (1918)

Produced in Canada
Directed by Alan Holubar
Cast includes: Erich Von Stroheim, Dorothy Phillips, Lloyd Hughes, Pat O'Malley
Category: War melodrama in which Von Stroheim plays a brutal, heartless, and sadistic military officer. Features the famous scene in which he throws a baby out the window.
Grapevine Video (#HOH12-111 / $19.95)
Nostalgia Family Video (#1379 / $19.95)
Video Yesteryear (#1223 / $39.95)

Heart of Texas Ryan (1916)

Selig Productions
Cast includes: Tom Mix
Category: Western
Grapevine Video (#36-4-1 / $16.95)
Nostalgia Family Video (#1214 / $19.95)

Heart's Haven (1922)

Directed by Benjamin B. Hampton
Cast includes: Robert McKim, Claire Adams, Garl Gantvoort, Claire McDowell, Jean Hersholt
Category: Romantic drama in which a man's wife runs off with another man.
Grapevine Video ($16.95)

Hearts of the World (1918)

Directed by D.W. Griffith
Cast includes: Lillian Gish, Dorothy Gish, Mary Gish, Robert Harron, Josephine Crowell, Erich Von Stroheim, Noel Coward, child star Ben Alexander
Category: Griffith's classic World War I propaganda drama, filmed on location in Europe. A portrayal of the ravages of war, both on and off the battlefield. Dorothy Gish steals the show as "the little disturber."
Grapevine Video (#HOWDWG / $19.95)
Nostalgia Family Video (#2026 / $19.95)
Republic Pictures Home Video (#1713 / $19.98)
Color tinted
Video Yesteryear (#1292 / $39.95)

Hell's Hinges (1916)

Produced by Thomas H. Ince
Directed by William S. Hart
Cast includes: William S. Hart, Louise Glaum, Clara Williams, Jack Standing, Jean Hersholt, John Gilbert (bit part)
Category: Serious, sentimental western featuring as the villain a hypocritical, evil minister. This movie is regarded by cinema scholars as the very best of Hart's early films, and as one of the greatest of all silent westerns.
Grapevine Video (#36-8-2 / $16.95)
Nostalgia Family Video (#1215 / $19.95)
Video Yesteryear (#1069 / $24.95)

Her Silent Sacrifice (1918)

Directed by Edward Jose
Cast includes: Alice Brady, Henry Clive
Category: Romantic melodrama about a woman who sacrifices true love

for wealth. One might remember the director, Edward Jose, as one of Theda Bara's victims in *A Fool There Was*.

Video Yesteryear (#273 / $19.95)

Hidden Aces (1927)

Louis T. Rogers Productions
Directed by Howard Mitchell
Cast includes: Charles Hutchinson, Alice Calhoun
Category: Crime-drama about an international jewel thief ring. One of the only two examples of serial king Charles Hutchinson's work on video.
Grapevine Video (#5-5-2 / $16.95)

His First Flame (1926)

Directed by Frank Capra, Harry Edwards
Cast includes: Harry Langdon, Natalie Kingston
Category: Early Langdon feature comedy which includes the famous sequence in which he hitchhikes in women's clothes.
Nostalgia Family Video (#2581 / $19.95)
Video Yesteryear (#1051 / $19.95)

His Majesty, the American (1919)

United Artists
Directed by Joseph Henabery
Cast includes: Douglas Fairbanks, Sr., Marjorie Daw, Boris Karloff (bit part)
Category: Delightful comedy-adventure, in which Fairbanks plays an heir to the throne who performs some miraculous stunt work to prevent a plot to overthrow the king. Fairbanks' very first film for United Artists, the company he cofounded.
Discount Video Tapes ($19.95)

Grapevine Video (#HMADF / $24.95)
Nostalgia Family Video (#2579 / $19.95)

His Majesty, the Scarecrow of Oz (1914)

Oz Film Company
Directed by L. Frank Baum
Cast includes: Mildred Harris, Violet McMillan, Frank Moore, Pierre Coudere, Vivian Reed (the "Oz" girl); Harold Lloyd and Hal Roach as extras
Category: Charming children's fantasy film, directed by L. Frank Baum, the original *Wizard of Oz* author, who made this as part of a series of three films based on his Oz characters. This is the most technically sophisticated of the series.
Discount Video Tapes ($19.95)
Grapevine Video (#HMSOO / $14.95)
Offers all three "Oz" films on one SP tape for $24.95
Nostalgia Family Video (#2037 / $19.95)
Includes *The Magic Cloak of Oz* on the same tape

His Picture in the Papers (1916)

Triangle Film Company
Cowritten by John Emerson and Anita Loos
Directed by John Emerson
Cast includes: Douglas Fairbanks, Sr., Loretta Blake, Erich Von Stroheim
Category: Hilarious comedy, in which Fairbanks goes to extraordinary lengths to get his picture in the newspaper as a prerequisite to marrying the girl of his dreams.
Grapevine Video (#2-11-2 / $16.95)
Nostalgia Family Video (#2578 / $19.95)
Video Yesteryear (#1126 / $24.95)

Hold Your Breath (1924)
Cast includes: Dorothy Devore
Category: A "female version" of *Safety Last.*
Nostalgia Family Video (#3244 / $19.95)

Home, Sweet Home (1914)
Mutual Film Company
Directed by D.W. Griffith
Cast includes: Lillian Gish, Dorothy Gish, Henry B. Walthall, Josephine Crowell, James Kirkwood, Sr., Donald Crisp, Jack Pickford, Robert Harron, Blanche Sweet, Miriam Cooper, Mary Alden, Owen Moore
Category: Early Griffith feature effort, which was a dramatic portrayal based on how the life of one song composer affected the lives of many people. Interesting to watch for the all-star cast alone.
Grapevine Video (#HSH / $16.95)
Video Yesteryear (#813 / $24.95)

The Homecoming (1928)
Produced in Germany
Cast includes: Lars Hanson, Dita Parlo
Foothill Video ($14.95)

Homer Comes Home (1920)
Cast includes: Charles Ray, Priscilla Bonner
Foothill Video ($7.95)

Hoodoo Ann (1916)
Directed by Lloyd Ingraham
Cast includes: Mae Marsh, Robert Harron, Mildred Harris, Elmo Lincoln
Category: Melodrama about a Cinderella-type orphan who feels she is cursed to have bad luck.
Video Yesteryear (#1811 / $24.95)

Hot Water (1924)
Directed by Sam Taylor and Fred Newmeyer

Cast includes: Harold Lloyd, Jobyna Ralston
Category: Funny Lloyd comedy, which finds him in "hot water" throughout a number of predicaments on a trolley car, with his new car, and in a haunted house.
Movies Unlimited (#44-1947 / $19.99)

Hotel Imperial (1927)
Paramount Pictures
Directed by Mauritz Stiller
Cast includes: Pola Negri, James Hall, George Siegmann, Nicholas Soussanin
Category: Classic romantic drama based on a stage play from Hungary, Negri plays a Polish maid who falls in love with a military officer during World War I, and risks her life to save him. This was the last film directed by Mauritz Stiller, who died a year later. This silent version was moderately successful at the box office; a 1939 talkie remake turned out to be one of the biggest flops in motion picture history.
Grapevine Video (#HIPN / $19.95)

Hula (1928)
Paramount Pictures
Directed by Victor Fleming
Cast includes: Clara Bow, Clive Brook, Arlette Marchal
Category: One of the first of a series of Polynesian South Pacific island beach movies popular in the late 1920s.
Discount Video Tapes ($19.95)
Grapevine Video (#H19-204 / $19.95)
Nostalgia Family Video (#1184 / $19.95)

Human Hearts (1922)
Universal Studios
Cast includes: Mary Philbin, House Peters, Gertrude Claire

Category: Romantic, melodramatic tear jerker.
Video Yesteryear (#1604 / $24.95)

The Hunchback of Notre Dame (1923)

Universal Studios
Directed by Wallace Worsley
Cast includes: Lon Chaney, Sr., Patsy Ruth Miller, Ernest Torrence, Norman Kerry, Tully Marshall, Raymond Hatton, Brandon Hurst
Category: One of Chaney's greatest roles, and the one that launched him to immortal stardom. Chaney went all out for the performance, using some crude, painful contraptions and devices to pull off his gruesome illusion as Quasimodo, the hunchback. In the author's opinion, this is the definitive adaptation of the Victor Hugo classic. Patsy Ruth Miller, who is best remembered for her performance as Esmeralda, resided in Palm Desert, California, until her death at age 91 on July 16, 1995.
Discount Video Tapes ($19.95)
Grapevine Video (#6-68 / $19.95)
Nostalgia Family Video (#1140 / $19.95)
Republic Pictures Home Video (#1933 / $19.98)
    Color tinted
Video Yesteryear (#23 / $39.95)

The Ice Flood (1927)

Columbia Pictures
Directed by George B. Seitz
Cast includes: Kenneth Harlan, Viola Dana, Fred Kohler
Category: Rare surviving performance of screen actress Viola Dana; one of two available on video.
Foothill Video ($7.95)

The Idol Dancer (1920)

Directed by D.W. Griffith

Cast includes: Richard Barthelmess, Clarine Seymour, George McQuarrie, Kate Bruce, Creighton Hale
Category: South Seas drama, which was also the last film completed by Clarine Seymour before she died as a result of pneumonia during the filming of the blizzard sequences in *Way Down East.*
Grapevine Video (#IDDWG / $19.95)

In the Days of the Thundering Herd (1914)

Directed by Colin Campbell
Cast includes: Tom Mix
Category: One of Mix's earliest westerns.
Discount Video Tapes ($19.95)
Grapevine Video (#IDOTH / $14.95)
    Also includes *Local Colour,* a 1916 short with Tom Mix.

In the Tentacles of the North (1926)

Rayart Pictures
Directed by Louis Chaudet
Cast includes: Gaston Glass, Alice Calhoun, Al Ferguson, Joseph Girard
Category: Rare drama about a frightened girl who is the only survivor on one of two ships caught in the Arctic Ocean.
Grapevine Video (#ITON / $14.95)

The Informer (1929)

(Part-talkie)
Produced in Great Britain
Directed by Arthur Robinson
Cast includes: Lars Hanson, Ray Milland, Lya dePutti
Grapevine Video (#ILH / $24.95)

Intolerance (1916)

See complete review on pages 11–14

The Irish Cinderella (192?)

Produced in Ireland

Cast includes: Pattie McNamara

Category: Irish adaptation of *Cinderella* interweaving statements of the Irish political climate of the time. The only Irish silent known to be available on video in the United States.

Video Yesteryear (#1140 / $12.95)

The Iron Mask (1929)

United Artists

Directed by Allan Dwan

Cast includes: Douglas Fairbanks, Sr., Marguerite de la Motte, Belle Bennett, Nigel DeBrulier, Dorothy Revier, child star Robert Parrish

Category: The classic tale of the rightful heir to the French throne being thrown into prison with a locked iron mask to hide his identity, and subsequent rescue by the four musketeers. Fairbanks portrays D'Artagnan in his last silent film.

Discount Video Tapes ($19.95)

Nostalgia Family Video (#1441 / $19.95)

Republic Pictures Home Video (#2025 / $19.98)
Color tinted

Video Yesteryear (#1125 / $12.95)

The Iron Rider (1920)

Goodwill Pictures

Directed by Jacques Jaccard

Cast includes: Yakima Canutt

Category: Western

Discount Video Tapes ($19.95)

Grapevine Video (#IRYC / $16.95)

Is Life Worth Living? (1921)

Selznick Pictures

Directed by Alan Crosland

Cast includes: Eugene O'Brien, Winifred Westover

Category: Drama in which a man who is unjustly imprisoned and unable to succeed prepares to commit suicide, but is saved when he meets a wonderful woman who is even more unfortunate than he is.

Discount Video Tapes ($19.95)

Grapevine Video (#ILWL / $16.95)
Color tinted

Island of Bliss (1913)

Produced in Germany by Max Reinhardt

Directed by Arthur Kahana

Category: One of Germany's first feature films.

Discount Video Tapes ($29.95)

Isn't Life Wonderful? (1924)

Directed by D.W. Griffith

Cast includes: Carol Dempster, Neil Hamilton, Lupino Lane, Frank Puglia

Category: One of Griffith's last important films, detailing the hardships suffered by families in Germany during the aftermath of World War I.

Grapevine Video (#ISWDWG / $19.95)

Nostalgia Family Video (#2027 / $19.95)

It! (1927)

Paramount Pictures

Directed by Clarence Badger and Josef Von Sternberg

Cast includes: Clara Bow, Antonio Moreno, Gary Cooper, Elinor Glyn, Priscilla Bonner

Category: The most famous of all of the flapper movies, and the movie that gave Bow the nickname of the "It" girl. A light, entertaining film that is fun to watch.

Discount Video Tapes ($19.95)

Grapevine Video (#IT17-176 / $19.95)

Nostalgia Family Video (#1462 / $19.95)

The Italian (1915)

Produced by Thomas H. Ince
Directed by Reginald Barker
Cast includes: George Beban
Category: Grim drama about the lives of a struggling family of Italian immigrants trying to make a new life for themselves in New York City.
Grapevine Video (#ITA / $19.95)
Nostalgia Family Video (#1463 / $19.95)

The Italian Straw Hat (1928)

Produced in France
Directed by René Clair
Cast includes: Albert Prejean
Category: Classic French comedy that helped to establish René Clair as one of the preeminent French directors. Acclaimed by critics and historians as the best of Clair's silent films.
Nostalgia Family Video (#3362 / $19.95)

It's the Old Army Game (1926)

Paramount Pictures
Directed by Edward Sutherland
Cast includes: W.C. Fields, Louise Brooks
Category: Classic comedy in which Fields plays a pharmacist relocating his family to the West Coast.
Nostalgia Family Video (#1269 / $19.95)

The Jack-Knife Man (1920)

Directed by King Vidor
Cast includes: Fred Turner, Florence Vidor, Claire McDowell
Category: Touching drama about a recluse who adopts an orphaned boy, bringing the main character out of his shell and turning him into a loving, outgoing person fighting to save the boy from being put in an orphanage. Vidor's fourth directorial credit.
Grapevine Video (#JKM-11 / $19.95)
Video Yesteryear (#1406 / $12.95)

The Jazz Singer (1927)

See complete review on pages 51–52

Jesse James Under the Black Flag (1921)

Cast includes: Jesse James, Jr., Harvey Hoffman
Category: Extremely rare, very interesting historical western about a millionaire who happens to accidentally land his airplane at the home of Jesse James, Jr., son of the famous outlaw, and his daughter. They read a book about Jesse James, Sr., and the film details some little known heroic deeds that James did in addition to robbing banks, including his involvement in the Civil War. A 1930s reissue print with voice narrative.
Grapevine Video (#JJUBF / $17.95)

Jesus of Nazareth (1928)

Category: Little-seen, rare biographical religious drama detailing the life of Christ, from birth to crucifixion. The death scene on the cross is especially well done.
Video Yesteryear (#1517 / $24.95)

The Joyless Street (1925)

Produced in Germany
Directed by G.W. Pabst
Cast includes: Greta Garbo, Asta Nielsen, Werner Krauss
Category: Grimly realistic German classic set in post–World War I Vienna, Austria, portraying the devastating aftermath while contrasting the lives of the rich and the lives of the average person. Garbo portrays a woman forced to go to work

to help support her family in a bleak job market. She holds out as long as she can, and finally takes a job as a cabaret dancer. G.W. Pabst's second directorial effort, and Garbo's last German feature before emigrating to the United States.

Discount Video Tapes ($29.95)
Kino Video ($29.95)
  Restored version
Nostalgia Family Video (#2639 / $19.95)
Video Yesteryear (#1274 / $24.95)

Judith of Bethulia (1913)

Biograph
Directed by D.W. Griffith
Cast includes: Blanche Sweet, Lillian Gish, Dorothy Gish, Mae Marsh, Elmo Lincoln, Robert Harron, Henry B. Walthall
Category: Griffith's first hour-long feature is a well-done biblical epic, featuring an all-star cast. This is probably the very best of the pre-*Birth of a Nation* American films. A must for cinema scholars.

Discount Video Tapes ($19.95)
Grapevine Video (#JOBDWG / $14.95)
Kino Video
  Includes *Home Sweet Home* on the same tape.
Nostalgia Family Video (#2638 / $19.95)
Republic Pictures Home Video (#2136 / $19.98)
  Color tinted
Video Yesteryear (#1682 / $24.95)

The Jungle Princess (1920)

Featurized Serial
Directed by E.A. Martin
Cast includes: Juanita Hansen, George Cheseborough, Frank Clark, Hector Dion

Category: Featurized version of the long-lost, complete 15-chapter serial *The Lost City*. This is also the only significant example of Juanita Hansen's work (her role in *The Patchwork Girl of Oz* was minor). Hansen was one of many Hollywood celebrities who suffered the horrible misfortune of drug/alcohol addiction, which led to her highly publicized arrest. Unlike Alma Rubens, Wallace Reid, Olive Thomas, Jeanne Eagels, Mabel Normand, and others who eventually died directly or indirectly as a result of their addiction, Hansen was fortunate enough to recover. Instead of returning to motion picture work, she formed the Juanita Hansen Foundation for the purpose of drug dependency treatment.

Grapevine Video (#6-1 / $16.95)

Just Tony (1922)

Fox Film Company
Directed by Lynn Reynolds
Cast includes: Tom Mix, Claire Adams, Tony (the horse)
Category: Western in which Mix's horse, Tony, is the featured attraction.

Discount Video Tapes ($19.95)
Grapevine Video (#1-3 / $19.95)
Nostalgia Family Video (#2161 / $19.95)

Juve Contre Fantomas (1913)

Produced in France
Directed by Louis Feuillade
Cast includes: Rene Navarre
Category: Early French feature about a cop chasing a villain. Features English titles, as do all foreign films in this book unless otherwise specified.

Nostalgia Family Video (#2161 / $19.95)

Kean (1927)

Produced in France
Cast includes: Ivan Moujouskine
Category: French feature film. This film has French title cards.
Nostalgia Family Video (#2003 / $19.95)
Color tinted

The Kid (1921)

Chaplin–First National
Directed by Charlie Chaplin
Cast includes: Charlie Chaplin, Jackie Coogan, Edna Purviance, Charles Reisner, Esther Ralson
Category: Chaplin's first feature film, as well as the feature debut of Jackie Coogan. In the author's opinion (which will face great dissent on the part of the established critics), this ranks as Chaplin's masterpiece over all of his other films. Esther Ralston appears as one of the angels in the dream sequence.
Movies Unlimited (#04-3041 / $19.99)

Kid Boots (1926)

Paramount Pictures
Directed by Frank Tuttle
Cast includes: Billie Dove, Clara Bow, Eddie Cantor, Lawrence Gray, Natalie Kingston
Category: The film debut of Eddie Cantor, which is also one of two Billie Dove movies available on video. Ms. Dove currently resides in California.
Foothill Video ($7.95)

The Kid Brother (1927)

Directed by Ted Wilde
Cast includes: Harold Lloyd, Jobyna Ralston, Constantine Romanoff
Category: Classic Lloyd comedy about the "weakling" of a sheriff's three sons trying to gain acceptance on the same level as his two brothers.

He gets the opportunity when crooks from a touring medicine show steal money entrusted with his father by the townspeople. The sequence on the ship in which Lloyd singlehandedly takes on a villainous murderer (played to the hilt by Constantine Romanoff) with a little help from a monkey is especially hilarious. Considered by many to be Lloyd's best.
Movies Unlimited (#44-1948 / $19.99)

Kidnapped in New York (1914)

Category: Exploitation film about the hazards of living in New York City. This one is so rare that the researchers at Grapevine Video solicited for information anybody might have on this film. This author's research was equally unsuccessful in the quest to find information.
Grapevine Video ($14.95)

King of Kings (1927)

Cecil B. DeMille Productions
Directed by Cecil B. DeMille
Cast includes: H.B. Warner, William Boyd, Jacqueline Logan, Joseph Schildkraut, Rudolph Schildkraut, Montague Love, Robert Edeson, Noble Johnson, Sam DeGrasse, Theodore Kosloff, Victor Varconi, Sally Rand, Bryant Washburn, Ernest Torrence, May Robson, Brandon Hurst, and many others.
Category: Beautifully done, lavish portrayal of the life of Jesus Christ. The Technicolor sequence is especially impressive. A masterpiece, and a must-see.
Discount Video Tapes ($19.95) (catalog does not specify if Technicolor sequence is intact)
Movies Unlimited (#62-7000 / $69.99) Restored version, with Technicolor sequence

King of the Kongo (1929)
Serial
Directed by Richard Thorpe
Cast includes: Walter Miller, Boris Karloff
Category: One of the last silent serials, this is one set in the jungle in which a secret agent attempts to bust a gang of ivory thieves.
Discount Video Tapes ($29.95)
Nostalgia Family Video (#2964 / $29.95)

King of Wild Horses (1924)
Cast includes: Charley Chase, Rex (the horse)
Category: Charley Chase in an atypical non-comedy role.
Nostalgia Family Video (#2625 / $19.95)

The King on Main Street (1925)
Directed by Monta Bell
Cast includes: Bessie Love, Greta Nissen, Adolphe Menjou
Category: Romantic film in which Bessie Love's character becomes romantically involved with a king on vacation in America. Historically important as the film in which Love introduced "the Charleston" to the screen.
Nostalgia Family Video (#1829 / $19.95)

Kismet (1920)
Robertson-Cole Productions
Directed by Louis Gasnier
Cast includes: Otis Skinner, Elinor Faire, Tom Kennedy
Category: "Arabian Nights" fantasy. When one sees this film, it is hard to believe that it came from the same director who in 1936 directed

Reefer Madness, the popular marijuana exploitation film which was so bad that it has become a cult classic.
Video Yesteryear (#1491 / $24.95)

The Kiss (1929)
MGM
Directed by Jacques Feyder
An MGM/UA Home Video Release
Cast includes: Greta Garbo, Conrad Nagel, Lew Ayres
Category: Romantic drama, which was Garbo's last silent, as well as one of her better performances. Also the film debut of Academy Award nominee Lew Ayres (for *Johnny Belinda* in 1948), who currently resides in California.
Movies Unlimited (#12-2220 / $29.99)

Kriemhilde's Revenge (1924)
Produced in Germany
Directed by Fritz Lang
Cast includes: Paul Richter, Margarette Schoen
Category: Spellbinding German masterpiece, which is the sequel to *Siegfried*, in which Kriemhilde seeks to avenge the murder of her husband. This is also referred to as the second part of *Die Niebelungen*, or *Neibelungenlied*, released in two parts. Highly recommended.
International Historic Films (#004 / $24.95)

The Lady of the Lake (1928)
Produced in Great Britain
Cast includes: Benita Hume, Percy Marmont
Category: Rare British adaptation of Sir Walter Scott's literary masterpiece.
Nostalgia Family Video (#1705 / $19.95)

Lady Windermere's Fan (1925)
Warner Bros.
Directed by Ernst Lubitsch
Cast includes: May McAvoy, Ronald Colman, Irene Rich, Burt Lytell
Category: Adaptation of the classic Oscar Wilde play dealing with adultery in upper class circles.
Grapevine Video (#21-222-1 / $19.95)
Nostalgia Family Video (#2655 / $19.95)
Video Yesteryear (#1084 / $24.95)

The Lamb (1915)
Triangle Film Company
Directed by William Christy Cabanne
Cast includes: Douglas Fairbanks, Sr., Seena Owen, Alfred Paget
Category: Romantic comedy which was Fairbanks' film debut.
Grapevine Video (#15-555-1 / $16.95)
Nostalgia Family Video (#2654 / $19.95)

Lash of the Law (1925)
Cast includes: Bill Bailey
Category: Western
Discount Video Tapes ($19.95)
Nostalgia Family Video (#3363 / $19.95)

The Last Command (1928)
See complete review on pages 48–49

The Last Laugh (1925)
Produced in Germany
Directed by F.W. Murnau
Cast includes: Emil Jannings
Category: Classic satire in which Jannings plays a snooty, elderly doorman of a high class, high society hotel, and is demoted to washroom attendant on account of his age. This film is known for the fact that the story was told without the use of title cards.
Discount Video Tapes ($29.95)
International Historic Films (#003 / $24.95)
Kino Video ($24.95)
Newly remastered, restored version
Nostalgia Family Video (#2650 / $19.95)

The Last of the Mohicans (1920)
Associated Producers
Directed by Maurice Tourneur and Clarence Brown
Cast includes: Wallace Beery, Barbara Bedford, Boris Karloff
Category: Excellent adaptation of Cooper's classic novel. The photography and scenery are absolutely breathtaking. This adaptation is action packed, and the story keeps moving, as opposed to the highly acclaimed 1992 version during which the author fell asleep halfway through. This 1920 version enjoyed a successful, well-received revival on American Movie Classics in early 1994.
Nostalgia Family Video (#2019 / $19.95)
Movies Unlimited (#80-5023 / $39.99)
Restored version

The Last Trail (1927)
Fox Film Company
Directed by Lewis Seiler
Cast includes: Tom Mix
Category: Western
Grapevine Video (#LTTM / $17.95)

Laugh, Clown, Laugh (1927)
MGM
Directed by Herbert Brenon
Cast includes: Lon Chaney, Sr., Nils Asther, Loretta Young

Category: Of all of Lon Chaney, Sr.'s movies, he regarded this one as his personal favorite. Features an early appearance by Loretta Young who went on to win an Academy Award for her performance in *The Farmer's Daughter* (1947), and is another one of the few silent film stars who is still alive at the time of book composition.
Foothill Video ($7.95)

Laughing at Danger (1924)
Carlos Productions
Directed by James W. Horne
Cast includes: Richard Talmadge, Eva Novak, Joe Girard
Category: Action movie in which Talmadge's character must save the U.S. military from a secret weapon.
Grapevine Video (#LAD6-2 / $14.95)

Leap Year (1921)
Paramount Pictures
Directed by James Cruze
Cast includes: Roscoe "Fatty" Arbuckle
Category: Exceedingly rare comedy, this is Fatty Arbuckle's only surviving feature film, which was never released in the United States.
Grapevine Video (#17-169-2 / $14.95)
Nostalgia Family Video (#2646 / $19.95)

Leaves from Satan's Book (1919)
Produced in Denmark
Directed by Carl-Theodore Dreyer
Cast includes: Helge Milsen, Halvart Hoft, Jacob Texiere
Category: Denounced by socialists at the time as hate propaganda against labor workers, this film was modeled after *Intolerance,* with Satan portrayed throughout different ages of human history.
Grapevine Video (#LSB / $24.95)

The Leopard Woman (1920)
Directed by Wesley Ruggles
Cast includes: Louise Glaum, House Peters, Noble Johnson
Category: Spy movie which was one of Louise Glaum's most popular and successful films. Glaum was one of Theda Bara's many "vamp" imitators.
Grapevine Video (#LWLG / $16.95)
Nostalgia Family Video (#2644 / $19.95)

Let 'Em Go, Gallagher (1928)
Directed by Elmer Clifton
Cast includes: Junior Coghlan, Harrison Ford, Elinor Faire, Ivan Lebedoff
Category: Comedy featuring child star Junior Coghlan in a variety of misadventures.
Discount Video Tapes ($19.95)
Grapevine Video (#5-49-1 / $16.95)

Let's Go (1923)
Directed by William K. Howard
Cast includes: Richard Talmadge, Tully Marshall, Eileen Percy
Category: Romantic adventure in which Talmadge (who used to work as a stunt double for Douglas Fairbanks, Sr.) pulls off some amazing stunts in an effort to save the family business.
Nostalgia Family Video (#2640 / $19.95)
Video Yesteryear (#1455 / $12.95)

The Light of Faith (1922)
Cast includes: Lon Chaney, Sr., Hope Hampton
Category: Rare Chaney vehicle which is a short (33 minutes) fantasy drama about an incurably ill woman who touches the Holy Grail and is cured.
Nostalgia Family Video (#1576$19.95)

Lighthouse by the Sea (1924)

Warner Bros.

Directed by Malcolm St. Clair

Cast includes: Rin-Tin-Tin, Louise Fazenda, William Collier

Category: Classic canine drama, and one of the first of the Rin-Tin-Tin movies.

Nostalgia Family Video (#2875 / $19.95)

Lightning Bryce (1919)

Serial

Cast includes: Jack Hoxie, Ann Little

Category: Complete, 15-chapter western serial.

Discount Video Tapes ($29.95)

Grapevine Video (#30-11/12 / $29.95)

Lilac Time (1928)

First National Pictures

Directed by George Fitzmaurice

Cast includes: Gary Cooper, Colleen Moore, Eugenie Besserer

Category: An interesting war film, complete with daredevil airplane stunts. Acclaimed as one of Colleen Moore's very best silent era performances.

Discount Video Tapes ($19.95)

Linda (1929)

Mrs. Wallace Reid Productions

Directed by Dorothy Davenport (Mrs. Wallace) Reid

Cast includes: Helen Foster, Warner Baxter, Noah Beery, Sr.

Category: Romantic melodrama, and a very rare find just recently made available on videocassette. One of the last of Dorothy Davenport Reid's silent era films.

Discount Video Tapes ($19.95)

Grapevine Video (#Lmwr / $19.95)

The Little American (1917)

Paramount Pictures

Directed by Cecil B. DeMille

Cast includes: Mary Pickford, Jack Holt, Raymond Hatton, Walter Long, child star Ben Alexander, Ramon Novarro (bit part)

Category: Wartime romantic melodrama, which was one of Pickford's more sentimental early films. One of Pickford's best performances.

Grapevine Video (#LAMP / $19.95)

Nostalgia Family Video (#2878 / $19.95)

Little Annie Rooney (1925)

United Artists

Directed by William Beaudine

Cast includes: Mary Pickford, William Haines

Category: One of Pickford's "tomboy" pictures, in which she is head of the household.

Grapevine Video (#11-105 / $19.95)

Nostalgia Family Video (#2777 / $19.95)

The Little Church Around the Corner (1923)

Directed by William Seiter

Cast includes: Claire Windsor, Kenneth Harlan, Hobart Bosworth, Pauline Starke, Walter Long

Category: Coal mining drama

Grapevine Video (#LCAC5-56-1 / $18.95)

Little Lord Fauntleroy (1921)

United Artists

Directed by Alfred E. Green and Jack Pickford

Cast includes: Mary Pickford, Dorothy Rosher (a.k.a. Joan Marsh)

Category: Classic "rags to riches" story in which Mary Pickford plays a double role as Little Lord Fauntleroy and "Dearest the mother."

Nostalgia Family Video (#1815 / $19.95)

The Live Wire (1925)
Cast includes: Johnny Hines
Category: Circus comedy
Nostalgia Family Video (#2870 / $19.95)

The Lodger (1926)
Produced in Great Britain
Directed by Alfred Hitchcock
Cast includes: Ivor Novello, Marie Ault, Malcolm Keen
Category: Hitchcock's early silent horror classic in which a London family takes in a boarder, whom they later suspect to be a serial killer after their daughter. Hitchcock's earliest film available on video.
Discount Video Tapes ($19.95)
Grapevine Video (#LAH / $18.95)
Nostalgia Family Video (#2109 / $19.95)
Video Yesteryear (#608 / $39.95)

Lorna Doone (1922)
Ince–First National
Directed by Maurice Tourneur
Cast includes: Madge Bellamy, John Bowers
Category: Romantic costume drama based on Blackmore's classic novel.
Nostalgia Family Video (#2158 / $19.95)

The Lost Express (1926)
Featurized Serial
Directed by J.P. McGowan
Cast includes: Helen Holmes, Henry Barrows
Category: One of Holmes' classic railroad dramas, this is a featurized version of the original lost serial.
Discount Video Tapes ($19.95)
Grapevine Video (#LEHH / $14.95)
Nostalgia Family Video (#2882 / $19.95)

The Lost World (1925)
See complete review on pages 34–35

Love (1927)
MGM
Directed by Edmund Goulding
An MGM/UA Home Video Release
Cast includes: Greta Garbo, John Gilbert, George Fawcett, Philippe De Lacy, Brandon Hurst
Category: Original silent adaptation of Leo Tolstoy's *Anna Karenina,* this, in the author's opinion, is the very best of the Garbo/Gilbert silents, as well as the best of all of the *Anna Karenina* adaptations. This video version shows two different endings — a happy ending that was tacked on for its United States release, and the other ending that was internationally distributed elsewhere.
Movies Unlimited (#12-2958 / $29.99)

Love 'Em and Leave 'Em (1927)
Paramount Pictures
Directed by Frank Tuttle
Cast includes: Louise Brooks, Lawrence Gray, Evelyn Brent
Category: Light flapper romantic comedy.
Discount Video Tapes ($19.95)
Grapevine Video (#LE&LE / $24.95)

The Love Flower (1920)
Directed by D.W. Griffith
Cast includes: Richard Barthelmess, Carol Dempster
Category: Griffith melodrama about the life of a murder fugitive and his daughter.
Nostalgia Family video (#2906 / $19.95)

Love Never Dies (1922)
Vidor–Associated Producers

Directed by King Vidor
Cast includes: Madge Bellamy, Lloyd Hughes, Claire McDowell
Category: One of Vidor's earlier efforts, this is a romantic action-drama of love, lust, and revenge.
Nostalgia Family Video (#2904 / $19.95)
Color tinted

The Love of Jeanne Ney (1927)

Produced in Germany
Directed by G.W. Pabst
Cast includes: Brigitte Helm, Vladimir Sokoloff
Category: Classic German melodrama about a blind girl who falls in love with a communist.
Kino Video ($24.95)
Nostalgia Family Video (#2130 / $19.95)

Lucky Devil (1925)

Paramount Pictures
Directed by Frank Tuttle
Cast includes: Richard Dix, Esther Ralston
Category: Light race car drama.
Grapevine Video (#LD3-33-2 / $16.95)

Lure of the Circus (1918)

Featurized Serial
Universal Studios
Directed by J.P. McGowan
Cast includes: Eddie Polo, Noble Johnson
Category: Extremely rare, featurized version of the 18-chapter serial, this is reconstructed from a print of eight surviving reels that were discovered in Europe. One of very few existing examples of Eddie Polo's work, and the only one on video.
Grapevine Video (#LOCEP / $12.95)

Lure of the Range (1924)

Cast includes: Dick Hatton

Category: Western comedy
Nostalgia Family Video (#2901 / $19.95)

The Mad Whirl (1925)

Universal Studios
Directed by William Seiter
Cast includes: May McAvoy, George Fawcett, Barbara Bedford, Grady Sutton (bit part)
Category: Jazz Age movie of life in the fast lane during the Roaring '20s.
Grapevine Video (#MW1-4 / $16.95)
Nostalgia Family Video (#1382 / $19.95)

Made for Love (1926)

DeMille Pictures–Producer's Distribution Corporation
Directed by Paul Sloane
Cast includes: Leatrice Joy, Edmund Burns, Ethel Wales, Frank Butler
Category: Romantic story set in Egypt about a couple trapped in a tomb.
Grapevine Video (#MFL5-57-2 / $16.95)

Mademoiselle Midnight (1924)

Directed and produced by Robert Z. Leonard
Cast includes: Mae Murray, Don Alvarado, Monte Blue, Nigel DeBrulier, Robert Edeson
Category: One of the rare surviving films of Mae Murray.
Nostalgia Family Video (#1280 / $19.95)

The Magic Cloak of Oz (1914)

Oz Film Company
Directed by L. Frank Baum
Cast includes: Mildred Harris, Violet McMillan, Fred Woodward; Harold Lloyd and Hal Roach were among the extras; Vivian Reed as the "Oz" girl
Category: One of the three "Oz"

movies produced by the original author of the novels. This is a delightful movie in which a magic cloak is invented which will grant any wish. Good trick photography for the time.

Discount Video Tapes ($19.95)

Grapevine Video (#MCOO / $14.95)
Offers all three "Oz" movies on one tape for $24.95)

Nostalgia Family Video (#2037 / $19.95)
Includes *His Majesty, the Scarecrow of Oz* on the same tape.

The Magician (1927)

Universal Studios

Directed by Rex Ingram

Cast includes: Conrad Veidt, Paul Wegener, Mary Philbin, Alice Terry

Category: Romantic melodrama, in which a crazed magician frames one of his employees for murder in a fit of jealousy. Unfortunately, this is one of only two Rex Ingram movies currently available on video. Erich Von Stroheim once referred to Ingram as "the world's greatest director."

Nostalgia Family Video (#1834 / $19.95)

The Magnificent Ambersons (1925)

See *Pampered Youth,* the title under which this particular adaptation was released

Male and Female (1919)

Paramount Pictures

Directed by Cecil B. DeMille

Cast includes: Gloria Swanson, Lila Lee, Bebe Daniels, Thomas Meighan, Raymond Hatton, Tom Moore, Wesley Barry, Theodore Roberts

Category: Interesting, all-star roman-tic drama about a spoiled brat heiress who falls in love with her servant, but will not admit "lowering" herself to fall in love with somebody outside her social class. All this changes once their party is shipwrecked on a deserted island for three years, during which Swanson's character marries the ex-servant in a private ceremony.

Grapevine Video (#M&F / $19.95)

Nostalgia Family Video (#1135 / $19.95)

The Man from Beyond (1922)

Houdini Picture Company

Written and produced by Harry Houdini

Directed by Burton King

Cast includes: Harry Houdini, Nita Naldi

Category: Rare, obscure film in which one can see Houdini's daredevil stunt work in which his character, after having been brought back to life after being frozen for 100 years, sets out to rescue the great-granddaughter of his fiancée from his past life.

Grapevine Video (#3-33-1 / $18.95)

Video Yesteryear (#965 / $24.95)

The Man from Headquarters (1928)

Cast includes: Cornelius Keefe, Edith Roberts

Category: Spy drama

Nostalgia Family Video (#3364 / $19.95)

The Man from Painted Post (1917)

Triangle Film Company

Directed by Joseph Henabery

Cast includes: Douglas Fairbanks, Sr., Eileen Percy, Frank Campeau, Monte Blue

Category: Comedy western
Discount Video Tapes ($19.95)
Nostalgia Family Video (#1842 / $19.95)

The Man from Texas (1915)
Selig Productions
Cast includes: Tom Mix
Category: Western
Discount Video Tapes ($19.95)
Grapevine Video (#MFTTM / $14.95)
    Color tinted
Nostalgia Family Video (#1814 / $19.95)
    Color tinted

The Man on the Box (1925)
Warner Bros.
Directed by Charles Reisner
Cast includes: Sydney Chaplin, Helene Costello, David Butler, Alice Calhoun, Kathleen Calhoun
Category: Romantic comedy in which Chaplin's character is a wealthy bachelor who accepts a job as a gardener to be near his girlfriend, and discovers that the butler is a spy.
Discount Video Tapes ($19.95)
Grapevine Video (#MOBSC / $16.95)
Nostalgia Family Video (#2198 / $19.95)

The Man Who Laughs (1928)
Universal Studios
Directed by Paul Leni
Cast includes: Conrad Veidt, Mary Philbin, Olga Baclanova, Frank Puglia, Josephine Crowell, Stuart Holmes, Brandon Hurst
Category: Romantic drama set in the early 1700s, in which Veidt plays an heir to British royalty who is surgically deformed, with his mouth permanently forced into a laughing grin. Mary Philbin plays a blind co-worker who loves him. Josephine Crowell, the old Griffith actress, is

fabulous as the queen. The story lags in some parts, but is worth watching for the performance of Veidt.
Foothill Video ($7.95)

The Man with the Movie Camera (1929)
Produced in Russia
Directed by Dziga Vertov
Category: Unusual avant-garde Russian movie which places the audience at the eye of the camera.
Discount Video Tapes ($29.95)
Movies Unlimited (#53-7013 / $29.99)

Manhandled (1924)
Paramount Pictures
Directed by Allan Dwan
Cast includes: Gloria Swanson, Tom Moore, Frank Morgan, Ian Keith, Lilyan Tashman
Category: Hard-to-find Swanson film about the era of working women on the rise. Also features Frank Morgan, who is famous for having played the title role in the 1939 version of The Wizard of Oz.
Nostalgia Family Video (#1990 / $19.95)

Manhattan Cowboy (1928)
Directed by J.P. McGowan
Cast includes: Bob Custer
Category: Western
Discount Video Tapes ($19.95)

Manhattan Madness (1916)
Triangle Film Company
Directed by Allan Dwan
Cast includes: Douglas Fairbanks, Sr., Jewel Carmen, Norman Kerry, Estelle Taylor
Category: Comedy-adventure contrasting New York City and the Midwest, which finds Fairbanks

involved in a series of misadventures and magnificent stunts to rescue an endangered girl. Norman Kerry's film debut.
Video Yesteryear (#1815 / $19.95)

Mantrap (1926)
Paramount Pictures
Directed by Victor Fleming
Cast includes: Clara Bow, Eugene Pallette, Ernest Torrence, Patricia "Miss" DuPont, Percy Marmont, Tom Kennedy
Category: Romantic feature in which Bow plays a semi-vampish flapper.
Discount Video Tapes ($19.95)
Grapevine Video (#M-6-69-1 / $19.95)
Nostalgia Family Video (#1185 / $19.95)

The Manxman (1928)
Produced in Great Britain
Directed by Alfred Hitchcock
Cast includes: Carl Brisson, Anny Ondra
Category: Early Hitchcock feature in which two best friends fall in love with the same woman. When one of the suitors is reported dead, the woman marries the other. When the "dead" suitor returns, chilling situations arise.
Discount Video Tapes ($19.95)
Nostalgia Family video (#1075 / $19.95)
Video Yesteryear (#1166 / $39.95)

The Mark of Zorro (1920)
See complete review on pages 16–17

Marked Money (1928)
Directed by Spencer Gordon Bennett
Cast includes: Junior Coghlan, Virginia Bradford, Tom Kennedy, George Duryea (a.k.a. Tom Keene, Richard Powers)

Category: Adventure
Discount Video Tapes ($19.95)
Grapevine Video (#JC-3 / $16.95)

The Marriage Circle (1924)
Warner Bros.
Directed by Ernst Lubitsch
Cast includes: Esther Ralston, Marie Prevost, Florence Vidor, Monte Blue, Creighton Hale, Harry Myers, Adolphe Menjou
Category: Classic, all-star romantic comedy, which was Lubitsch's first in America.
Discount Video Tapes ($19.95)
Nostalgia Family Video (#2753 / $19.95)
Video Yesteryear (#1197 / $24.95)

Married? (1925)
Jans Productions
Directed by George Terwilliger
Cast includes: Owen Moore, Constance Bennett
Category: Romantic comedy about marriage for the convenience of inheriting money. Very entertaining, and one of the few Constance Bennett silent features which survives.
Grapevine Video (#13-123-2 / $16.95)
Nostalgia Family Video (#2266 / $19.95)

Martin Luther: His Life and Times (1924)
Produced by the Lutheran Film Association
Category: Well-done biopic of the great founder of the Lutheran Church.
Video Yesteryear (#533 / $24.95)

The Master of the House (1925)
Produced in Denmark
Directed by Carl-Theodore Dreyer
Category: A rare film, this is an early

women's lib propaganda drama which satirizes a story of a male chauvinist's awful treatment of his wife.

Video Yesteryear (#526 / $39.95)

The Matrimaniac (1916)

Triangle Film Corporation

Directed by Paul Powell

Cast includes: Douglas Fairbanks, Sr., Constance Talmadge, Winifred West-over, Monte Blue

Category: Hilarious comedy in which Fairbanks' character performs a variety of daredevil stunts to marry the girl of his dreams against her father's will. Constance Talmadge's only surviving non-*Intolerance* performance available on video.

Grapevine Video (#MDF2-11-1 / $16.95)

Nostalgia Family Video (#2924 / $19.95)

Video Yesteryear (#961 / $24.95)

Merry-Go-Round (1925)

Universal Studios

Directed by Erich Von Stroheim and Rupert Julian

Cast includes: Mary Philbin, Norman Kerry, Anton Vaverka, Maude George, Spottiswoode Aitken

Category: Romantic melodrama, for which Erich Von Stroheim was fired from Universal Studios for extravagant spending. The film was finished by Rupert Julian.

Nostalgia Family Video (#1224 / $19.95)

Messenger of the Blessed Virgin (1930)

Category: Religious drama set in the 1850s, billed as "the world's greatest Catholic photoplay."

Video Yesteryear (#1526 / $24.95)

Metropolis (1926)

Produced in Germany

Directed by Fritz Lang

Cast includes: Brigitte Helm, Rudolf Klein-Rogge, Alfred Abel

Category: The classic German science fiction masterpiece, well over 50 years ahead of its time. Some great photography and futuristic settings, including robots, airplanes, space-ships, and magnificent special effects. The versions listed here are the traditional version as it was meant to be seen, not the 1980s re-release which ruined the movie in an attempt to update it with a contemporary rock music score. Along with the futuristic effects, the film also has a great story line, concerning the revolt of workers against a tyrannical entrepreneur. Highly recommended.

International Historic Films (#001 / $24.95)

94 minutes

Kino Video ($29.95)

90 minutes

MC Film Festival ($39.95)

Video Yesteryear's 131-minute version

Mickey (1918)

Mabel Normand Productions

Directed by Richard Jones, James Young

Cast includes: Mabel Normand, Lew Cody, George Nichols, Minta Durfee, Wheeler Oakman, Tom Kenney

Category: Classic comedy, this is one of Normand's best films. One of her co-stars, Lew Cody, was to become Normand's husband later in her life.

Grapevine Video (#24-257 / $24.95)

Nostalgia Family Video (#1886 / $19.95)

Mid-Channel (1920)

Garson Studios

Directed by Harry Garson

Cast includes: Clara Kimball Young, William Marion, Edward M. Kimball, Milla Davenport

Category: One of Young's few surviving films on video, she plays a married woman neglected by her husband.

Discount Video Tapes ($19.95)

Grapevine Video (#Mccky / $16.95)

Nostalgia Family Video (#2948 / $19.95)

Midnight Faces (1926)

Cast includes: Francis X. Bushman, Jr., Kathryn McGuire

Category: Mystery-suspense movie set in a deserted Florida mansion.

Discount Video Tapes ($19.95)

Nostalgia Family Video (#2288 / $19.95)

Video Yesteryear (#1453 / $12.95)

The Midnight Girl (1925)

Directed by Wilfred Noy

Cast includes: Bela Lugosi, Lila Lee, Dolores Cassinelli

Category: Drama in which Lugosi plays the villain.

Grapevine Video (#MGBL / $16.95)

Nostalgia Family Video (#2947 / $19.95)

Video Yesteryear (#1147 / $12.95)

The Million Dollar Mystery (1927)

Cast includes: James Kirkwood, Sr., Lila Lee

Category: Classic film with mystery and suspense, taking place in a haunted-looking house. Features husband-wife acting team Kirkwood and Lee in a rare joint film appearance. Kirkwood, Sr., and Lee were the parents of famed musical writer James Kirkwood, Jr., who wrote *A Chorus Line*.

Nostalgia Family Video (#1136 / $19.95)

The Miracle Man (1919) and The Oubliette (1914)

Cast includes: Lon Chaney, Sr.

Category: Two rare finds, including *The Oubliette* which is the oldest Chaney film in existence, and the 5 minutes of remaining footage of the long lost movie *The Miracle Man* (which launched Betty Compson's career to stardom) still in existence.

Nostalgia Family Video (#2212 / $19.95)

Miss Lulu Bett (1921)

Paramount Pictures

Directed by William C. DeMille

Cast includes: Milton Sills, Lois Wilson, Theodore Roberts, Helen Ferguson, Mabel Van Buren

Category: Entertaining comedy directed by the talented, though largely forgotten, brother of Cecil B. DeMille.

Nostalgia Family Video (#2042 / $19.95)

Mistaken Orders (1925)

Directed by J.P. McGowan

Cast includes: Helen Holmes, Jack Perrin

Category: Railroad drama

Foothill Video ($7.95)

Moana (1926)

Paramount Pictures

Directed by Robert J. Flaherty

Category: Early South Seas documentary of the Samoan people, this was Flaherty's follow-up to *Nanook of the North*. Also referred to as *Moana of the South Seas*.

Nostalgia Family Video (#1929 / $19.95)

Mockery (1927)
MGM
Directed by Benjamin Christensen
Cast includes: Lon Chaney, Sr., Barbara Bedford, Ricardo Cortez, Mack Swain
Category: Chaney plays a peasant who saves the life of Barbara Bedford's character, a member of royalty during national revolutionary times. Long thought to be lost, this is one of Benjamin Christensen's rare American films.
Foothill Video ($7.95)

A Modern Musketeer (1918)
Paramount Artcraft
Directed by Allan Dwan
Cast includes: Douglas Fairbanks, Sr., Marjorie Daw, ZaSu Pitts, Tully Marshall
Category: Fairbanks' first really serious costume role in a rare, atypical appearance.
Nostalgia Family Video (#2942 / $19.95)

Modern Times (1936)
Chaplin–United Artists
Directed by Charlie Chaplin
Cast includes: Charlie Chaplin, Paulette Goddard
Category: Chaplin's last silent comedy, which satirizes modern technology, industry, and government. Rated by some critics as Chaplin's masterpiece.
Columbia House (#0059006 / $19.95)
Movies Unlimited (#04-3045 / $19.99)

The Mollycoddle (1920)
United Artists
Directed by Victor Fleming
Cast includes: Douglas Fairbanks, Sr., Wallace Beery

Category: Comedy in which Fairbanks demonstrates remarkable versatility by playing three roles.
Nostalgia Family Video (#2940 / $19.95)

Monsieur Beaucaire (1924)
Paramount Pictures
Directed by Sidney Olcott
Cast includes: Rudolph Valentino, Bebe Daniels, Lois Wilson, Doris Kenyon, Lowell Sherman, Flora Finch, Brian Donlevy (bit part)
Category: Costume drama set in eighteenth century France. Although this was meant to be Valentino's comeback film after a two-year absence from the screen, it was not well-received in rural areas of the country in part because of the beauty mark on the side of his face.
Discount Video Tapes ($19.95)
Grapevine Video (#26-320 / $19.95)
    Contains a rare audio-track on which one can hear Valentino sing
Nostalgia Family Video (#1121 / $19.95)

Moran of the Lady Letty (1922)
Paramount Pictures
Directed by George Melford
Cast includes: Rudolph Valentino, Dorothy Dalton, Walter Long, ZaSu Pitts, cameos by George O'Brien, William Boyd
Category: Adventure romance based on Frank Norris' classic 1898 novel.
Discount Video Tapes ($19.95)
Grapevine Video (#MOLLRV / $24.95)
    Also includes the rare 1918 Valentino short A Society Sensation
Nostalgia Family video (#1120 / $19.95)

A Mormon Maid (1917)
Directed by Robert Z. Leonard and Cecil B. DeMille

Cast includes: Mae Murray, Noah Beery, Sr., Frank Borzage, Hobart Bosworth

Category: Highly controversial, anti–Mormon drama featuring Mae Murray in one of her earlier screen appearances. Also features an early screen appearance of Frank Borzage as an actor, who won the very first Best Director Oscar for *Seventh Heaven.*

Nostalgia Family Video (#2939 / $19.95)

Video Yesteryear (#1475 / $24.95)

Mother (1926)

Produced in Russia

Directed by Vsevolod (V.I.) Pudovkin

Category: Russian dramatic masterpiece about a mother who turns her son in to law enforcement authorities, only to regret it when he is sent to prison.

Discount Video Tapes ($29.95)

Movies Unlimited (#53-7470 / $29.99)

The Mother and the Law (1914)

Wark Producing Company

Directed by D.W. Griffith

Cast includes: Mae Marsh, Robert Harron, Miriam Cooper, Walter Long

Category: The Modern Story from *Intolerance,* this was filmed in 1914 and worked into the complete *Intolerance.* It was released separately in 1919, along with the Babylon Story, in an attempt to recoup some of the losses of *Intolerance.*

Grapevine Video ($19.95)

Moulin Rouge (1928)

Produced in Great Britain

Directed by E.A. DuPont

Cast includes: Olga Chekova, Eve Gray, Jean Bradin

Category: Romantic drama about a man who falls in love with his girlfriend's mother. Very risqué at the time of release.

Grapevine Video (#18-888 / $19.95)

Nostalgia Family Video (#2936 / $19.95)

Video Yesteryear (#1957 / $14.95)

Mr. Wu (1927)

MGM

Directed by William Nigh

Cast includes: Lon Chaney, Sr., Renée Adorée, Louise Dresser, Anna May Wong, Ralph Forbes, Gertrude Olmstead, Holmes Herbert

Category: Chaney horror film with Chaney in one of his simplest, yet most gruesome, disguises as an old, bespectacled man with a shriveled face.

Foothill Video ($7.95)

My Best Girl (1927)

United Artists

Directed by Sam Taylor

Cast includes: Mary Pickford, Charles "Buddy" Rogers, Hobart Bosworth, Lucien Littlefield

Category: Hailed as one of Pickford's better performances, this was the last silent featuring the "Old Mary" before she bobbed off the long curls and started playing more mature roles. Pickford plays a young salesgirl whose family depends on her for everything. When she unknowingly falls in love with the son of the department store owner, it seems that everything that could go wrong does. Pickford married her costar Rogers in 1937, two years after her divorce from Douglas Fairbanks, Sr.

Nostalgia Family Video (#2758 / $19.95)

My Boy (1921)

First National Pictures

Directed by Victor Herman and Albert Austin

Cast includes: Jackie Coogan

Category: Touching drama in which Coogan plays an orphaned boy fighting deportation. This film was thought to have been lost for many years.

Grapevine Video (#MBJC / $16.95)

Nostalgia Family Video (#1278 / $19.95)

My Four Years in Germany (1918)

Directed by William Nigh

Cast includes: Halbert Brown, Earl Schenk, Louis Dean, Karl Dane

Category: Anti-German propaganda film.

Discount Video Tapes ($19.95)

Grapevine Video (#MFYIG / $19.95)

Nostalgia Family Video (#1934 / $19.95)

My Lady of Whims (1925)

Arrow Productions

Directed by Dallas Fitzgerald

Cast includes: Clara Bow, Lee Moran, Francis McDonald, Donald Keith

Category: Jazz Age film in which Bow plays a flapper trying to have more fun than her stern father will allow.

Grapevine Video (#MLOWCB / $14.95)

Nostalgia Family Video (#3256 / $19.95)

The Mysterious Island (1929)

Part-talkie

MGM

Directed by Lucien Hubbard

Cast includes: Lionel Barrymore, Jane Daly, Montague Love, Gibson Gowland, Lloyd Hughes

Category: Big-budget adaptation of the Jules Verne science fiction classic about the discovery of an underwater civilization. A part-talkie, this film was originally filmed in 2-strip Technicolor. Black and white prints are all that remain today. Recommended.

Foothill Video ($7.95)

The Mysterious Lady (1928)

MGM

Directed by Fred Niblo

An MGM/UA Home Video Release

Cast includes: Greta Garbo, Conrad Nagel, Gustav Von Seyffertitz

Category: Spy movie in which Garbo's character falls in love with the man she is supposed to be spying on, and has to choose between love and loyalty to her country.

Movies Unlimited (#12-2224 / $29.99)

The Mystery of the Double Cross (1917)

Serial

Pathé Pictures

Directed by Louis Gasnier

Cast includes: Molly King, Leon Barry, Clarine Seymour

Category: Complete, 15-chapter Pathé serial, this is not the typical cliffhanger type, but one that encourages audience participation, presenting it as a mystery and challenging the audience to solve it. Very unique and different, this is one of the most interesting of the few existing silent serials that remain in complete form. 5 hours, 50 minutes.

Discount Video Tapes ($29.95)

Grapevine Video (#36-10/12 / $34.95)

Nostalgia Family Video (#1401 / $29.95)

The Mystery of the Leaping Fish (1916)
Triangle Film Corporation
Directed by John Emerson
Cast includes: Douglas Fairbanks, Sr., Alma Rubens, Bessie Love
Category: Comedy spoof with Fairbanks portraying "Coke Ennyday," an hallucinating detective with a few bad habits. It is ironic that this comedy satirizing drug abuse starred Alma Rubens, who would later suffer the misfortune of a fatal drug dependency. This tape also includes the Russian comedy short *Chess Fever,* which was V.I. Pudovkin's second directorial credit.
Video Yesteryear (#1160 / $24.95)

Nanook of the North (1922)
Pathé Pictures
Directed and produced by Robert J. Flaherty
Category: Although credited widely as the first documentary, that is not quite true. However, this realistic feature documentary on Eskimo life in the Arctic regions was the very first documentary feature to become a box office success. It is highly acclaimed by film critics as one of the greatest documentaries of all time. When one sees the breathtaking outdoor photography and expert editing, one can see why this remains the most famous of all documentary features.
Movies Unlimited (#22-5168 / $29.99)

Napoleon (1927)
See complete review on pages 43–44

The Narrow Trail (1918)
William S. Hart Productions
Directed by Lambert Hillyer
Cast includes: William S. Hart, Sylvia Breamer

Category: Western
Grapevine Video (#NTWSH4-42-2 / $16.95)
Nostalgia Family Video (#2949 / $19.95)

The Navigator ((1924)
Joseph Schenk Productions
Directed by Buster Keaton, Donald Crisp
Cast includes: Buster Keaton, Kathryn McGuire, Noble Johnson
Category: One of Keaton's most famous features finds him and McGuire stranded aboard a runaway ocean liner. One of Keaton's funniest; recommended.
Discount Video Tapes ($19.95)

The Nervous Wreck (1926)
Cast includes: Harrison Ford, Phyllis Haver, Hobart Bosworth
Category: Comedy in which Ford (not in any way related to the modern-day Harrison Ford of the *Star Wars* trilogy) plays a hypochondriac.
Nostalgia Family Video (#2849 / $19.95)

Nevada (1927)
Paramount Pictures
Directed by John Waters
Cast includes: Gary Cooper, Thelma Todd, William Powell
Category: Star-studded western featuring the legendary Thelma Todd in a rare, early silent western role — long before she was ever costarred with the Marx Brothers or ZaSu Pitts in comedies.
Grapevine Video (#Ngc / $18.95)

The New School Teacher (1923)
Directed by Gregory LaCava
Cast includes: Chic Sale
Category: Riotous comedy with Sale

cast as a professor in the class of rowdy, uncooperative kids.

Discount Video Tapes ($19.95)

Nostalgia Family Video (#2822 / $19.95)

Video Yesteryear (#1217 / $24.95)

The Nickel Hopper (1926)

Produced by Hal Roach

Cast includes: Mabel Normand, Boris Karloff, Oliver Hardy

Category: Delightful comedy which was also one of Mabel Normand's last films.

Grapevine Video (#MN#3 / $19.95) Comes as part of a compilation including four other shorts made from 1913 to 1916.

Nostalgia Family Video (#2773 / $19.95)

The Night Club (1925)

Paramount Pictures

Directed by Frank Urson and Paul Iribe

Cast includes: Raymond Griffith, Vera Reynolds, Louise Fazenda, Wallace Beery

Category: Romantic film in which a man has to demonstrate to his girlfriend that he is interested in more than her money.

Grapevine Video (#NC4-39 / $16.95)

Nostalgia Family Video (#2868 / $19.95)

The Night Cry (1926)

Warner Bros.

Cast includes: Rin-Tin-Tin, June Marlowe, Johnnie Harron (younger brother of Robert)

Category: Canine drama

Nostalgia Family Video (#2867 / $19.95)

The Night Riders (1922)

Produced in Canada

Cast includes: Albert Ray, Russel Gordon

Category: Drama about terrorists who are harassing ranchers in a farm village.

Grapevine Video (#NRAR / $14.95)

Color tinted

No Man's Law (1926)

Cast includes: Oliver Hardy, Barbara Kent, James Finlayson

Category: Western comedy in which Hardy plays a villain role.

Nostalgia Family Video (#2233 / $19.95)

Noah's Ark (1929)

Warner Bros.

Produced by Daryl F. Zanuck

Directed by Michael Curtiz

Cast includes: Dolores Costello, George O'Brien, Noah Beery, Sr., Myrna Loy, Guinn "Big Boy" Williams, Louise Fazenda, Nigel DeBrulier, Noble Johnson

Category: The last of the silent biblical epic spectacles, this was originally filmed as a silent, but then had some talking sequences added. It was filmed on a colossal scale, using thousands of extras. Three of the extras in the flood sequence were killed during filming. This was also the first film produced by Daryl F. Zanuck, who was 27 years old at the time of production.

Discount Video Tapes ($19.95)

Nomads of the North (1920)

Produced by Hal Roach

Directed by David M. Hartford

Cast includes: Lon Chaney, Sr., Lewis Stone, Betty Blythe, Spottiswoode Aitken, Francis McDonald

Category: Romantic drama (a rarity for Hal Roach) in which Chaney's character's fiancée receives unwanted advances from the son of a store-keeper that her family owes money to. Filled with edge-of-your-seat suspense.

Grapevine Video (#NONLC / $19.95)

Nostalgia Family Video (#2211 / $19.95)

Video Yesteryear (#1189 / $24.95)

Nosferatu (1922)

Produced in Germany

Directed by F.W. Murnau

Cast includes: Max Schreck

Category: Excellent German version of the classic horror story by Bram Stoker. This remains as probably the best of all adaptations and has stood the test of time well. In order to avoid paying royalties to the Bram Stoker estate, Murnau changed some of the names and places. However, Murnau remained so faithful to the story line in the novel that a copyright infringement suit forced Nosferatu to be withdrawn from distribution in 1925.

Grapevine Video (#19-204 / $19.95)

Kino Video ($29.95)

Color tinted, and restored with new intertitles based on the original script.

Nostalgia Family Video (#1891 / $19.95)

Republic Pictures Home Video (#3029 / $19.98)

Color tinted

Video Yesteryear (#530 / $24.95)

The Notorious Lady (1927)

First National Pictures

Directed by King Baggot

Cast includes: Lewis Stone, Barbara Bedford, Francis McDonald, Ann Rorke (at one time married to J. Paul Getty)

Category: Romantic drama in which a woman takes the blame for a murder committed by her husband.

Grapevine Video (#NLLS / $19.95)

The Nut (1921)

United Artists

Directed by Ted Reed

Cast includes: Douglas Fairbanks, Sr., Barbara LaMarr, Marguerite de la Motte

Category: The last of Fairbanks' light comedy spoofs before he went exclusively into action/swashbuckling features. In this one, he plays a demented inventor.

Nostalgia Family Video (#3537 / $19.95)

Officer 444 (1926)

Serial

Directed by Francis Ford

Cast includes: Walter Miller, Ben Wilson, Neva Gerber

Category: Complete, 10-chapter, cops and robbers serial. Action-packed and great fun, living up to the tradition of the great cliffhanger silent serials at their best. Directed by Francis Ford, the older brother of highly renowned director John Ford.

Discount Video Tapes ($29.95)

Grapevine Video (#26-284-5 / $24.95)

Nostalgia Family Video (#2863 / $29.95)

Old Heidelberg (1915)

Triangle Film Corporation

Directed by John Emerson

Cast includes: Dorothy Gish, Wallace Reid, Erich Von Stroheim

Category: The earliest available version of the romantic drama about the student prince attending classes at Old Heidelberg University. The prince (played by Wallace Reid) falls in love with a commoner (played by Dorothy Gish) only to be told that he cannot marry out of his social class. Remade in 1927 as The Student Prince in Old Heidelberg, and as a 1953 musical called *The Student Prince.* This video combines three rarities into one movie: (1) the only solo feature film appearance (without Lillian) of Dorothy Gish on video; (2) one of Wallace Reid's few surviving films; and (3) the earliest film appearance of Erich Von Stroheim on video.

Nostalgia Family Video (#1353 / $19.95)

Old Ironsides (1926)

Paramount Pictures
Directed by James Cruze
A Paramount Home Video Release
Cast includes: Charles Farrell, Esther Ralston, Wallace Beery, Johnny Walker, Fred Kohler
Category: Lavishly produced historical sea adventure with some great battle scenes. This is about an American ship called the USS *Constitution*, which was the first to defy a band of pirates by refusing to pay them not to attack their ships. The video box identifies Boris Karloff as a cast member. This author has not yet spotted Karloff anywhere in this film, or in any other published cast list for *Old Ironsides.*

Columbia House Video Club (#03067042 / $29.95)

Movies Unlimited (#06-1436 / $29.99)

The Old Swimmin' Hole (1921)

Charles Ray Productions–First National
Directed by Joseph DeGrasse
Cast includes: Charles Ray, Laura LaPlante, Marjorie Prevost (Marie's sister)
Category: According to Joe Franklin in *Classics of the Silent Screen* (1959), this is among the best of the Ray films. This is also one of the experimental films that did not use title cards, and the role that got Laura LaPlante noticed.

Discount Video Tapes ($19.95)

Oliver Twist (1922)

First National Pictures
Directed by Frank Lloyd
Cast includes: Lon Chaney, Sr., Jackie Coogan, George Siegmann, Esther Ralston, Carl Stockdale
Category: Early adaptation of Charles Dickens' literary masterpiece. Chaney and Coogan achieved wide critical acclaim for their performances.

Discount Video Tapes ($19.95)

Grapevine Video (#OTLC / $19.95)

Nostalgia Family Video (#2890 / $19.95)

On the Night Stage (1915)

Produced by Thomas H. Ince
Directed by Reginald Barker
Cast includes: William S. Hart, Robert Edeson, Rhea Mitchell
Category: Western

Grapevine Video (#14-139-1 / $16.95)

Video Yesteryear (#1500 / $24.95)

One Arabian Night (1920)

Produced in Germany
Directed by Ernst Lubitsch
Cast includes: Pola Negri, Ernst Lubitsch
Category: Fantasy drama with a touch of comedy and romance, in which Lubitsch stars as well as directs. Based on the "Arabian Nights" fantasies.

Nostalgia Family Video (#2889 / $19.95)

Video Yesteryear (#1064 / $24.95)

One Punch O'Day (1926)

Directed by Harry Joe Brown, Sr.
Cast includes: Billy Sullivan, Charlotte Merriem

Category: Boxing drama
Nostalgia Family Video (#2836 / $19.95)
Video Yesteryear (#1746 / $12.95)

The Open Switch (1925)

Cast includes: Helen Holmes, Jack Perrin, Mack Wright, Charles Whittaker
Category: Railroad drama
Discount Video Tapes ($19.95)
Grapevine Video (#OSFF5-56-2 / $14.95)

Orchids and Ermine (1926)

First National Pictures
Directed by Alfred Santell
Cast includes: Colleen Moore, Mickey Rooney, Hedda Hopper, Kate Price, Jed Prouty, Jack Mulhall
Category: Romantic comedy which was one of Moore's better pictures for First National. This was also Mickey Rooney's feature debut, in which he plays an adult midget. Light, entertaining, and fun.
Nostalgia Family Video (#2152 / $19.95)

Orphans of the Storm (1922)

See complete review on pages 19–20.

Othello (1922)

Produced in Germany
Directed by Dimitri Buschowetzki
Cast includes: Emil Jannings, Werner Krauss
Category: German silent version of Shakespeare's literary classic.
Discount Video Tapes ($29.95)
Nostalgia Family Video (#2894 / $19.95)
Video Yesteryear (#771 / $24.95)

The Oubliette (1914)

See *The Miracle Man* (1919)

Our Dancing Daughters (1928)

MGM
Directed by Harry Beaumont
An MGM/UA Home Video Release
Cast includes: Joan Crawford, Anita Page, Johnny Mack Brown, Sam DeGrasse, Niles Asther, Kathlyn Williams
Category: Classic "Jazz Age" melodrama which established Joan Crawford's late '20s flapper image. Also features a fabulous performance by Anita Page, who currently resides in California.
Movies Unlimited (#12-222 / $19.99)

Our Hospitality (1923)

Directed by Buster Keaton, John Blystone
An HBO Home Video Release
Cast includes: Buster Keaton, Natalie Talmadge, Joseph Keaton
Category: One of Keaton's finest early feature comedies, which includes some impressive stunt work by Keaton. Among the examples is a sequence depicting a last-minute rescue from the edge of a waterfall, reminiscent of the *Way Down East* sequence.
Movies Unlimited (#44-1668 / $39.99)
Color tinted with orchestral score

Our Modern Maidens (1929)

MGM
Directed by Jack Conway
An MGM/UA Home Video Release
Cast includes: Douglas Fairbanks, Jr., Joan Crawford, Rod LaRocque, Anita Page
Category: Romantic melodrama in which two women are in love with the same man (Fairbanks, Jr.), one of whom is engaged to him — the other pregnant with his child. Which one will he choose? Crawford's last

silent appearance, and a favorite among many silent movie buffs.
Movies Unlimited (#12-2623 / $19.99)

The Outlaw and His Wife
(1917)
Produced in Sweden
Directed by Victor Seastrom
Cast includes: Victor Seastrom
Category: Classic Swedish melodrama directed by and starring Victor Seastrom. One of his earlier directorial credits.
Kino Video ($29.95)
Color tinted

Outside the Law (1921)
Directed by Tod Browning
Cast includes: Lon Chaney, Sr., Priscilla Dean, Ralph Lewis, Wheeler Oakman
Category: Rare Chaney drama thought for years to have been among the many lost films of the silent era. In this one, Chaney plays two roles as an evil villain and as a Chinese servant.
Discount Video Tapes ($19.95)
Grapevine Video (#OLLC / $19.95)
Nostalgia Family Video (#3365 / $19.95)
Video Yesteryear (#1198 / $24.95)

The Pace That Kills (1928)
Directed by Norton Parker
Cast includes: Florence Turner, Owen Gorin
Category: Well-done anti-drug exploitation movie, far better than some of its successors.
Nostalgia Family Video (#1130 / $19.95)
Video Yesteryear (#1556 / $12.95)

Pampered Youth (1925)
Vitagraph
Cast includes: Cullen Landis, Alice Calhoun, Ben Alexander

Category: Early little-known, little-seen silent adaptation of *The Magnificent Ambersons*. This was also one of Vitagraph's last films before the takeover by Warner Bros.
Nostalgia Family Video (#1131 / $19.95)

Pandora's Box (1928)
Produced in Germany
Directed by G.W. Pabst
Cast includes: Louise Brooks, Fritz Kortner, Alice Roberts
Category: One of the two silent German collaborations of Louise Brooks and renowned director G.W. Pabst. This is a drama that has it all — lesbianism, promiscuity, blackmail, murder, and prostitution. Quite scandalous, especially for the time it was released. Louise Brooks plays Lulu, a woman who seems to destroy the lives of every man she comes into contact with. Alice Roberts portrays the screen's first lesbian, who is actually presented in a positive light as yet another person taken for a ride by Lulu. Highly recommended.
Discount Video Tapes ($29.95)
Grapevine Video (#PBLB / $19.95)

Passion (a.k.a. DuBarry)
(1919)
Produced in Germany
Directed by Ernst Lubitsch
Cast includes: Emil Jannings, Pola Negri
Category: German historical costume drama, this is a lavish version of the story of Madame DuBarry. The plot is laced with elements of aristocracy, adultery, scandal, and rebellion — all the ingredients necessary for an enticing film.
Nostalgia Family Video (#1044 / $19.95)
Video Yesteryear (#520 / $29.95)

The Passion of Joan of Arc
(1928)
Produced in France
Directed by Carl-Theodore Dreyer
Cast includes: Renee Falconetti, Michel Simon
Category: Excellently produced biopic detailing the trial of and burning of the great French martyr whom many believe was a lesbian. The story is told mostly in facial close-ups, one of the traits that makes it unique. This is also Renee Falconetti's one and only screen performance.
Discount Video Tapes ($29.95)
MC Film Festival ($24.95)
Nostalgia Family Video (#2168 / $19.95)

The Patchwork Girl of Oz
(1914)
Oz Film Company
Directed by J. Farrell McDonald
Cast includes: Midred Harris, Violet McMillan, Juanita Hansen, Frank Moore, Pierre Coudere, Raymond Russell, Fred Woodward; Vivian Reed as the "Oz" girl; Harold Lloyd and Hal Roach as extras
Category: The first of the three "Oz" movies produced by the short-lived Oz Film Company. This is a charming children's fantasy film in which a doll is brought to life to be used as a slave. Although not as sophisticated as that in the later Oz movies, the trick photography of the doll assembling itself, the cast disappearing into a wall, and a table setting itself are quite impressive for the time and well done.
Discount Video Tapes ($19.95)
Grapevine Video (#PGOO / $14.95) Offers all 3 Oz films on one SP tape for $24.95)

Nostalgia Family Video (#1443 / $19.95)
Video Yesteryear (#1201 / $24.95)

Paths to Paradise (1925)
Paramount Pictures
Directed by Clarence Badger
Cast includes: Raymond Griffith, Betty Compson, Tom Santschi
Category: Crime drama about two arch-criminals' plot to steal a large diamond.
Grapevine Video (#PTP12-112 / $17.95)
Nostalgia Family Video (#2245 / $19.95)

The Peacock Fan (1929)
Directed by Phillip E. Rosen
Cast includes: Dorothy Dwan, Lucien Prival
Category: Late silent murder mystery.
Nostalgia Family Video (#3366 / $19.95)
Video Yesteryear (#969 / $24.95)

Peck's Bad Boy (1921)
First National Pictures
Directed by Sam Wood
Titles by Irvin S. Cobb
Cast includes: Jackie Coogan, James Corrigan, Raymond Hatton
Category: Delightful comedy in which Coogan's wonderful performance as a brat getting into trouble every time he turns around carries the whole movie. Includes the famous scene in which Coogan lets a lion loose at the circus. Light, entertaining fun that the whole family can enjoy.
Discount Video Tapes ($19.95)
Grapevine Video (#PBBJC / $16.95)
Nostalgia Family Video (#2118 / $19.95)
Video Yesteryear (#457 / $24.95)

The Penalty (1920)

Directed by Wallace Worsley

Cast includes: Lon Chaney, Sr., Kenneth Harlan

Category: Chaney's follow-up to his well-received performance in *The Miracle Man*. This was probably the role which was the most difficult for Chaney to do, as he portrays a man with both legs amputated at the knee. His legs were tied behind him to create this illusion, and he even did some scenes which required that he jump from high places and land on his knees.

Foothill Video ($7.95)

The Perfect Clown (1925)

Chadwick Pictures

Directed by Fred Newmeyer

Cast includes: Larry Semon, Dorothy Dwan, Oliver Hardy

Category: Slapstick comedy

Grapevine Video (#PCLS / $14.95)

Nostalgia Family Video (#1837 / $19.95)

Video Yesteryear (#1299 / $24.95)

The Perils of Pauline (1914)

See complete review on pages 6–7

Perils of the Rail (1925)

Directed by J.P. McGowan

Cast includes: Helen Holmes, Edward Hearn, J.P. McGowan

Category: One of the best of the Helen Holmes railroad dramas.

Discount Video Tapes ($19.95)

Grapevine Video (#PORHH / $16.95)

The Phantom Bullet (1926)

Universal Studios

Directed by Clifford S. Smith

Cast includes: Hoot Gibson, Eileen Percy, Alan Forrest

Category: Western

Grapevine Video (#PBHG24-258-1 / $16.95)

The Phantom Chariot (a.k.a. The Phantom Carriage) (1920)

Produced in Sweden

Directed by Victor Seastrom

Cast includes: Victor Seastrom

Category: Swedish classic about death and morality, with Seastrom as a man who meets death.

Grapevine Video (#PCVS / $16.95)

The Phantom Flyer (1928)

Cast includes: Al Wilson

Category: Western featuring impressive stunt work.

Video Yesteryear (#1400 / $12.95)

The Phantom of the Opera (1925)

See complete review on pages 31–33

Picking Peaches (1924)

Cast includes: Harry Langdon

Category: Comedy

Foothill Video ($7.95)

Playing Dead (1915)

Vitagraph

Directed by Sidney Drew

Cast includes: Mr. and Mrs. Sidney Drew, Alice Lake

Category: Rare romantic comedy of the husband-wife team, who were very popular in the teens. Also stars Alice Lake, another popular Vitagraph star of the teens.

Grapevine Video (#PDSD / $16.95)

Pollyanna (1920)

United Artists

Directed by Paul Powell

Cast includes: Mary Pickford, Helen Jerome Eddy, Dorothy Rosher (a.k.a. Joan Marsh)

Category: Hard to find, original version of the story of the orphan girl who brings happiness to her cold, stern, rich aunt and everybody else around her. A heart-warming family film, this was Pickford's first release through United Artists.
Nostalgia Family Video (#1059 / $19.95)

Pony Express (1925)
Paramount Pictures
Directed by James Cruze
Cast includes: Betty Compson, Ricardo Cortez, Ernest Torrence, Wallace Beery, George Bancroft
Category: Western with an all-star cast, this was Cruze's follow-up to *The Covered Wagon*.
Grapevine Video (#7-60-2 / $14.95)

The Poor Little Rich Girl (1916)
Directed by Maurice Tourneur
Cast includes: Mary Pickford
Category: Pickford's first feature length classic about a little girl who is unhappy despite the extraordinary wealth of her parents. With a touch of comedy added, the moral of this movie is that money isn't everything. Some great camerawork, with oversize sets having been built to make Pickford look even younger and smaller than she really was.
Grapevine Video (#PLRG / $16.95)
Nostalgia Family Video (#1444 / $19.95)
Video Yesteryear (#411 / $24.95)

Pop Goes the Cork (192?)
Cast includes: Max Linder
Category: Comedy
Foothill Video ($7.95)

Power (1928)
MGM
Cast includes: Alan Hale, William Boyd, Joan Bennett, Carole Lombard, Jacqueline Logan
Category: The only silent era performances of Joan Bennett or Carole Lombard on video.
Discount Video Tapes ($19.95)
Nostalgia Family Video (#1357 / $19.95)

The Power God (1926)
Serial
Cast includes: Ben Wilson
Category: Complete 15-chapter serial. Fast paced, action packed cliffhanger mystery.
Discount Video Tapes ($29.95)

The Power of the Press (1914)
Cast includes: Alan Hale, Lionel Barrymore
Category: Drama of false imprisonment of a man for a crime he did not commit, who is finally exonerated with the help of a news reporter's investigation.
Nostalgia Family Video (#2820 / $19.95)

The Prairie King (1927)
Universal Studios
Directed by B. Reeves Eason
Cast includes: Hoot Gibson
Category: Western
Grapevine Video (#PKHG39-1 / $16.95)

The Prairie Pirate (1925)
Hunt Stromberg Corporation
Directed by Edmund Mortimer
Cast includes: Harry Carey
Category: Western
Grapevine Video (#PPHC28-312 / $16.95)

The Pride of the Clan (1916)

Artcraft Pictures

Directed by Maurice Tourneur

Cast includes: Mary Pickford, Matt Moore, Leatrice Joy

Category: Romance film in which Pickford's character falls in love with a boy whose parents disapprove of the relationship.

Grapevine Video (#POCMP / $19.95)

Nostalgia Family Video (#2819 / $19.95)

The Primrose Path (1925)

Arrow Pictures

Directed by Harry Hoyt

Cast includes: Clara Bow, Tom Santschi, Stuart Holmes

Foothill Video ($7.95)

The Prince of Pep (1925)

Cast includes: Richard Talmadge

Foothill Video ($7.95)

Pursued (1928)

Cast includes: Art Acord

Category: Western

Discount Video Tapes ($19.95)

Nostalgia Family Video (#2826 / $19.95)

Q-Ships (1928)

Produced in Great Britain

Directed by Geoffrey Barkas and Michael Barringer

Cast includes: Roy Travers, Douglas Herald, Jack McErwin

Category: Classic semi-documentary war drama about a World War I German soldier torn between his own personal moral beliefs and loyalty to his country.

Discount Video Tapes ($19.95)

Grapevine Video (#QSB / $19.95)

Queen Elizabeth (1912)

See complete review on pages 4–5

Queen Kelly (1929)

See complete review on pages 49–51

Queen of the Chorus (1928)

Cast includes: Virginia Brown Fair, Rex Lease, Betty Francisco

Category: Romantic flapper drama

Video Yesteryear (#1557 / $12.95)

Raffles, the Amateur Cracksman (1917)

Independent Motion Picture Company (IMP)

Directed by George Irving

Cast includes: John Barrymore, Nigel Bruce, Evelyn Brent, Frank Morgan

Category: In this story reminiscent of a Robin Hood–type tale, this was one of a series of pre–1920 comedies that Barrymore starred in. It is the earliest example on video not only of John Barrymore's work, but that of Frank Morgan and Evelyn Brent as well.

Nostalgia Family Video (#2080 / $19.95)

Raggedy Rose (1926)

Hal Roach Studios

Directed by Stan Laurel

Cast includes: Mabel Normand, James Finlayson, Anita Garvin

Category: One of Normand's last films, this is an enchanting romantic comedy in which Normand, playing a peasant, meets the man of her dreams.

Discount Video Tapes ($19.95)

Grapevine Video (#RRMN / $14.95)

Nostalgia Family Video (#2056 / $19.95)

Ranchers and Rascals (1925)

William Steiner Productions

Cast includes: Leo Maloney, Josephine Hill, Bullet (the dog)

Category: Western
Grapevine Video (#R&R14-141-1 /
$16.95)

Ranson's Folley (1926)
Directed by Sidney Olcott
Cast includes: Richard Barthelmess,
Dorothy MacKaill
Category: One of Barthelmess' most
popular mid–1920s movies, in
which he plays a member of the
U.S. Cavalry who poses on a dare
as a famous outlaw.
Discount Video Tapes ($19.95)
Nostalgia Family Video (#2835 /
$19.95)

The Raven (1915)
Directed by Charles J. Brabin
Cast includes: Henry B. Walthall,
Warda Howard, Ernest Malone
Category: Biopic in which Walthall
portrays literary genius Edgar Allan
Poe. Charles J. Brabin, the direc-
tor, was the husband of Theda
Bara. He also directed the Italian
location footage of Ben-Hur (1927),
having been the original director
before he was replaced by Fred
Niblo.
Discount Video Tapes ($19.95)
Grapevine Video (#RHBW / $14.95)
Nostalgia Family Video (#2305 /
$19.95)

Reaching for the Moon (1917)
Paramount Artcraft
Cowritten by Anita Loos and John
Emerson
Directed by John Emerson
Cast includes: Douglas Fairbanks, Sr.,
Eileen Percy, Erich Von Stroheim
Category: Fantasy-comedy about a
daydreaming desk clerk in a button
factory. No connection whatsoever
with Fairbanks' 1931 talkie of the
same title.

Nostalgia Family Video (#2833 /
$19.95)
Video Yesteryear (#1130 / $12.95)

Rebecca of Sunnybrook Farm (1917)
Paramount Pictures
Directed by Marshall Neilan
Cast includes: Mary Pickford, Eugene
O'Brien, Wesley Barry, ZaSu Pitts,
Marjorie Daw
Category: Another hard-to-rind Pickford classic, this is a film in which
Pickford plays a poor orphan girl,
based on the classic novel of the
same title. This movie is also a rarity in the fact that it is one of the
few films directed by Marshall
Neilan (at one time the husband of
Blanche Sweet, who divorced him
because of his chronic alcoholism)
which is available on video. To clear
up any. misconceptions, the 1938
Shirley Temple movie of the same
name was not based on the novel,
and has no connection or relation
to this version in any way.
Nostalgia Family Video (#1060 /
$19.95)

Red Blood (1926)
Directed by J.P. McGowan
Cast includes: Al Hoxie, J.P. McGowan
Category: Western
Video Yesteryear (#1646 / $24.95)

The Red Kimona (1925)
See complete review on pages 29–31

Red Raiders (1927)
Charles P. Rogers Productions
Directed by Albert Rogell
Cast includes: Ken Maynard, J.P. Mc-
Gowan
Category: Western
Grapevine Video (#RRKM16-166-1 /
$16.95)

The Regeneration (1915)

Directed by Raoul Walsh

Cast includes: Rockliffe Fellowes, Anna Q. Nilsson, John McCann

Category: The first feature-length gangster movie, this is about a woman who attempts to reform a gangster criminal. Filmed on location in the slums of Bowery, this was Walsh's first directorial effort after having left D.W. Griffith's company as an actor.

Discount Video Tapes ($19.95)

Kino Video ($29.95)

Restored version also includes the 1910 Edison short *The Police Force of New York City*

Reggie Mixes In (1916)

Triangle Film Corporation

Directed by William Christy Cabanne

Cast includes: Douglas Fairbanks, Sr., Bessie Love, Alma Rubens

Category: Romantic comedy

Grapevine Video (#6-56-2 / $16.95)

Nostalgia Family Video (#2831 / $19.95)

The Return of Boston Blackie (1927)

Directed by Harry Hoyt

Cast includes: Strongheart (the dog), Raymond Glenn, Rosemary Cooper, Corliss Palmer

Category: Mystery-adventure about an ex-con trying to reform his ways, with the assistance of his canine.

Grapevine Video (#ROBB / $14.95)

Video Yesteryear (#1484 / $24.95)

The Return of Draw Egan (1916)

Triangle Film Corporation

Directed by William S. Hart

Cast includes: William S. Hart, Louise Glaum

Category: Western

Video Yesteryear (#1441 / $24.95)

The Return of Grey Wolf (1922)

Cast includes: Leader (the dog), James Pierce, Helen Lynch

Category: Early canine adventure

Video Yesteryear (#1129 / $12.95)

Riders of the Law (1922)

Directed by Robert North Bradbury

Cast includes: Jack Hoxie

Category: Western about bootleg liquor.

Nostalgia Family Video (#2838 / $19.95)

Video Yesteryear (#1651 / $24.95)

Riders of the Purple Sage (1925)

Fox Film Company

Directed by Lynn Reynolds

Cast includes: Tom Mix, Warner Oland, Fred Kohler, Marion Nixon, Wilfred Lucas, Dawn O'Day (a.k.a. Anne Shirley)

Category: Western based on the Zane Grey novel, this is one of the best of the many movie adaptations. Tom Mix's most famous western.

Discount Video Tapes ($19.95)

Grapevine Video (#ROPSTM / $19.95)

Nostalgia Family Video (#1889 / $19.95)

Riders of the Range (1924)

See complete review on pages 28–29

Riding for Life (1927)

Cast includes: Bob Reeves, Bob Fleming

Category: Western

Video Yesteryear (#1616 / $12.95)

Rien Que les Heures (1926)

Produced in France

Directed by Albert Calvalcanti

Category: French avant-garde documentary representing 24 hours of life in Paris using experimental special effects as freeze frames, split-screen photography, etc.
Discount Video Tapes ($29.95)
Nostalgia Family Video (#3243 / $19.95)

The Ring (1927)
Produced in Great Britain
Directed by Alfred Hitchcock
Cast includes: Carl Brisson, Ian Hunter, Lillian Hall-Davis, Gordon Harker
Category: Early Hitchcock silent filmed in Britain, and unavailable on video until very recently.
Discount Video Tapes ($19.95)

Rip Van Winkle (1914)
Cast includes: Thomas Jefferson (son of Joseph Jefferson, original coauthor of the 1865 play)
Category: The third known silent adaptation (previously filmed in 1902 and 1910) of the Washington Irving classic.
Discount Video Tapes ($19.95)
Grapevine Video (#RVW / $14.95)

Rip Van Winkle (1921)
Cast includes: Thomas Jefferson
Category: 1921 remake of the 1914 version, also featuring Jefferson in the leading role.
Nostalgia Family Video (#1706 / $19.95)

Risky Business (1926)
Directed by Alan Hale
Cast includes: Vera Reynolds, ZaSu Pitts, Ethel Clayton
Category: Vera Reynolds plays a girl who wants to marry a country doctor, as opposed to her mother's wishes that she marry for wealth.
Grapevine Video (#RBVR / $16.95)

Road Agent (1926)
Cast includes: Al Hoxie
Category: Western
Discount Video Tapes ($19.95)
Nostalgia Family Video (#3367 / $19.95)
Video Yesteryear (#1412 / $12.95)

Road to Mandalay (1926)
Cast includes: Lon Chaney, Sr.
Category: One of Chaney's MGM features directed by Tod Browning, and costarring Lois Moran, Henry B. Walthall, and Owen Moore.
Foothill Video ($7.95)

The Road to Ruin (1928)
Cast includes: Grant Withers, Helen Foster, Virginia Roye, Florence Turner
Category: Prostitution exploitation drama.
Discount Video Tapes ($19.95)
Nostalgia Family Video (#2930 / $19.95)
Video Yesteryear (#1065 / $12.95)

The Road to Yesterday (1925)
Paramount Pictures
Directed by Cecil B. DeMille
Cast includes: Jetta Goudal, William Boyd, Vera Reynolds, Junior Coghlan, Joseph Schildkraut, Sally Rand, Chester Morris
Category: Fantasy melodrama in which a train wreck causes a time warp for the main characters, who are sent back to their past lives of 300 years earlier.
Grapevine Video (#RTYWB / $19.95)
Nostalgia Family Video (#2047 / $19.95)
Video Yesteryear (#275 / $39.95)

The Roaring Road (1919)
Paramount Pictures
Directed by James Cruze

Cast includes: Wallace Reid, Ann Little, Theodore Roberts
Category: One of the very few of Reid's race car movies still in existence. The reader will also recognize the name of Theodore Roberts, who played Moses in the 1923 version of *The Ten Commandments.*
Grapevine Video (#RRWR / $14.95)
Nostalgia Family Video (#2197 / $19.95)
Video Yesteryear (#1466 / $19.95)

Robin Hood (1922)
United Artists
Directed by Allan Dwan
Cast includes: Douglas Fairbanks, Sr., Enid Bennett (wife of Fred Niblo), Wallace Beery, Alan Hale, Sam De-Grasse
Category: Adventure film, which was the most elaborate and biggest of all of the Fairbanks features. The castle set in this movie remains the only movie set to have possibly equaled the size of the Belshazzar Banquet Hall set in *Intolerance.* Neither set has been topped since. An awesome, action-packed adventure with death-defying, daredevil stunt work.
Discount Video Tapes ($29.95)
Grapevine Video (#5-47 / $19.95)
Nostalgia Family Video (#1177 / $19.95)

A Romance of Happy Valley (1918)
Directed by D.W. Griffith
Cast includes: Lillian Gish, Robert Harron, Carol Dempster, George Fawcett
Category: Romantic drama
Foothill Video ($7.95)

Romola (1924)
Inspiration-Metro-Goldwyn Pictures

Directed by Henry King
Cast includes: Lillian Gish, Dorothy Gish, William Powell, Ronald Colman, Frank Puglia
Category: Classic romantic melodrama with an all-star cast, filmed in location in Italy. This was one of Gish's better box office silent successes after she left D.W. Griffith's company. William Powell turns in a great performance as the villain of the story. Received worldwide critical acclaim and praise.
Discount Video Tapes ($19.95)
Nostalgia Family Video (#1046 / $19.95)

Rounding Up the Law (1922)
Cast includes: Guinn "Big Boy" Williams
Category: Western
Video Yesteryear (#1485 / $19.95)

Rubber Tires (1927)
Cecil B. DeMille Productions
Directed by Alan Hale
Cast includes: Harrison Ford, Bessie Love, Junior Coghlan, May Robson
Category: Light comedy about big city residents trying to make a quiet trip to the country in an uncooperative car.
Discount Video Tapes ($29.95)
Grapevine Video (#26-277-2 / $16.95)
Nostalgia Family Video (#3368 / $19.95)

Running Wild (1927)
Paramount Pictures
Directed by Gregory LaCava
A Paramount Home Video Release
Cast includes: W.C. Fields, Mary Brian
Category: Fields is at his best in this hilarious comedy in which he plays an unassertive father who is bullied

by his second wife and step-son, as well as at work. It all changes when he accidentally throws a horseshoe through a window, and runs into a hypnotist's show, where he is hypnotized to think he is a lion. His luck changes, and he gains everybody's respect. This is one of the funniest silent comedies the author has ever seen.

Columbia House Video Club (#03068032 / $19.95)

Movies Unlimited (#06-1433 / $29.95)

The Rush Hour (1927)

Directed by E. Mason Hopper

Cast includes: Marie Prevost, Seena Owen, Harrison Ford

Category: Comedy in which Prevost finds herself in a variety of misadventures after stowing away on a boat to France.

Discount Video Tapes ($19.95)

The Sacred Mountain (1926)

Produced in Germany

Directed by Arnold Fanck

Cast includes: Leni Riefenstahl

Category: German mountain drama featuring Riefenstahl in one of her earlier film appearances.

Nostalgia Family Video (#1042 / $19.95)

Sadie Thompson (1928)

United Artists

Directed by Raoul Walsh

1928-29 Best Actress Academy Award Nominee

Cast includes: Gloria Swanson, Lionel Barrymore, Raoul Walsh

Category: Classic melodrama in which Swanson earned a Best Actress nomination for her portrayal of a prostitute who is blackmailed into having sex with a hypocritical, evangelist reformer played to the

hilt by Lionel Barrymore. Walsh not only directed, but also played the Marine that Swanson's character falls in love with. For years, this film was not seen because the sole surviving print was missing the last reel. The print was restored for Kino using stills, title cards, and extant footage to finish the story. This was Swanson's answer to the Hays office, and her greatest dramatic silent era performance. Highly recommended.

Kino Video ($29.95)

Nostalgia Family Video (#1658 / $19.95)

Safety Last (1923)

See complete review on pages 26–27

The Saga of Gosta Berling (1924)

See *Gosta Berling's Saga* for description

Discount Video Tapes ($29.95)

Nostalgia Family Video (#1721 / $19.95)

A Sailor-Made Man (1921)

Hal Roach Productions

Directed by Fred Newmeyer

Cast includes: Harold Lloyd, Mildred Davis

Category: Lloyd's first feature length comedy.

Foothill Video ($7.95)

Sally of the Sawdust (1925)

Paramount Pictures

Directed by D.W. Griffith

Cast includes: W.C. Fields, Carol Dempster, Alfred Lunt

Category: Fields' first major movie was this comedy in which he plays a big hearted con artist juggler who adopts and helps a girl down on her luck. Also features an appearance by Alfred Lunt, who received a

1931-32 Oscar nominaton for *The Guardsman*.

Discount Video Tapes ($19.95)
Grapevine Video (#SOSDWG / $19.95)
Nostalgia Family Video (#1279 / $19.95)
Video Yesteryear (#399 / $24.95)

Salome (1923)

See complete review on pages 25–26

The Sands of Sacrifice (1921)

Neal Hart Productions
Directed by Charles Bartlett
Cast includes: Neal Hart, Violet Palmer
Category: Western
Grapevine Video (#SOSNH / $16.95)

Savages of the Sea (1925)

Cast includes: Frank Merrill, Marguerite Snow
Category: Two of the biggest stars of silent serials team up in this drama about a castaway on a deserted island. Snow was famous for her early serials in the teens, most notably *The Million Dollar Mystery* and its sequel serial *Zudora*. Merrill was in late silent and early talkie serials.
Nostalgia Family Video (#2975 / $19.95)

Scar of Shame (1927)

Colored Players Film Company
Directed by Frank Peregrini
Cast includes: Harry Henderson, Lucia Lynn Moses
Category: All-black melodrama which was the very first production of the Colored Players Film Company in Philadelphia, Pennsylvania. One of the few all-black silents known to exist.
Discount Video Tapes ($29.95)

The Scarlet Car (1917)

Directed by Joseph DeGrasse
Cast includes: Lon Chaney, Sr., Edith Johnson, Sam DeGrasse, Franklyn Farnum
Category: Early Chaney drama in which Chaney portrays a bank cashier who discovers embezzlers within the bank. Sam DeGrasse is the younger brother of the director.
Grapevine Video (#SCLC / $16.95)
Nostalgia Family Video (#3087 / $19.95)
Video Yesteryear (#1585 / $19.95)

The Scarlet Letter (1926)

MGM
Directed by Victor Seastrom
Cast includes: Lillian Gish, Lars Hanson, Henry B. Walthall, Karl Dane
Category: Fantastic adaptation of the Hawthorne novel, and one in which Lillian Gish turns in a stellar performance as Hester Prynne. Print condition is fair, but this is the only known available version.
Foothill Video ($7.95)

The Sea Lion (1921)

Directed by Rowland Lee
Cast includes: Hobart Bosworth, Bessie Love
Category: Viking sea drama.
Video Yesteryear (#532 / $24.95)

Secrets of a Soul (1926)

Produced in Germany
Directed by G.W. Pabst
Cast includes: Werner Krauss, Ruth Weyher
Category: Bizarre psychological drama in which Krauss gives a performance as a man who is jealous of his wife's cousin who is also his best friend, and is therefore tempted to kill his wife. Many reviewers of the time felt this to be a propaganda drama in support of Freudian philosophy.
Grapevine Video (#SOSG / $14.95)

Seven Chances (1925)
Directed by Buster Keaton
Cast includes: Buster Keaton, Jean Arthur (unbilled bit part)
Category: Comedy
Discount Video Tapes ($19.95)

Seven Keys to Baldpate (1917)
Artcraft
Cast includes: Anna Q. Nilsson, George M. Cohan, Hedda Hopper
Category: Mystery in which strange happenings ruin an author's plans to check into a nice, quiet inn to finish his novel.
Discount Video Tapes ($19.95)
Nostalgia Family Video (#1307 / $19.95)

Seven Years' Bad Luck (1920)
Robertson-Cole Productions
Directed and written by Max Linder
Cast includes: Max Linder
Category: Classic comedy featuring French comedian Max Linder, whom Chaplin was inspired by. In this one, Linder accidentally breaks a mirror, and finds out the truth to the superstition, "seven years' bad luck." This is one of three feature length comedies Linder made in the United States during the 1920-1922 time period. He and his wife tragically committed suicide in a Paris hotel room on October 30, 1925.
Grapevine Video (#SYBL / $16.95)
Nostalgia Family Video (#1292 / $19.95)
Video Yesteryear (#124 / $24.95)

Seventh Heaven (1927)
Fox Film Corporation
Directed by Frank Borzage
1927-28 Best Director Academy Award Winner
1927-28 Best Actress Academy Award Winner
Cast includes: Janet Gaynor, Charles Farrell, Marie Mosquini, Brandon Hurst, David Butler, George E. Stone
Category: Hailed as the greatest romantic story of all time by some. Winner of two Academy Awards — for best director, and one of three films for which Janet Gaynor won the first Best Actress Oscar.
Discount Video Tapes ($19.95)

Sex (a.k.a. The Spider Woman) (1920)
Hodkinson Productions
Directed by Fred Niblo
Cast includes: Louise Glaum, Irving Cummings
Category: A typical vamp movie, this picture was extremely controversial during the time of its release for the title alone. Some localities refused to show it under Sex, which is why it is also known as The Spider Woman. This is one of vamp imitator Louise Glaum's biggest roles, in which she plays an exotic dancer out to get any man who suits her fancy at the time — even if he is married. When she finally does settle down with a nice man, all of her past comes back to haunt her.
Discount Video Tapes ($19.95)
Nostalgia Family Video (#2676 / $19.95)
Video Yesteryear (#503 / $24.95)

Shadows (1922)
Directed by Tom Forman
Cast includes: Lon Chaney, Sr., Marguerite de la Motte, Walter Long, Harrison Ford, John Sainpolis, Priscilla Bonner
Category: Drama of romance, blackmail, and religious conversion, this

is one in which Chaney gives a great performance in a double role as a fisherman and as a Chinese heathen.

Grapevine Video (#SLC / $19.95)

Video Yesteryear (#1200 / $24.95)

The Shamrock and the Rose (1927)

Cast includes: Maurice Costello, Mack Swain, Olive Hasbrook

Category: Cultural comedy about immigrant families in New York. This was the introductory comedy of which *The Cohens and the Kellys* was a spinoff. One of the few performance of Maurice Costello (Dolores' and Helene's father) on video.

Nostalgia Family Video (#2962 / $19.95)

Video Yesteryear (#1215 / $12.95)

She (1911)

Cast includes: James Cruze, Marguerite Snow, Marie Eline (billed as the "Thanhouser kidlet")

Category: The earliest version of several screen adaptations of H. Rider Haggard's novel on video. This is a 20-minute version which was long thought to be lost.

Nostalgia Family Video (#2963 / $19.95)

She (1925)

Produced in Great Britain

Artlee Productions

Cast includes: Betty Blythe, Carlisle Blackwell, Mary Odette

Category: The most famous of all of the silent versions of this "lost race" fantasy adventure.

Grapevine Video (#14-135-1 / $19.95)

Nostalgia Family Video (#2964 / $19.95)

Video Yesteryear (#774 / $24.95)

She Goes to War (1929)

(Part-talkie)

Inspiration Pictures

Directed by Henry King

Cast includes: Eleanor Boardman, Alma Rubens, Al St. John (nephew of Roscoe "Fatty" Arbuckle)

Category: Powerful, moving portrayal of the ravages of World War I and its devastating aftereffects. A great performance by Eleanor Boardman, who plays a spoiled rich girl given a rude awakening by the war. Also notable as the very last performance of Alma Rubens, who died in 1931. Released after the talkie era was in full swing, some brief dialogue sequences were added in order to bill it as a "part-talkie."

Grapevine Video (#SGTW / $14.95)

Nostalgia Family video (#2754 / $19.95)

Video Yesteryear (#1516 / $19.95)

The Sheik (1921)

Paramount Pictures

Directed by George Melford

Cast includes: Rudolph Valentino, Agnes Ayres, Patsy Ruth Miller, Frank Butler, George Wagner, Walter Long, Lucien Littlefield, Adolphe Menjou, Loretta Young (bit)

Category: This romantic adventure film was the one that launched Valentino to stardom overnight, and established his reputation as "Great Lover of the Silver Screen." As a direct result of this film, the word "sheik" became a part of everybody's vocabulary for an entire generation, as did "vamp" from Theda Bara's *A Fool There Was*.

Critic's Choice Video (#DQPAR002680 / $19.95)

Paramount Home Video Release

Discount Video Tapes ($19.95)

Sherlock, Jr. (1924)
Metro Pictures
Directed by Buster Keaton
Cast includes: Buster Keaton, Kathryn McGuire, Joe Keaton
Category: Hilarious comedy in which Keaton plays a movie projectionist who is also a "wanna-be" detective. A spoof on Sherlock Holmes.
Discount Video Tapes ($19.95)

Shifting Sands (1918)
Directed by Albert Parker
Cast includes: Gloria Swanson, Lillian Langdon
Category: Melodrama in which Swanson plays a poor artist whose happy romance may be ruined due to the fact that she served time in prison as an unjustly accused prostitute.
Grapevine Video (#SSGS / $14.95)
Nostalgia Family Video (#3369 / $19.95)
Video Yesteryear (#1248 / $12.95)

A Ship Comes In (1928)
Cecil B. DeMille Productions
Directed by William K. Howard
1928-29 Academy Award Nominee for Best Actress
Cast includes: Louise Dresser, Rudolph Schildkraut, Lucien Littlefield, Robert Edeson, Fritz Feld
Category: The struggles of an immigrant Hungarian family are portrayed. Louise Dresser won an Academy Award nomination for Best Actress.
Grapevine Video (#SCIRS / $17.95)

Ships in the Night (1919)
Cast includes: Sidney Franklin
Foothill Video ($7.95)

Ships in the Night (1928)
Cast includes: Jacqueline Logan, Andy Clyde

Category: South Seas drama
Nostalgia Family Video (#2993 / $19.95)

The Shock (1923)
Universal Studios
Directed by Lambert Hillyer
Cast includes: Lon Chaney, Sr., Virginia Valli, Walter Long, Christine Mayo
Category: Drama of blackmail, revenge, and redemption about good winning out over evil. Chaney plays a cripple.
Grapevine Video (#S11-101-1 / $19.95)
Nostalgia Family Video (#2992 / $19.95)
Video Yesteryear (#227 / $24.95)

Shore Leave (1925)
First National Pictures
Directed by John S. Robertson
Cast includes: Richard Barthelmess, Dorothy MacKaill
Category: Light romantic comedy
Discount Video Tapes ($19.95)
Nostalgia Family Video (#2991 / $19.95)
Video Yesteryear (#1456 / $24.95)

Show People (1928)
MGM
Directed by King Vidor
An MGM/UA Home Video Release
Cast includes: Marion Davies, William Haines, Charlie Chaplin, John Gilbert, Douglas Fairbanks, Sr., Louella Parsons, Leatrice Joy, Rod LaRocque, Mae Murray, Norma Talmadge, William S. Hart, Elinor Glyn, Lew Cody, William Randolph Hearst, and others.
Category: The last of the big, all-star silent extravaganzas. Marion Davies, the lead actress in this comedy spoof on Hollywood, gave what is regarded as her best performance

ever. Not only is this entertaining to watch, but also gives a "behind-the-scenes" look at Hollywood during the silent era. Highly recommended.
Movies Unlimited (#12-1137 / $29.99)

Siegfried (1924)
(Part 1 of Die Niebelungen*)*
Produced in Germany
Directed by Fritz Lang
Cast includes: Paul Richter, Margaretta Schoen
Category: This is the first part of the great German masterpiece, *Die Niebelungen,* directed by legendary director Fritz Lang. Considered by some critics as the best of all of the German silents. Recommended.
International Historic Films (#430 / $24.95)

The Silent Enemy (1930)
Cast includes: Chief Yellow Robe
Category: Documentary in which the plight of Indian civilization in America is portrayed, this is well worth watching for the historic value alone. Silent with a sound introductory prologue.
Video Yesteryear (#458 / $24.95)

Silent Movie (1976)
Directed by Mel Brooks
Cast includes: James Caan, Anne Bancroft, Mel Brooks, Paul Newman, Burt Reynolds, Liza Minnelli, Dom DeLuise
Category: Comedy spoof about a recovering alcoholic director trying to save a major studio from bankruptcy by filming the first silent movie in 40 years.
Movies Unlimited (#04-1859 / $14.99)

Silk Husbands and Calico Wives (1920)
Directed by Alfred E. Green
Cast includes: House Peters, Mary Alden, Eva Novak
Category: Drama about a marriage in which the husband, a male chauvinist pig, demands that his wife's life revolve around him. A portrayal of the philosophy that women belong in the kitchen barefoot and pregnant.
Nostalgia Family Video (#2988 / $19.95)

The Single Standard (1929)
MGM
Directed by John S. Robertson
An MGM/UA Home Video Release
Cast includes: Greta Garbo, Nils Asther, Johnny Mack Brown, Lane Chandler, Kathlyn Williams, Joel McCrea, Robert Montgomery (bit part)
Category: Romantic drama in which Garbo plays a woman who turns down a rich and handsome man's generous marriage proposal, only to regret it later.
Movies Unlimited (#12-2221 / $29.99)

Sir Arne's Treasure (1919)
Swedish Biograph Company
Directed by Mauritz Siller
Cast includes: Mary Johnson
Category: Romantic drama set in the late 1500s in northern Europe, this is about a woman who falls in love with the murderer of her younger sister, and gives her life for him in the end. Features some beautiful photography in comparing photos of frozen-over ice, etc., to run concurrently with the story. Listed in Discount Video Tapes' catalogue as *The Treasue of Arne.*
Discount Video Tapes ($19.95)

Skinner's Dress Suit (1926)
Universal Studios
Directed by William Seiter
Cast includes: Reginald Denny, Laura LaPlante, Arthur Lake (famous in the 1930s for playing Dagwood in the "Blondie" movies), Hedda Hopper, Grady Sutton (bit part)
Category: Comedy
Grapevine Video (#37-1 / $19.95)

Sky High (1922)
Fox Film Corporation
Directed by Lynn Reynolds
Cast includes: Tom Mix, Eva Novak, J. Farrell McDonald
Category: Western
Grapevine Video (#SHTM / $19.95)

The Sky Pilot (1922)
First National Pictures
Directed by King Vidor
Cast includes: Colleen Moore, John Bowers, David Butler
Category: Western in which a young minister saves Moore's character from a stampede and helps her to walk again.
Grapevine Video (#1-18-1 / $16.95)
Nostalgia Family Video (#2995 / $19.95)

The Sky Rider (1927)
Cast includes: Champion, the wonder dog
Category: Canine drama
Nostalgia Family Video (#2996 / $19.95)

Sky's the Limit (1925)
Cast includes: Jack Geddings, Jane Starr, Bruce Gordon, Mary Jane Irving
Category: Gangster movie, with many airplane sequences.
Video Yesteryear (#534 / $12.95)

Skyscraper (1928)
Directed by Howard Higgins
Cast includes: William Boyd, Alan Hale, Sue Carol
Category: Drama in which men risk their lives to build the tallest buildings.
Discount Video Tapes ($19.95)
Grapevine Video (#28-306 / $16.95)
Nostalgia Family Video (#2997 / $19.95)

Slow as Lightning (1923)
Cast includes: Kenneth McDonald, Edna Pennington
Category: Drama in which a lazy bum has a difficult time learning to accept responsibility.
Video Yesteryear (#1652 / $12.95)

The Smiling Madam Buedet (1927)
Produced in France
Directed by Germaine Dulac
Cast includes: Germaine Dumoy, Madeline Gultty
Category: French avant-garde feature using experimental film techniques. The plot is about a woman who escapes her neglectful husband through daydreams and fantasies. French title cards with English subtitles.
Movies Unlimited (#10-8228 / $29.99)

Smouldering Fires (1924)
Universal Studios
Directed by Clarence Brown
Cast includes: Laura LaPlante, Pauline Frederick, Tully Marshall, Malcolm McGregor, Wanda Hawley
Category: Melodrama portraying the conflicts of love and the corporate ladder.
Discount Video Tapes ($19.95)
Grapevine Video (#SFpf / $17.95)
Nostalgia Family Video (#2251 / $19.95)

Advertised as the uncensored British print never shown in the United States.
Video Yesteryear (#990 / $24.95)

Snarl of Hate (1926)
Cast includes: Flash (the wonder dog), Johnnie Walker
Category: Canine western in which Walker plays a double role.
Nostalgia Family Video (#3071 / $19.95)

So This Is Paris (1928)
Warner Bros.
Directed by Ernst Lubitsch
Cast includes: Myrna Loy, Patsy Ruth Miller, Monte Blue, Lilyan Tashman
Category: Marital infidelity comedy
Grapevine Video (#STIP / $24.95)

The Soilers (1923)
(Stan Without Ollie Vol. #2)
Cast includes: Stan Laurel
Category: Comedy in which Laurel plays a gold prospector fighting off a scoundrel who tries to intrude on his claim. Their fight is interrupted by a gay cowboy. A parody of The Spoilers.
MC Film Festival ($19.95)

Sold for Marriage (1916)
Triangle Film Company
Directed by William Christy Cabanne
Cast includes: Lillian Gish, Walter Long, A.D. Sears, Olga Grey
Category: Lillian Gish plays a waif fleeing to America from Russia after she thinks she's killed a rapist in self-defense. She is exploited by a group of people trying to sell her in an illegal marriage market. This is not among Gish's stronger performances, but important in that it is her only performance from the 1910s not directed by D.W. Griffith which is available for comparison.
Nostalgia Family Video (#1354 / $19.95)

Son of a Gun (1919)
Cast includes: Broncho Billy Anderson
Category: Western
Nostalgia Family Video (#1217 / $19.95)

Son of Man (1915)
Presented in color
Category: Biopic of Jesus Christ, in which each individual frame was colored by hand.
Nostalgia Family Video (#2145 / $19.95)

Son of the Sheik (1926)
See complete review on pages 38–39

The Sorrows of Satan (1926)
Paramount Pictures
Directed by D.W. Griffith
Cast includes: Ricardo Cortez, Carol Dempster, Lya DePutti, Ivan Lebedoff, Adolphe Menjou
Category: Drama in which a man about to commit suicide makes a deal with the devil instead.
Discount Video Tapes ($19.95)
Grapevine Video (#SOSDWG / $24.95)
Nostalgia Family Video (#2289 / $19.95)

Soul-Fire (1925)
First National Pictures
Directed by John S. Robertson
Cast includes: Richard Barthelmess, Bessie Love
Category: Drama in which Richard Barthelmess plays a composer who remembers events that inspired his music during the first concert recital. Bessie Love appears in a South Seas flashback.

Nostalgia Family Video (#1610 / $19.95)

Soul of the Beast (1923)
Ince-Metro
Directed by John Griffith Wray
Cast includes: Oscar (the elephant), Madge Bellamy, Cullen Landis, Noah Beery, Sr.
Category: Similar to the canine dramas — except the hero in this film is a circus elephant.
Grapevine Video (#SOBMB / $16.95)
Video Yesteryear (#1461 / $12.95)

South of Panama (1928)
Cast includes: Carmelita Geraghty, Edouardo Roquello
Category: Gangster drama in which the leader of a gang has to choose between true love or his gangster friends.
Video Yesteryear (#1645 / $12.95)

Spangles (1926)
Universal Studios
Cast includes: Marion Nixon, Pat O'Malley, Hobart Bosworth
Foothill Video ($7.95)

The Spanish Dancer (1923)
Paramount Pictures
Directed by Herbert Brenon
Cast includes: Pola Negri, Wallace Beery, Antonio Moreno, Gareth Hughes, Kathlyn Williams, Dawn O'Day (a.k.a. Anne Shirley), Adolphe Menjou
Category: Romantic adventure in which Negri plays a damsel in distress rescued by her lover from an evil king.
Nostalgia Family Video (#2057 / $19.95)

Sparrows (1926)
United Artists

Directed by William Beaudine
Cast includes: Mary Pickford, Gustav von Seyffertitz, Roy Stewart, Milton Berle (bit part)
Category: One of Mary Pickford's more serious silent dramas, in which she plays the oldest of a group of orphans with a tyrannical headmaster who treats them as slaves. The scenes toward the end in which Pickford attempts to lead the other orphans on an escape mission through alligator-infested swamps is especially good.
Grapevine Video (#12-166-1 / $19.95)
Nostalgia Family Video ($2046 / $19.95)
Video Yesteryear (#968 / $24.95)

The Speed Spook (1924)
East Coast Films
Directed by Charles Hines
Cast includes: Johnny Hines
Category: Adventures of a ghost on the loose in a race car.
Grapevine Video (#16-167 / $16.95)
Nostalgia Family Video (#3370 / $19.95)

Speedy (1928)
Cast includes: Harold Lloyd, Babe Ruth (cameo)
Category: Lloyd's last silent comedy, portraying his misadventures in trying to save the city's doomed horse-drawn trolley system.
Movies Unlimited (#44-1946 / $19.99)

The Spider Woman (1920)
See Sex

Spiders (1919)
Produced in Germany
Directed by Fritz Lang
Category: Classic serial adventure in which a mob of gangsters plot to take over the world.

Kino Video ($29.95)
Color tinted

The Spieler (1928)

Directed by Tay Garnett
Cast includes: Renée Adorée, Alan Hale, Clyde Cook, Fred Kohler
Category: Circus drama of murder, mayhem, and jealousy — in some ways similar to Joan Crawford's 1967 movie *Berserk!*
Nostalgia Family video (#2675 / $19.95)

Spies (1928)

Produced in Germany
Directed by Fritz Lang
Cast includes: Rudolph Klein-Rogge, Nerda Maurus, Lien Deyers, Louis Ralph
Category: Action packed German spy drama of all spy dramas.
Discount Video Tapes ($29.95)
Grapevine Video (#SFL-29 / $19.95)
Kino Video ($29.95)
Nostalgia Family Video (#1229 / $19.95)
Video Yesteryear (#44 / $39.95)

Spite Marriage (1929)

MGM
Directed by Edward Sedgwick
An MGM/UA Home Video Release
Cast includes: Buster Keaton, Dorothy Sebastian, Edward Brophy, Hank Mann, Edward Earle
Category: Keaton's last silent.
Movies Unlimited (#12-2223 / $29.99)

The Spoilers (1914)

Selig Polyscope Company
Directed by Colin Campbell
Cast includes: William Farnum, Tom Santschi, Kathlyn Williams, Bessie Eyton, Wheeler Oakman
Category: Classic western, this may seem a bit primitive, but was rela-
tively well done for its time. It has been remade at least five times since, and the brawl between Farnum and Santschi has not been topped by any of the remakes. One of the most historically important westerns in motion picture history.
Discount Video Tapes ($19.95)
Grapevine Video (#SWF / $19.95)
This video version includes rare film clips from Cecil B. DeMille's *The Squaw Man* (1914), starring Dustin Farnum.

A Sporting Chance (1919)

Directed by George Melford
Cast includes: William Russell
Category: One of the few surviving films of William Russell, who started in serials in the teens, and was at one time a roommate of the ill-fated Paramount director William Desmond Taylor. He is perhaps best remembered for his role in *Anna Christie* (1923) opposite Blanche Sweet (see page 54).
Foothill Video ($7.95)

Square Shoulders (1929)

Directed by E. Mason Hopper
Cast includes: Junior Coghlan, Louis Wolheim, Anita Louise
Category: This film finds child star Junior Coghlan in a military academy. Mr. Coghlan currently lives in California.
Grapevine Video (#5-49-2 / $16.95)

The Star Prince (1918)

Little Players Film Company of Chicago
Directed by Madeline Brandeis
Cast includes: Zoe Rae, Dorphia Brown, John Dorland, Edith Rothschild, Marjorie Claire Bowden (an all-child cast)

Category: Rare children's fairy tale adventure

Grapevine Video (#SPZR / $14.95)

Steamboat Bill, Jr. (1928)

United Artists

Directed by Charles F. Reisner

Cast includes: Buster Keaton, Ernest Torrence, Marion Byron, Tom Lewis

Category: Classic Keaton comedy in which Keaton plays a college student trying to impress his father. Includes the famous cyclone sequence. A favorite of many silent film buffs.

Discount Video Tapes ($19.95)

Grapevine Video (#19-197 / $16.95)

Video Yesteryear (#573 / $24.95)

Stella Maris (1918)

Paramount Artcraft

Directed by Marshall Neilan

Cast includes: Mary Pickford, Conway Tearle, Irene Rich (bit part)

Category: Pickford demonstrates her versatility as an actress by playing a double role in this romantic melodrama. The bit part by Irene Rich was her film debut.

Nostalgia Family Video (#2668 / $19.95)

Stop at Nothing (1922)

Cast includes: George Larkin

Foothill Video ($7.95)

Storm Over Asia (1928)

Produced in Russia

Directed by V.I. Pudovkin

Cast includes: Boris Barnet, Anna Sten

Category: Historical drama set in the Soviet Union in 1920. This is one of the Russian masterpieces which helped establish Pudovkin's reputation as one of Russia's preeminent movie directors. The movie is about a young Mongol who is captured by capitalists and then finds out he is the heir of Genghis Khan. He rejects their offer of an easy life, and leads a rebellion against them.

Video Yesteryear (#1407 / $39.95)

Straight Shooting (1917)

Directed by John Ford

Cast includes: Harry Carey, Milly Malone, Hoot Gibson

Category: Western which was one of John Ford's earlier directorial credits.

Grapevine Video (#SS17-178-2 / $16.95)

The Street (1923)

Produced in Germany

Directed by Karl Grune

Cast includes: Max Schreck

Category: German expressionistic drama which was the first in the series of 1920s "street" films (*Street of Forgotten Women, Dream Street, Joyless Street,* etc.) that explored various social problems of the time. Features Max Schreck, who is best known for playing the title role in *Nosferatu* (1922).

Video Yesteryear (#268 / $24.95)

The Street of Forgotten Women (1927)

Category: Low budget, prostitution exploitation movie. This is another that is so bad, it is funny.

Video Yesteryear (#1429 / $19.95)

Strike! (1925)

Produced in Russia

Directed by Sergei Eisenstein

Category: This was the very first of the great Sergei Eisenstein's series of historical films he made at the request of the Russian government. This one depicts a 1912 incident in which factory workers revolted against the Czarist regime, and the strike which resulted, adding fuel to the movement for the Russian Revolution

Discount Video Tapes ($29.95)

Kino Video ($29.95)

Nostalgia Family Video (#1225 / $19.95)

Video Yesteryear (#1418 / $24.95)

The Strong Man (1926)

Directed by Frank Capra

An HBO Home Video Release

Cast includes: Harry Langdon, Priscilla Bonner, Robert McKim, Gertrude Astor

Category: Critically acclaimed as Langdon's best silent comedy feature, and perhaps one of the top ten silent comedies produced.

Movies Unlimited (#44-1669 / $39.99)

A Student of Prague (1913)

Produced in Germany

Directed by Stellan Rye

Cast includes: Paul Wegener

Category: Perhaps the earliest German feature in existence, this is the first version of the film based on *Doppengager* about a man who makes a deal with the devil to make his prospective romance work out. Note: German titles.

Discount Video Tapes ($29.95)

Nostalgia Family Video (#2661 / $19.95)

The Student of Prague (1926)

Produced in Germany

Directed by Paul Wegener and Henrik Galeen

Category: Remake of the 1913 film, by the same duo who directed *The Golem* (1920).

Nostalgia Family Video (#1073 / $19.95)

The Student Prince in Old Heidelberg (1927)

MGM

Directed by Ernst Lubitsch

An MGM/UA Home Video Release

Cast includes: Ramon Novarro, Norma Shearer, Jean Hersholt, Philippe DeLacy, Otis Harlan, Gustav von Seyffertitz

Category: Remake of Emerson's 1915 *Old Heidelberg* in which Ramon Novarro plays the prince, and Norma Shearer plays the part formerly played by Dorothy Gish in the 1915 version.

Movies Unlimited (#12-2145 / $29.99)

Submarine (1928)

Columbia Pictures

Directed by Frank Capra

Cast includes: Jack Holt, Ralph Graves, Dorothy Revier

Category: Underwater sea drama

Discount Video Tapes ($19.95)

Suds (1920)

Paramount Artcraft Pictures

Directed by Jack Dillon

Cast includes: Mary Pickford, Dorothy Rosher (a.k.a. Joan Marsh), Albert Austin, Harold Goodwin

Category: Light romantic drama

Grapevine Video (#28-302-2 / $19.95)

Nostalgia Family Video (#1381 / $19.95)

Sunny Side Up (1928)

Cecil B. DeMille Productions

Directed by Donald Crisp

Cast includes: Vera Reynolds, ZaSu Pitts, Sally Rand, Ethel Clayton

Category: Reynolds plays a pickle factory worker-turned-stage performer.

Grapevine Video (#SSUVR / $16.95)

Sunrise (1927)

Fox Film Company

Directed by F.W. Murnau
1927-28 Academy Award Winner for Best Artistic Quality of Production
1927-28 Best Actress Academy Award Winner
Cast includes: Janet Gaynor, George O'Brien, Margaret Livingston, J. Farrell McDonald, Jane Winton, Barry Norton, Sally Eilers
Category: Touching romantic film in which O'Brien plays a farmer who cheats on his wife (Janet Gaynor) with a vamp from the big city (Margaret Livingston). Features an "edge-of-your seat" ending. This was the "other" Best Picture Academy Award winner in the only year that two awards were given out — for best production, and for best artistic quality of production.
Foothill Video ($7.95)

Surrender (1927)

Universal Studios
Directed by Edward Sloman
Cast includes: Mary Philbin, Ivan Mosjoukine, Nigel DeBrulier
Category: Ivan Mosjoukine's only American film appearance was in this World War I melodrama set in Russia.
Nostalgia Family Video (#1079 / $19.95)

The Swan (1925)

Paramount Pictures
Cast includes: Ricardo Cortez, Frances Howard (married Sam Goldwyn shortly after this movie was produced), Adolphe Menjou
Category: Romantic drama. Elsie Ferguson had been the first choice for the role played by Frances Howard Goldwyn, but she turned down the role.
Discount Video Tapes ($19.95)

Sweeping Against the Wind (1928)

Cast includes: Theodore Von Eltz, Dorothy Lee, Florence Lawrence
Category: Romantic melodrama, with a later appearance by Florence Lawrence, the original "Biograph Girl" from the pioneering days of filmmaking.
Video Yesteryear (#1558 / $12.95)

Tabu (1931)

Paramount Pictures
Directed by F.W. Murnau
Category: Classic docu-drama of life in the South Seas islands, this was originally begun as a collaboration between Murnau and Robert Flaherty. The two had different techniques and styles and found that they could not work together, and Flaherty dropped out in the early stages of production. This was Murnau's last film before a tragic 1931 automobile accident in which he was killed.
Movies Unlimited (#80-5000 / $39.99)

A Tale of Two Cities (1911)

Vitagraph
Directed by J. Stuart Blackton
Cast includes: Maurice Costello, Florence Turner, Norma Talmadge, William J. Humphrey, Charles Kent, John Bunny, Earle Williams
Category: The earliest existing adaptation of the Charles Dickens classic on video. Also included on the same tape is In the Switch Tower (1915) with an early performance by Frank Borzage.
Video Yesteryear (#1158 / $24.95)

Tarzan of the Apes (1918)

Hollywood Film Enterprises
Directed by Scott Sidney
Cast includes: Elmo Lincoln, Enid Markey, Thomas Jefferson

Category: The very first screen adaptation of Edgar Rice Burroughs' *Tarzan*.
Grapevine Video (#35-3-2 / $16.95)
Nostalgia Family Video (#2208 / $19.95)
Video Yesteryear (#529 / $24.95)

Tarzan the Tiger (1929)
Serial
Universal Studios
Directed by Henry McRay
Cast includes: Frank Merrill, Natalie Kingston, Al Ferguson
Category: Complete 15-chapter serial with Frank Merrill as Tarzan.
Grapevine Video (#10-11-12 / $29.95)

The Taxi Mystery (1926)
Cast includes: Robert Agnew, Phillip Snaley
Foothill Video ($7.95)

Tell It to the Marines (1927)
MGM
Directed by George W. Hill
Cast includes: Lon Chaney, Sr., William Haines, Eleanor Boardman, Carmel Myers
Category: One of Chaney's few "straight" roles in which he plays a marine sergeant teaching Haines' new recruit character the facts of life. George W. Hill, the director, is best known for directing *Min and Bill*, which won Marie Dressler the 1930-31 Best Actress Oscar.
Foothill Video ($7.95)

The Tempest (1927)
United Artists
Directed by Sam Taylor
Cast includes: John Barrymore, Camilla Horn, Louis Wolheim
Category: Classic melodrama in which Barrymore plays a peasant-turned-military officer in the days of the Russian Revolution. Camilla Horn, the leading actress in this film, currently resides in Germany.
Nostalgia Family Video (#2689 / $19.95)
Video Yesteryear (#1205 / $39.95)

The Ten Commandments (1923)
See complete review on pages 22–24

Ten Days That Shook the World (a.k.a. October) (1927)
Produced in Russia
Directed by Sergei Eisenstein and G.V. Alexandrov
Category: Classic Russian docu-drama masterpiece, this was Eisenstein's follow-up to *Battleship Potemkin*, portraying the Russian Revolution in Leningrad during October of 1917.
Video Yesteryear (#461 / $24.95)

The Test of Donald Norton (1926)
Chadwick Pictures
Directed by B. Reeves Eason
Cast includes: George Walsh, Tyrone Power, Sr., Eugenia Gilbert
Category: Well-done drama in which Walsh plays a man who is half-Indian, half-white dealing with racial prejudice.
Grapevine Video (#TODN / $16.95)
Video Yesteryear (#1156 / $12.95)

That Certain Thing (1928)
Columbia Pictures
Directed by Frank Capra
Cast includes: Viola Dana, Ralph Graves, Burr McIntosh
Category: Rare romantic comedy which is the best example of Viola Dana's work on video.
Grapevine Video (#9-87 / $18.95)

The Thief of Bagdad (1924)
United Artists
Directed by Raoul Walsh
Cast includes: Douglas Fairbanks, Sr., Anna May Wong, Julanne Johnston, Charles Belcher, Snitz Edwards, Noble Johnson, Brandon Hurst
Category: Fantasy-adventure in which Fairbanks plays a thief who undergoes a change of heart to win a princess. Features some excellent and innovative special effects for the time.
Discount Video Tapes ($19.95)
Nostalgia Family Video (#2729 / $19.95)
Republic Pictures Home Video (#4160 / $19.98)
  Color tinted
Video Yesteryear (#519 / $39.95)

Thomas Graal's Best Child (1917)
Produced in Sweden
Directed by Mauritz Stiller
Cast includes: Victor Seastrom, Karin Molander
Category: Satirical comedy on marriage and family life.
Grapevine Video (#TGBC / $19.95)

Thomas Graal's Best Film (1917)
Produced in Sweden
Directed by Mauritz Stiller
Cast includes: Victor Seastrom, Karin Molander
Category: Comedy spoof on movie making.
Grapevine Video (#TGBF / $16.95)

The Three Ages (1923)
See complete review on pages 21–22

The Three Brothers (1918)
Cast includes: Wallace Reid
Category: Rare Reid film in which he plays one of three brothers in love with their new adopted sister.
Nostalgia Family Video (#1466 / $19.95)

The Three Musketeers (a.k.a. D'Artagnan) (1916)
Produced by Thomas H. Ince
Cast includes: Orrin Johnson, Dorothy Dalton, Louise Glaum, Walt Whitman
Category: Swashbuckling adventure filmed many times throughout the silent and talkie eras, based on Alexander Dumas' literary classic. This is the earliest version available on video.
Nostalgia Family Video (#2463 / $19.95)
Video Yesteryear (#1546 / $24.95)

The Three Musketeers (1921)
United Artists
Directed by Fred Niblo
Cast includes: Douglas Fairbanks, Sr., Marguerite de la Motte, Barbara LaMarr, Eugene Pallette, George Siegmann, Adolphe Menjou
Category: Fairbanks' classic swashbuckling adventure, this is the most elaborately produced of the silent versions of the Dumas novel. Also includes a rare surviving film appearance by Barbara LaMarr, often referred to as "the girl who is too beautiful," and another Hollywood star who suffered the tragedy of alcohol/drug addiction which led to her premature death in 1926 at the age of 29.
Discount Video Tapes ($19.95)
Grapevine Video (#3-31 / $19.95)
Nostalgia Family Video (#1558 / $19.95)

The Three Must-Get-Theirs (1921)

Robertson-Cole Productions
Directed by Max Linder
Cast includes: Max Linder, Jobyna Ralston
Category: Comedy spoof of Fairbanks' *The Three Musketeers,* this was one of three features produced by Linder during his brief stay in America from 1920 to 1922. Also features the earliest performance of Jobyna Ralston (Harold Lloyd's leading lady in the mid–1920s) on video. Titles are in French, as all that seems to have survived is a print released for circulation in France.
Grapevine Video (#TMGT / $14.95)

Three Songs of Lenin (1934)

Produced in Russia
Directed by Dziga Vertov
Category: Classic Russian biopic portraying the life of Vladimir Lenin, leader of Communist Russia from 1917 until his death in 1924. Vertov's last directorial effort.
Kino Video ($29.95)

Three Word Brand (1921)

Directed by Lambert Hillyer
Cast includes: William S. Hart, Jane Novak
Category: Western in which Hart plays three roles — father and twin sons.
Grapevine Video (#TWBWSH / $18.95)
Video Yesteryear (#809 / $12.95)

Three's a Crowd (1927)

Cast includes: Harry Langdon
Category: Comedy
Foothill Video ($7.95)

Through the Breakers (1928)

Cast includes: Margaret Livingston
Foothill Video ($7.95)

Thundering Hoofs (1924)

Monogram Pictures
Directed by Albert Rogell and Francis Ford
Cast includes: Fred Thomson, Francis Ford, Silver King
Category: Western
Grapevine Video (#13-128 / $19.95)
Nostalgia Family Video (#1464 / $19.95)

Tillie Wakes Up (1917)

Directed by Harry Davenport
Cast includes: Marie Dressler, Johnny Hines
Category: One of the comedy sequels to *Tillie's Punctured Romance.* The other was *Tillie's Tomato Surprise,* which is not currently available on video. Director Harry Davenport was the father of Dorothy Davenport (Mrs. Wallace) Reid.
Discount Video Tapes ($19.95)
Grapevine Video (#TWUMD / $16.95)

Tillie's Punctured Romance (1914)

Produced by Mack Sennett
Cast includes: Marie Dressler, Charlie Chaplin, Mabel Normand, Mack Swain, Charlie Chase, Chester Conklin, Al St. John, Slim Summerville, Hank Mann, Edgar Kennedy, bit part by Milton Berle at age 6
Category: The first feature-length, all star comedy extravaganza. Chaplin plays a city slicker looking for somebody to swindle, which happens to be Tillie Banks, niece of "Old Money" Banks, played by Marie Dressler. Normand plays Chaplin's city girlfriend who helps him steal the money. Swain plays Tillie's father. Chase, Conklin, St. John, and Summerville are the Keystone Cops.
Discount Video Tapes ($19.95)

Kino Video ($29.95)
  Includes *Mabel's Married Life* on the same tape.
Nostalgia Family Video (#2722 / $19.95)
Republic Pictures Home Video (#4212 / $19.98)
  Color tinted
Video Yesteryear (#75 / $24.95)

Tol'able David (1921)
First National Pictures
Directed by Henry King
Cast includes: Richard Barthelmess, Edmund Gurney, Marion Abbott
Category: Barthelmess' classic melodrama set in the Appalachian mountains in the early 19th century. Barthelmess plays a boy who comes of age to combat three evil men who terrorize their small mountain village, killing his dog and his father, and crippling his older brother. Also features the film debut of Ernest Torrence, who played many villain roles during the silent era.
Discount Video Tapes ($19.95)
Nostalgia Family Video (#1178 / $19.95)
Video Yesteryear (#872 / $24.95)

The Toll Gate (1920)
Directed by Lambert Hillyer
Cast includes: William S. Hart, Anna Q. Nilsson
Category: Western
Grapevine Video (#TGWSH / $19.95)

Toll of the Sea (1922)
Presented in Two-Strip Technicolor
Technicolor Motion Picture Company
Distributed by Metro Pictures
Directed by Chester M. Franklin
Cast includes: Anna May Wong, Kenneth Harlan
Category: Romantic drama in which Wong (at age 15) plays a Chinese woman who falls in love with an American sailor and "marries" him Chinese fashion. She bears him a son, and he returns two years later to inform her that he has married another American woman. This was the first feature film to be presented entirely in two-strip Technicolor.
Nostalgia Family Video (#2115 / $19.95)

The Tomboy (1924)
Cast includes: Dorothy Devore
Category: Comedy
Foothill Video ($7.95)

The Tong Man (1919)
Directed by William Worthington
Cast includes: Sessue Hayakawa, Helen Jerome Eddy
Category: Hayakawa plays a drug smuggler who is targeted for murder by the Chinese mafia.
Discount Video Tapes ($19.95)
Grapevine Video (#TMSH / $16.95)

Too Wise Wives (1921)
Directed by Lois Weber
Cast includes: Claire Windsor, Louis Calhern, Phillip Smalley
Category: Romantic story in which strange, coincidental circumstances lead to accusations of adultery.
Nostalgia Family Video (#1995 / $19.95)

The Torture of Silence (1917)
Produced in France
Directed by Abel Gance
Category: Rare, early French psychological drama directed by Abel Gance, best known for his grand bio-epic *Napoleon* (1927). This is the only other Gance silent known to be available on video in the United States.

Nostalgia Family Video (#2714 / $19.95)

Tracked by the Police (1927)

Warner Bros.
Cast includes: Rin-Tin-Tin, Jason Robards, Sr., Virginia Brown Fair, Tom Santschi
Category: Canine drama
Nostalgia Family Video (#2530 / $19.95)

Traffic in Souls (1913)

Universal Studios
Directed by George Loane Tucker
Cast includes: Matt Moore, Jane Gail, Howard Crampton, Ethel Grandin, William Turner, Irene Wallace
Category: Rare, early feature film which deals with the trade of white slave trafficking. The very first feature-length film from Universal Studios.
Grapevine Video (#TIS-13 / $24.95)
Kino Video ($29.95)

Trailing the Killer (1930)

(Part-talkie)
Cast includes: Tom London
Category: Canine western in which a dog is accused of killing sheep.
Grapevine Video (#TKTL / $14.95)

Tramp, Tramp, Tramp (1926)

Directed by Harry Edwards and Frank Capra
Cast includes: Harry Langdon, Joan Crawford, Alec B. Francis
Category: Early Langdon comedy feature.
Foothill Video ($17.95)

Transcontinental Limited (1926)

Cast includes: Johnnie Walker, Eugenia Gilbert
Discount Video Tapes ($19.95)

The Trap (1922)

Universal Studios
Cast includes: Lon Chaney, Sr., Irene Rich, Alan Hale
Category: Chaney feature in which he plays a man betrayed when his girlfriend marries a man who stole from him.
Nostalgia Family Video (#1575 / $19.95)

Trapped by the Mormons (1922)

Produced in Great Britain
Cast includes: Evelyn Brent, Lewis Willoughby
Category: British anti–Mormon exploitation film which was banned for many years.
Grapevine Video (#21-221-1 / $18.95)
Nostalgia Family Video (#2136 / $19.95)
Video Yesteryear (#1507 / $24.95)

Trilby (1915)

World Film Company
Directed by Maurice Tourneur
Cast includes: Clara Kimball Young, Wilton Lackaye
Category: The original silent version of George de Maurier's Svengali.
Grapevine Video (#TCKY / $16.95)

Trouble Busters (192?)

Cast includes: Jack Hoxie
Category: Western
Discount Video Tapes ($19.95)

True Heart Susie (1919)

Directed by D.W. Griffith
Cast includes: Lillian Gish, Robert Harron, George Fawcett, Clarine Seymour, Carol Dempster, Kate Bruce
Category: Heart-rending romantic drama in which Gish's character

sacrifices everything for the love of her life, only to be betrayed when he falls for a vampish city girl. Based on the Dora/Agnes story from Charles Dickens' *David Copperfield*. One of Robert Harron's last screen performances before his tragic death in 1920 from a gunshot wound, the cause (accident or suicide) which remains unknown.

Discount Video Tapes ($19.95)
Nostalgia Family Video (#1355 / $19.95)
Video Yesteryear (#462 / $24.95)

Tumbleweeds (1925)

United Artists
Directed by William S. Hart and King Baggot
Cast includes: William S. Hart, Barbara Bedford, Lucien Littlefield
Category: The last of William S. Hart's westerns, this was not only his farewell to the screen, but also the last of what is considered the "old breed" of westerns. Some of the video versions contains a sound prologue that Hart filmed and added for a 1939 re-issue of the movie, seven years prior to his death in 1946. A must for all western enthusiasts.

Discount Video Tapes ($19.95)
Critic's Choice Video (#EPRPC004206 / $19.98)
    Republic Pictures Home Video color tinted version
Grapevine Video (#TWWSH24-264 / $19.95)
    Includes sound prologue by Hart
Nostalgia Family Video (#2970 / $19.95)
    Includes sound prologue by Hart
Video Yesteryear (#598 / $29.95)
    Includes sound prologue by Hart

20,000 Leagues Under the Sea (1916)

Directed by Stuart Paton

Cast includes: Alan Holubar, Jane Gail, Matt Moore, Noble Johnson
Category: Early adaptation of the Jules Verne classic, which was the first to feature actual underwater photography.

Discount Video Tapes ($19.95)
Grapevine Video (#23-241 / $19.95)
Kino Video ($29.95)
    Color tinted
Nostalgia Family Video (#1447 / $19.95)
    Color tinted

The Unchastened Woman (1925)

Chadwick Pictures
Directed by James Young
Cast includes: Theda Bara, Wyndham Standing, Dale Fuller, Eileen Percy, John Miljan
Category: Comedy spoof of the vamp movies, this was one of Theda Bara's last two screen appearances (the other was in *Madame Mystery* directed by Stan Laurel)

Discount Video Tapes ($19.95)
Grapevine Video (#4-45-2 / $14.95)
Nostalgia Family Video (#2761 / $19.95)

Uncle Tom's Cabin (1903, 1914)

Directed by Edwin S. Porter (1903)
Directed by William Robert Daly (1914)
Cast includes: Sam Lucas, Marie Eline, Irving Cummings (1914 version)
Category: Two early versions of the Harriet Beecher Stowe novel, with the 1914 version featuring Sam Lucas, the very first black man to play a leading role in a motion picture. Edwin S. Porter's version was produced by the Edison Company.

Discount Video Tapes ($19.95)
Grapevine Video (#16-166-2 / $14.95)

Contains 1914 version only
Nostalgia Family Video (#1812 / $19.95)

The Unholy Three (1925)
MGM
Directed by Tod Browning
Cast includes: Lon Chaney, Sr., Lila Lee, Mae Busch, Ivan Linow, Matt Moore, Victor McLaglen, William Humphrey
Category: Crime-drama about a group of career criminals. Chaney uses four different disguises, one of which is as an old woman.
Foothill Video ($7.95)
Also carries the 1930 sound version directed by Jack Conway at the same price, which was Chaney's only talkie before his death from cancer in 1930.

The Unknown (1927)
MGM
Directed by Tod Browning
Cast includes: Lon Chaney, Sr., Joan Crawford, Norman Kerry
Category: Horror
Grapevine Video (#ULC / $19.95)

The Untameable (1923)
Directed by Herbert Blaché
Cast includes: Gladys Walton, Malcolm McGregor, John Sainpolis
Category: Walton plays the lead in this bizarre movie about a schizophrenic woman.
Grapevine Video (#UGW / $16.95)
Nostalgia Family Video (#3017 / $19.95)

Up in Mabel's Room (1926)
Producer's Distribution Company
Directed by E. Mason Hopper
Cast includes: Marie Prevost, Harrison Ford, Sylvia Breamer, Harry Myers
Category: Hilarious romantic comedy

in which Prevost's character has second thoughts about her divorce, and does everything she can to wreak havoc.
Discount Video Tapes ($19.95)
Nostalgia Family Video (#2756 / $19.95)
Color tinted

The Vanishing American (1925)
Paramount Pictures
Directed by George B. Seitz
Cast includes: Richard Dix, Lois Wilson, Noah Beery, Sr., Malcolm McGregor
Category: Classic, star-studded western epic which explores the mistreatment of the Indians. Based on the Zane Grey novel, this western is in a category by itself, and is still considered one of the better westerns of the silent era.
Discount Video Tapes ($19.95)
Grapevine Video (#7-74 / $19.95)
Nostalgia Family Video (#1935 / $19.95)
Video Yesteryear (#970 / $39.95)

Vanity Fair (1911)
Vitagraph
Directed by Charles Kent
Cast includes: John Bunny, Helen Gardner, Alec B. Francis
Category: One of the earliest screen versions of the classic novel by William Makepeace Thackeray, and the only silent version available on video. In this one, Bunny plays an atypical dramatic role, as he was known for being primarily a comedy star.
Video Yesteryear (#1586 / $12.95)

Variety (1925)
Paramount Pictures
Directed by E.A. DuPont

Cast includes: Emil Jannings, Werner Krauss, Lya DePutti

Category: Drama of adultery, betrayal, revenge, and murder among circus performers.

Nostalgia Family Video (#2156 / $19.95)

Video Yesteryear (#782 / $24.95)

The Viking (1928)
See complete review on pages 44–45

The Virginian (1923)
Preferred Motion Pictures

Cast includes: Kenneth Harlan, Florence Vidor, Tom Forman, Pat O'Malley, Raymond Hatton

Category: Early silent adaptation of the western novel by Owen Wister. Cecil B. DeMille directed the 1914 version as one of his earlier directorial credits.

Nostalgia Family Video (#2280 / $19.95)

Virtue's Revolt (1924)
Cast includes: Edith Thornton

Category: Drama depicting the trials and tribulations of an aspiring actress.

Discount Video Tapes ($19.95)

Le Voyage Imaginaire (1925)
Produced in France

Directed by René Clair

Cast includes: Albert Prejean, cameos by Charlie Chaplin and Jackie Coogan

Category: A very rare avant-garde film directed by René Clair.

Grapevine Video (#LVI / $16.95)

Wagon Tracks (1919)
William S. Hart Productions

Directed by Lambert Hillyer

Cast includes: William S. Hart, Jane Novak, Robert McKim, Lloyd Bacon

Category: Western

Grapevine Video (#WT2-16-2 / $16.95)

Walking Back (1928)
Directed by Rupert Julian

Cast includes: Sue Carol (wife of Alan Ladd), Richard Walling, Robert Edeson, Florence Turner, James Bradbury, Sr., Ivan Lebedoff

Category: Gangster movie

Discount Video Tapes ($19.95)

Grapevine Video (#26-311 / $16.95)

The Walloping Kid (1926)
Cast includes: Kit Carson

Category: Western

Video Yesteryear (#1479 / $12.95)

The Wandering Jew (1920)
Produced in Great Britain

Directed by Maurice Elvey

Cast includes: Rudolph Schildkraut, Joseph Schildkraut, Belle Bennett, Tyrone Power, Sr., Matheson Lang, Isobel Elsom

Category: Filmed in Austria, this is a religious drama about a Jewish man condemned to wander the world forever.

Nostalgia Family Video (#1707 / $19.95)

Wanted by the Law (1924)
Cast includes: J.B. Warner

Category: Western

Foothill Video ($7.95)

Warning Shadows (1923)
Produced in Germany

Directed by Arthur Robinson

Cast includes: Fritz Kortner, Ruth Weyher

Category: German psychological expressionist drama.
Grapevine Video (#WS-22 / $19.95)
Nostalgia Family Video (#1228 / $19.95)
Video Yesteryear (#1604 / $24.95)

Waxworks (1922)
Produced in Germany
Directed by Paul Leni
Cast includes: Emil Jannings, Conrad Veidt, Werner Krauss
Category: Wax museum drama in which the figures come to life and tell their stories.
Grapevine Video (#WEJ / $19.95)
Nostalgia Family Video (#1448 / $19.95)

Way Down East (1920)
See complete review on pages 18–19

The Wedding March (1928)
Paramount Pictures
Directed by Erich Von Stroheim
A Paramount Home Video Release
Cast includes: Erich Von Stroheim, Fay Wray, ZaSu Pitts, Maude George, George Fawcett
Category: Classic romantic drama of unrequited love between a prince and a commoner, featuring Fay Wray in her biggest silent era role. Has some very interesting symbolism, such as the Iron Man, the hands of "death" playing the organ, etc. Includes a two-strip Technicolor sequence. This is a masterpiece which, unfortunately, will likely never be seen in its complete form again. The movie was released in its complete form in Europe only. This version of *The Wedding March* was the first part, and the second part was called *The Honeymoon*. The last known existing print of *The Honeymoon* was held by the Paris Cinémathèque while Henri Langlois was its director. It was lost due to negligent handling. Fay Wray currently divides her time between her homes in California and New York.
Columbia House Video Club (#0306308 / $19.95)
Movies Unlimited (#06-1434 / $29.99)

We're in the Navy Now (1927)
Paramount Pictures
Directed by Edward Sutherland
Cast includes: Wallace Beery, Raymond Hatton, Chester Conklin, Tom Kennedy
Category: Comedy satire on military life.
Grapevine Video (#WINN / $16.95)
Nostalgia Family Video (#3037 / $19.95)

The West Bound Limited (1923)
Cast includes: Johnny Harron, Ella Hall, Claire McDowell
Category: Railroad drama
Video Yesteryear (#228 / $24.95)

West of Zanzibar (1929)
MGM
Directed by Tod Browning
Cast includes: Lon Chaney, Sr., Mary Nolan, Lionel Barrymore, Warner Baxter, Noble Johnson
Category: One of Chaney's last silents, in which he plays a paralyzed man.
Discount Video Tapes ($19.95)

What Happened to Rosa? (1923)
Directed by Victor Schertzinger
Cast includes: Mabel Normand
Category: Funny feature comedy in which Normand's character falls overboard on a ship and is presumed dead.
Discount Video Tapes ($19.95)

Nostalgia Family Video (#2265 / $19.95)

What Price Glory? (1927)
Fox Film Company
Directed by Raoul Walsh
Cast includes: Victor McLaglen, Edmund Lowe, Dolores Del Rio, Phyllis Haver, Barry Norton, J. Carroll Naish, Leslie Fenton
Category: Spectacular war extravaganza, this was the Fox Film Company's answer to MGM's *The Big Parade.*
Discount Video Tapes ($19.95)

When the Clouds Roll By (1919)
United Artists
Directed by Victor Fleming
Cast includes: Douglas Fairbanks, Sr., Kathleen Clifford, Frank Campeau, Bull Montana, Ralph Lewis
Category: Fairbanks' second movie for United Artists, this is a hilarious romantic comedy in which Fairbanks goes up against a psychiatrist (actually an escaped lunatic) who is trying to make people insane. One of the earliest directorial credits of Victor Fleming, who brought us *Gone with the Wind* and *The Wizard of Oz* in 1939.
Grapevine Video (#WCRRDF / $19.95)
Nostalgia Family Video (#1826 / $19.95)

Where East Is East (1929)
MGM
Directed by Tod Browning
Cast includes: Lon Chaney, Sr., Lupe Velez, Estelle Taylor, Lloyd Hughes
Category: Another of Chaney's last silents, this is also one of the few surviving silent era performances of Lupe Velez.
Foothill Video ($7.95)

While the City Sleeps (1928)
MGM
Cast includes: Lon Chaney, Sr., Carroll Nye, Anita Page
Category: Chaney plays a tough detective
Foothill Video ($7.95)

The Whip (1917)
Directed by Maurice Tourneur
Cast includes: Irving Cummings, June Elvidge
Category: Drama about horse racing and the attempt to head off a villainous scam.
Nostalgia Family Video (#3024 / $19.95)
Video Yesteryear (#1723 / $24.95)

The Whistle (1921)
William S. Hart Productions
Directed by Lambert Hillyer
Cast includes: William S. Hart
Category: One of Hart's few non-western films, in which he plays a father out to get revenge for the death of his son in a mill accident.
Grapevine Video (#WWSH8-90-1 / $19.95)

The White Flame (1921)
Produced in Germany
Cast includes: Leni Riefenstahl
Category: German ski drama, featuring the renowned German director Leni Riefenstahl in an early role ten years before her directorial debut.
Nostalgia Family Video (#1043 / $19.95)

White Gold (1927)
Cecil B. DeMille Productions
Directed by William K. Howard
Cast includes: Jetta Goudal, George Bancroft, George Nichols, Clyde Cook

Category: Romantic drama considered by many as William K. Howard's masterpiece. This rare movie was believed to have been lost. In the early 1950s, plans for Charles Laughton to direct a talkie re-make fell through because no print of the original could be found at that time.
Grapevine Video (#4-45-1 / $19.95)
Nostalgia Family Video (#2196 / $19.95)

The White Hell of Pitz Palu (1929)
Produced in Germany
Directed by Arnold Fanck and G.W. Pabst
Cast includes: Leni Riefenstahl, Gustav Diessl, Ernst Petersen
Category: German mountain adventure praised for its superior photography.
Grapevine Video (#WHPP / $19.95)

The White Outlaw (1929)
J. Charles Davis Productions
Directed by Robert J. Horner
Cast includes: Art Acord, Vivian May, Bill Patton, Art Hoxie
Category: Western
Grapevine Video (#WOAA / $16.95)

The White Rose (1923)
Directed by D.W. Griffith
Cast includes: Mae Marsh, Carol Dempster, Ivor Novello, Neil Hamilton, Lucille LaVerne, Kate Bruce
Category: Excellent romantic drama in which Marsh plays a part similar to that of Lillian Gish in *Way Down East,* except the man she falls in love with and bears a child to is a priest played by Ivor Novello (best remembered for *The Lodger*). Marsh's last great silent era role. One of the best of D.W. Griffith's post-war independent productions.

Grapevine Video (#WRDWG / $19.95)

White Shadows in the South Seas (1928)
MGM
Directed by W.S. Van Dyke
Cast includes: Monte Blue, Racquel Torres, Robert Anderson, Renee Bush
Category: South Seas adventure film renowned for its magnificent outdoor photography, this is a portrayal of the negative effects of the white civilization's invasion of the South Seas. One of Monte Blue's best performances.
Foothill Video ($7.95)

The White Sin (1924)
F.B.O. Productions
Directed by William Seiter
Cast includes: Madge Bellamy, John Bowers, Billy Bevan
Category: Romantic melodrama in which Bellamy plays a girl tricked into a mock marriage, which turns out not to be a mock marriage at all — much to the surprise of her husband.
Video Yesteryear (#1454 / $12.95)

The White Sister (1923)
Inspiration–Metro Pictures
Directed by Henry King
Cast includes: Lillian Gish, Ronald Colman
Category: Romantic drama in which Gish plays a woman who enters a convent upon hearing about her fiancée's supposed death. Filmed on location in Italy, this was Colman's first major role, and Gish's first feature film after leaving D.W. Griffith's company.
Nostalgia Family Video (#1045 / $19.95)

White Tiger (1923)

Universal Studios
Directed by Tod Browning
Cast includes: Raymond Griffith, Wallace Beery, Matt Moore, Priscilla Dean
Category: Crime drama
Discount Video Tapes ($19.95)
Grapevine Video (#WTtb / $19.95)
Nostalgia Family Video (#3022 / $19.95)

Why Change Your Wife? (1920)

Directed by Cecil B. DeMille
Cast includes: Gloria Swanson, Bebe Daniels, Thomas Meighan, Sylvia Ashton, Lucien Littlefield, William Boyd (bit part), Theodore Kosloff
Category: The best of Swanson's infidelity comedies for Cecil B. DeMille.
Grapevine Video (#WCYW / $24.95)
Nostalgia Family Video (#1221 / $19.95)

Wild and Woolly (1917)

Paramount Artcraft
Photographed by Victor Fleming
Cowritten by John Emerson and Anita Loos
Directed by John Emerson
Cast includes: Douglas Fairbanks, Sr., Eileen Percy, Sam DeGrasse, Tom Wilson, Monte Blue
Category: Classic satire comedy on western frontier life.
Grapevine Video (#W&WDF8-69-2 / $16.95)
Nostalgia Family Video (#3771 / $19.95)
Video Yesteryear (#152 / $24.95)

Wild Horse Canyon (1925)

Cast includes: Yakima Canutt
Category: Western featuring impressive stunt work by Canutt, who would later become a renowned action film director in the talkie era. It was Canutt who directed the chariot race sequences in the 1959 version of Ben-Hur.
Nostalgia Family Video (#3040 / $19.95)
Video Yesteryear (#783 / $24.95)

Wild Orchids (1929)

MGM
Directed by Sidney Franklin
An MGM/UA Home Video Release
Cast includes: Greta Garbo, Lewis Stone, Nils Asther
Category: Romantic drama in which Garbo has a brief fling with a prince in Java while she and her husband are on a business trip. Her husband (played by Stone) finds them out and seeks revenge on the prince (played by Nils Asther). Garbo's character must choose between the two. A fair Garbo vehicle — she has done better and she has done worse.
Movies Unlimited (#12-1392 / $29.99)

Wings (1927)

Paramount Pictures
Directed by William Wellman
A Paramount Home Video Release
1927-28 Best Production Academy Award Winner
Cast includes: Clara Bow, Richard Arlen, Charles "Buddy" Rogers, Jobyna Ralston, Henry B. Walthall, Richard Tucker, Arlette Marchal, Hedda Hopper, George Irving, Nigel DeBrulier, Gary Cooper (cameo)
Category: Classic war movie, this is considered one of the best aviation war movies of all time. Features some impressive aerial sequences.
Columbia House Video Club (#0208405 / $19.95)
Movies Unlimited (#06-1235 / $19.99)

The Winning of Barbara Worth (1926)

United Artists
Directed by Henry King
Cast includes: Gary Cooper, Ronald Colman, Vilma Banky, Clyde Cook
Category: This is the western in which Cooper had his first leading screen appearance. He did so well in it that Samuel Goldwyn signed him on the spot.
Foothill Video ($7.95)

The Wishing Ring (1914)

Directed by Maurice Tourneur
Cast includes: Vivian Martin, Alec B. Francis, Johnny Hines
Category: Fantasy film about a girl who gets a ring that she believes has magic powers, and the resulting changes in her life. This is a very rare film of which the only surviving print was rescued by Kevin Brownlow. Tourneur's earliest film on video.
Grapevine Video (#WRMT / $18.95)
Nostalgia Family Video (#3042 / $19.95)

Witchcraft Thru the Ages (1922)

Produced in Sweden
Directed by Benjamin Christensen
Category: Weird, bizarre Swedish horror film hailed as a masterpiece. This controversial film of the occult was banned in several countries for many years. It explores satanism, witchcraft, blasphemy in respect to Christianity, and graphic portrayals of satanistic and witchcraft rituals. Although meant simply to be a docu-drama of witchcraft without necessarily endorsing such activity this is not recommended for those easily offended by graphic material.

Discount Video Tapes ($19.95)
Video Yesteryear (#274 / $39.95)

With Buffalo Bill on the U.P. Trail (1925)

Cast includes: Roy Stewart, Cullen Landis, Kathryn McGuire
Category: Western
Video Yesteryear (#963 / $12.95)

With Kit Carson Over the Great Divide (1925)

Cast includes: Roy Stewart, Henry B. Walthall, Marguerite Snow
Category: Excellent western featuring Henry B. Walthall and the last film appearance of serial-queen-turned-western-heroine Marguerite Snow.
Video Yesteryear (#1134 / $24.95)

Wizard of Oz (1925)

See complete review on pages 35–37

Wolf Blood (1925)

Ryan Pictures
Directed by George Cheseborough and George Mitchell
Cast includes: Marguerite Clayton, George Cheseborough
Category: After a life-saving blood transfusion with blood from a wolf, a man starts transforming into a werewolf and developing wolf-like characteristics.
Grapevine Video (#WBGC / $17.95)
Nostalgia Family Video (#2290 / $19.95)

Wolfheart's Revenge (1925)

Cast includes: Yakima Canutt, Guinn "Big Boy" Williams, Wolfheart (the dog)
Category: Canine western
Grapevine Video (#14-134-1 / $14.95)
Nostalgia Family Video (#3372 / $19.95)

The Wolves of Kultur (1918)
Serial
Cast includes: Charles Hutchinson, Leah Baird
Category: Extremely rare, abridged 7-chapter version of the complete action serial with Charles Hutchinson. Hutchinson was known for his death-defying stunts in a number of popular action serials of the late 1910s and early 1920s. Unfortunately, virtually all of his work seems to have disappeared. This is one of the rare surviving examples of his work in existence, and the only video of any of his serial work offered.
Grapevine Video (#WOK-Serial / $19.95)

A Woman in Grey (1919)
Serial
Serico Producing Company
Directed by James Vincent
Cast includes: Arline Pretty, Henry G. Sell, John Heenan, Margaret Fielding, Fred Jones, Ann Brody
Category: This is probably the best available complete example of the typical silent "cliffhanger" serials from the mid-to-late 1910s, chock-full of falls out of building windows and off bridges, close calls with quicksand and speeding locomotives, narrow escapes from burning houses, as well as other near fatalities. Arline Pretty stars as the mysterious "woman in grey."
Discount Video Tapes ($29.95)
Nostalgia Family Video (#1305 / $29.95)

The Woman in the Moon (1929)
Produced in Germany
Directed by Fritz Lang
Cast includes: Rudolph Klein-Rogge
Category: German science fiction classic, portraying a voyage to the moon and what might be found there. The film in which the backwards countdown was invented. Surprisingly, Lang was quite accurate with some of the details in this film made 40 years before the actual voyage.
Discount Video Tapes ($29.95)
Grapevine Video (#WIMFL / $19.95)
International Historic Films (#008 / $35.95)
Video Yesteryear (#989 / $39.95)

The Woman Men Yearn For (1928)
Produced in Germany
Cast includes: Marlene Dietrich
Category: Marlene Dietrich's only silent film appearance as a leading actress on video. Advisory: German titles.
Nostalgia Family Video (#2282 / $19.95)

A Woman of Affairs (1928)
MGM
Directed by Clarence Brown
An MGM/UA Home Video Release
Cast includes: Greta Garbo, John Gilbert, Douglas Fairbanks, Jr., Lewis Stone, Johnny Mack Brown, Dorothy Sebastian, Hobart Bosworth, Anita Fremault (a.k.a. Anita Louise)
Category: Romantic melodrama in which Garbo loses the love of her life as a result of meddling parents. This is a rather slow-moving film in which one waits for the moment something finally happens but never really materializes. However, Douglas Fairbanks, Jr.'s great performance as Garbo's younger alcoholic brother salvages the movie and makes it worth watching.

Columbia House Video Club (#0917104 / $29.95)

Movies Unlimited (#12-2146 / $29.99)

A Woman of Paris (1923)

Charlie Chaplin–United Artists

Written, produced, and directed by Charlie Chaplin

Cast includes: Edna Purviance, Adolphe Menjou, Bess Flowers

Category: Charlie Chaplin's only full-scale drama, which he directed but did not star in.

Movies Unlimited (#04-3042 / $19.99)

Also includes the 1919 short *Sunnyside*

A Woman of the World (1925)

Directed by Ernst Lubitsch

Cast includes: Pola Negri, Chester Conklin, Holmes Herbert

Category: Lubitsch-Negri collaboration in which Negri's character meets her American cousin, portrayed by Chester Conklin.

Nostalgia Family Video (#2808 / $19.95)

The Worldly Madonna (1922)

Harry Garson Studios

Directed by Harry Garson

Cast includes: Clara Kimball Young

Category: Rare Clara Kimball Young film, in which she plays a nun who changes places with her sister who is a cabaret dancer.

Discount Video Tapes ($19.95)

Grapevine Video (#WMcky / $14.95)

The Yankee Clipper (1927)

Cecil B. DeMille Productions

Directed by Rupert Julian

Cast includes: William Boyd, Elinor Faire, Junior Coghlan, John Miljan, Walter Long

Category: Adventure film which takes place during a ship race from China to Boston, with plenty of action. Includes a charming performance by child star Junior Coghlan as a young stowaway.

Grapevine Video (#YCWB / $19.95)

Video Yesteryear (#1054 / $24.95)
    Contains a recently taped prologue by Coghlan

Yankee Doodle in Berlin (1916)

Mack Sennett Production Company

Directed by Richard Jones

Cast includes: Ben Turpin, Charles Murray, Marie Prevost, Chester Conklin, Ford Sterling, Malcolm St. Clair, Bert Roach, Bothwell Browne

Category: All-star comedy set during World War I in which a spy dresses in drag as a woman to steal enemy secrets.

Grapevine Video (#5-41-1 / $14.95)

Young April (1926)

Cecil B. DeMille Productions

Directed by Donald Crisp

Cast includes: Bessie Love, Joseph Schildkraut, Rudolph Schildkraut, Bryant Washburn

Category: Romantic comedy

Nostalgia Family Video (#3004 / $19.95)

Video Yesteryear (#1829 / $24.95)

Three: Silent
Shorts on Video

Although the primary concentration of this book has been silent features of three reels or more, there are hundreds of important short films as well. Some of the more important shorts are listed alphabetically in this section, as well as representative short compilation videos for some of the better known short-film artists.

American Primitive Compilation (1903–1908)
Directed by Edwin S. Porter
Dream of a Rarebit Fiend (1906)
The Great Train Robbery (1903; starring Broncho Billy Anderson)
Life of an American Fireman (1903)
Rescued from an Eagle's Nest (1908; starring D.W. Griffith)
Discount Video Tapes ($29.95)

Charlie Chaplin, Volume 2 (1916–1917)
The Count (1916)
The Immigrant (1917)
The Floorwalker (1916)
The Rink (1916)
Nostalgia Family Video (#2110 / $19.95)

Early Comedies (1910–1921)
Tin Type Romance (1910)
A Suffragette in Spite of Himself (1912)
His Second Childhood (1914; with Charles Murray)

Deuces and Dangers (1917; with Larry Semon)
Chief Cook (1918; with Oliver Hardy)
Frauds and Frenzies (1918; with Stan Laurel, Larry Semon)
His Day Out (1918; with Oliver Hardy, Billy West)
Big Game (1921; with Snub Pollard)
Grapevine Video (#4-44 / $19.95)

Early Subjects, Volume 1 (circa 1907–1923)
Conquest of the North Pole (190?; starring Max Linder)
Max and the Statue (190?; starring Max Linder)
Max's Mother-in-Law (190?; starring Max Linder)
Auntie's Portrait (1914; with Mr. and Mrs. Sidney Drew)
Mabel's Dramatic Career (190?; Mabel Normand's earliest performance on video)
An Angelic Attitude (1916; with Tom Mix)

Cowboy Ambrose (190?; with Mack Swain)
Just Neighbors (1919; with Harold Lloyd)
Take the Air (1923; with Paul Parrot)
Nostalgia Family Video (#2085 / $19.95

The Eyes of Turpin Are Upon You (1918, 1921)
Featuring Ben Turpin
Idle Eyes (1918)
A Small Town Idol (1921; starring Ramon Novarro)
Video Yesteryear (#1122 / $19.95)

Films of Harold Lloyd — Volume #1 (1916–1920)
Cinema Director (1916; a rare "Lonesome Luke" short)
Non Stop Kid (1918)
On the Fire (1919)
Ring Up the Curtain (1919)
Just Neighbors (1919)
Count Your Change (1919)
Haunted Spooks (1920)
Grapevine Video (#34-4 / $18.95)

Hail ... Hail ... "Our Gang's" All Here! (1921–1926)
The Pickaninny (1921; the first "Our Gang" comedy)
Monkey Business (1926)
The Fraidy Cat (1924)
Video Yesteryear (#273 / $19.95)

A Happily Married Couple (1916)
Earliest Betty Compson appearance on video
Also includes *Hot Foot* (1925) with Bobbie Dunn
51 minutes total
Video Yesteryear (#1155 / $19.95)

Harold Lloyd Silents, Volume 1 (1919–1920)
Haunted Spooks (1920)
High and Dizzy (1920)
His Royal Slyness (1919)
Number, Please (1919)
Movies Unlimited (#10-8949 / $19.99)

A History of Color in Silent Films (1898–1914)
Compilation of early hand-colored short films
Life of Christ
Nobleman's Dog
Bob's Electric Theatre
Slave's Love
New Ways of Traveling
David and Saul
Death and Saul
Anne Boleyn
Hunting Mariboo in Abyssinia
Haunted Kitchen
Medium Wanted at Son-in-Law
Abuss of Bonau
Butterflies
Death of Christ
El Espectro Rojo
Discount Video Tapes (VS53 / $19.95)

Keystone Comedies, Volume 1 (1915)
Featuring Roscoe "Fatty" Arbuckle
Fatty's Faithful Fido
Fatty's Tintype Tangle
Fatty's New Role
Nostalgia Family Video (#1710 / $19.95)

Laurel & Hardy Silent Classics #1 (late 1920s)
Battle of the Century
Unaccustomed as We Are
Double Whoopee
45 Minutes from Hollywood
Slipping Wives
Discount Video Tapes ($19.95)

Laurel & Hardy Silent Classics #4 (late 1920s)

Angora Love
Putting Pants on Phillip
Two Tars
Discount Video Tapes ($19.95)

Mabel Normand — Volume 2 (1911–1913)

Troublesome Secretaries (1911; with John Bunny)
Cohen Saves the Flag (1913)
Barney Oldfield's Race for a Life (1913)
Mabel's New Hero (1913)
A Muddy Romance (1913)
Grapevine Video (#MN#2 / $16.95)

The Origins of Cinema Volume 1 (1898–1905)

Elopement on Horseback (1898)
Strange Adventures of New York Drummer (1899)
Uncle Josh's Nightmare (1900)
Terrible Teddy, the Grizzly King (1901)
Love by the Light of the Moon (1901)
Circular Panorama of Electric Tower (1901)
Panorama of Esplanade by Night (1901)
Martyred Presidents (1901)
Uncle Josh at the Moving Picture Show (1902)
The Twentieth Century Strap (1902)
Fun in a Baker Shop (1902)
Jack and the Beanstalk (1902)
Life of an American Fireman (1903)
Uncle Tom's Cabin (1903)
The Gay Shoe Clerk (1903)
A Romance of the Rail (1903)
Rounding Up the "Yeggemen" (1904)
European Rest Cure (1904)
The Ex-Convict (1904)
The Kleptomaniac (1905)
The Seven Ages (1905)
How Jones Lost His Roll (1905)
The Whole Dam Family and the Dam Dog (1905)
Nostalgia Family Video (#1066 / $19.95)

Our Gang, Volume #1 (1922–1924)

Young Sherlocks (1922)
The Big Show (1923)
Back Stage (1923)
Dogs of War — July Days (1923)
Big Business (1924)
Grapevine Video (#26-294 / $19.95)

Rudolph Valentino Short Subjects (1910s, 1920s)

The Sheik's Physique
His 88 American Beauties
Production Footage from *The Sheik* and *Blood and Sand*
Home Movies
Documentary Footage
Grapevine Video (#RVS / $16.95)

The Short Films of D.W. Griffith, Vol. 2 (1911–1918)

An Unseen Enemy (1911; film debut of Lillian and Dorothy Gish)
The Little Tease (1918)
Man's Genesis (1912; with Mae Marsh and Robert Harron)
The Musketeers of Pig Alley (1912; with Lillian Gish)
The Switchtower (1912; with Henry B. Walthall, Lionel Barrymore)
The Lonedale Operator (1911; with Blanche Sweet)
Discount Video Tapes ($29.95)

The Short Films of Mary Pickford (1909–1912)

In Old Madrid (1911)
The Lonely Villa (1909; directed by D.W. Griffith)
Sweet Memories (1911)
Her First Biscuits (1909)
Female of the Species (1912; directed by D.W. Griffith)
100% Canadian (circa 1917; footage of Pickford selling bonds for World War I)

The New York Hat (1912; written by Anita Loos), directed by D.W. Griffith)
Violin Maker of Cremona (1909)

1776, or the Hessian Renegades (1909; directed by D.W. Griffith)
Discount Video Tapes ($29.95)

Directory:
Silent Film Video Sources

BOISE STATE UNIVERSITY

The Bookstore
Hemingway Western Studies Center
1910 University Drive
Boise, ID 83725
Phone: (800) 992-TEXT

Boise State University is the exclusive American source for video copies of the early silents directed by pioneer female movie producer Nell Shipman. Professor Tom Trusky took it upon himself to recover copies of the Shipman films from different areas of the world.

Payment Methods: Visa, Master-Card, personal check, or money order.

Shipping Charges: For one to five items, add $3.00 for UPS ground shipping. For 2nd Day Air shipping, add $5.50.

COLUMBIA HOUSE VIDEO CLUB

1400 North Fruitridge Avenue
P.O. Box 1114
Terre Haute, IN 47811-1114
Phone: (800) 262-2001
8:00 a.m.–12:00 a.m., 7 days

This company specializes in silents produced by the big companies like MGM/UA and Paramount Home Video. If you do not have an account with them, you can start one over the telephone if you have a credit card. If you do not have a credit card, you can establish an account by sending prepayment in the form of check or money order. The process of starting an account in this fashion takes about six weeks *for your first order.* Once an account is established, they usually ship within 24 hours.

Payment Methods: Visa, Master-Card, personal check, or money order.

Average Delivery Time: One to four weeks, after you have an established account. All orders sent 4th class mail.

Shipping Charges: Usually around $3.19 for the first tape, $1.60 for each additional tape on the same order.

Appropriate sales tax collected in all 50 states.

Additional Comments: Columbia House has a dividend dollars program; for every tape you buy priced at $19.95 or above, you are given "dividend dollars" toward your account which will let you take up to 50 percent off on future videos priced at $19.95 or higher. In addition, they run some great closeout deals from time to time. Another option offered is the membership enrollments that are advertised in magazines, which give the buyer six tapes for 29¢ each upon signing an agreement to buy a certain number of videos at full price within a specified number of years.

CRITIC'S CHOICE VIDEO

P.O. Box 749

Itasca, IL 60143-0749

Phone: (800) 367-7765, 24 hours, orders only

Phone: (800)544-9852, info line, 8–6 CT

This company provides a catalogue subscription free with your first order. Not only can you buy videos that they have in stock, but you can also special-order videos from those put out by companies which do not sell directly to the public (i.e., Republic Pictures Home Video and Home Box Office [HBO] Video). Special orders for those titles not carried in stock usually take 6–12 weeks.

Payment Methods: Visa, Master-Card, Discover, American Express, personal check, or money order. No COD's.

Average Shipping Time: Two to five days (allow 14) on those orders in stock. Up to 12 weeks on special orders.

Shipping Charges: $5.50 flat rate per order via UPS 2nd Day Air. Add $8.00 per order for UPS next-day air.

Sales tax collected in Illinois.

Return Policy: Unconditional money back guarantee.

DISCOUNT VIDEO TAPES

833 "A" North Hollywood Way

P.O. Box 7122

Burbank, CA 91510

Phone: (818) 843-3366 (8–4 PT)

Fax: (818) 843-3821

Payment Methods: Visa, Master-Card, personal check, money order.

Average Delivery Times: Six to ten days (allow three weeks).

Shipping Charges: None, included in video prices. CANADIAN RESIDENTS: $3.00 per order.

Return Policy: Defective video cassettes exchanged for new cassette *of same title only,* if returned within ten days.

Additional Info: Free catalogue with order, $2.00 without. Color tinting is not necessarily specified on all of their videos; the author has ordered some that were not specifically advertised as color tinted, and received a pleasant surprise to find that they were.

8.25 percent sales tax collected from California residents.

FOOTHILL VIDEO

P.O. Box 547

Tujunga, CA 91043

Phone: (818) 353-8591 (8–5 PT)

Fax: (818) 353-7242

Payment Methods: Visa, Master-Card, American Express, personal check, money order.

Average Delivery Time: About two weeks.

Shipping Charges: $3.50 for first tape, 50¢ each additional tape per order.

8.25 percent sales tax collected in California.

Additional Info: Foothill has one of the largest selections of public domain silent titles available for purchase on video. They offer many titles that cannot be found anywhere else. All videos are shipped in a plastic case. Complete catalogues available for $5.00, refunded with first order.

GRAPEVINE VIDEO

P.O. Box 46161

Phoenix, AZ 85063

Phone: (602) 973-3661 7-7 MT
Fax: (602) 973-0060, 24 hours

Payment Methods: Visa, Master-Card, personal check, money order, and COD. COD $2.50 extra for U.S. mail; $5.00 extra for UPS.

Shipping Charges: $3.00 for first tape U.S. mail; $4.00 for first tape UPS; 50¢ for each additional tape on same order.

Average Delivery Time: About two weeks.

Return Policy: 100 percent satisfaction guaranteed; return privilege with option of credit, replacement, or refund. Sales tax collected in Arizona.

Additional Comments: All silent films transferred to video at correct projection speed. All videos are sent in a plastic video case.

HOME BOX OFFICE (HBO) VIDEO

This company does not sell directly to the public. Most of their videos are listed under Movies Unlimited's heading as a source of distribution. However, their excellent version of *Intolerance* does not seem to be in stock with any of the major mail order distribution companies. You can special order this video one of two ways if it is not in stock at your local retailer. The first option is to special order it through Critic's Choice Video (whom HBO recommended as a source when asked), which takes up to 12 weeks. The second option is to find a retailer near you that has an account with Major Video Concepts. Instructions on how to order through them are listed elsewhere in this section. All HBO Legendary Silents videos are part of the Thames Silents Series, and feature orchestral accompaniment by Carl Davis.

HOME FILM FESTIVAL

P.O. Box 2032
Scranton, PA 18501
Phone: (800) 258-3456

This company specializes in offbeat, hard-to-find classics of all genres, including the silent era. They specialize in rentals, but most of the titles they carry are also available for purchase.

INTERNATIONAL HISTORIC FILMS

Box 29035
Chicago, IL 60629
Phone: (312) 927-2900, 8-6 CT
Fax: (312) 927-9211

Payment Methods: Visa, Master-Card, money order, personal check.

Shipping Charges: $4.50 for orders up to four videos; 75¢ for each additional video on same order.

Additional Info: Offers selections in VHS and Beta format. Also available in PAL (Europe) or Secam L (France) television standards. Specify which format you prefer. Most orders shipped within 72 hours of receipt.

KINO ON VIDEO

333 West 39th Street, Suite 503
New York, NY 10018
Phone: (800) 562-3330, 9-5 ET
(212) 629-6880
Fax: (212) 714-0871

Payment Methods: Credit card, personal check, or money order.

Shipping Charge: $4.50 for the first tape; $1.00 for each additional tape on the same order. Overseas shipping $7.50 for first tape, $3.50 for each additional tape.

8.25 percent sales tax collected in New York State.

Additional Info: All of this company's videos are in individually designed packaging. Kino is known for its outstanding quality. They recently released their long-awaited "Art of Buster Keaton" series, featuring remastered versions of most of Keaton's major titles. Also released in 1995 was a series of restored and remastered titles of Lon Chaney, Sr. Another recent release is a series of remastered Douglas Fairbanks, Sr., titles. Some titles available on laser disc.

LS VIDEO, INC.
P.O. Box 415
Carmel, IN 46032

This video company specializes in rare, hard-to-find titles. They offer a few extremely rare early Conrad Veidt German films. They also have a wide variety of films featuring Boris Karloff, Bela Lugosi, Lon Chaney, Sr., and many others.

MC FILM FESTIVAL
(54561 Corporation)
P.O. Box 20071
Tampa, FL 33622-0071
Phone: (800) 445-7134
Fax: (813) 251-2628

Payment Methods: Visa, Master-Card, American Express, personal check, money order.

Shipping Charge: $5.75 per order flat rate.

Average Delivery Time: Four to six weeks.

Additional Info: This is a gay owned and operated company specializing in non-pornographic movies from all time periods (silent era included) with major or minor gay themes, characters, or influence. Carries many hard-to-find titles.

MAJOR VIDEO CONCEPTS
NATIONAL OFFICE

7998 Georgetown Road, Suite 1000
Indianapolis, IN 46268
(800) 365-0150

This company is another that does not sell directly to the public. Orders from them must be placed with a local retailer that has an account with them. If you call the corporate office, they will give you a toll-free number of the branch office nearest you, who can in turn tell you which local retailers have accounts with them. Major Video Concepts distributes most of the HBO "Legendary Silents" videos, and is also a good source for Republic Pictures Home Video's "Silent Classics" titles.

MGM/UA HOME VIDEO RE-
LEASES

All MGM/UA Home Video Releases contain orchestral accompaniment. Most of the orchestral accompaniments are the new Carl Davis scores, or from the original Vitaphone discs. They are beautifully packaged and taken from excellent condition prints.

MILESTONE FILM AND
VIDEO

275 West 96th Street, Suite 28C
New York, NY 10025
Phone: (212) 865-7449

Payment Methods: Personal check or money order.

Shipping Charges: $5.00 for the first tape; 75¢ for each additional tape on same order. CANADA AND OVERSEAS: $6.00 for first tape; $3.00 for each additional tape.

Sale tax collected in New York State.

Additional Info: This company specializes in early Russian cinema, as well as some of the American nature documentary-type films as *Chang* (1927), *Grass* (1925), *The Silent Enemy*

(1930), and *Tabu* (1931). Most titles also available on laser disc.

MOVIES UNLIMITED

6736 Castor Avenue
Philadelphia, PA 19149
Phone: (800) 523-0823, orders only, 24 hours
Phone: (215) 722-8398, info line 9–5 CT, M–F
Fax: (215) 725-3683
Payment Methods: MasterCard, Visa, Discover, money order, personal check (allow four weeks for personal check to clear)
Average Delivery Time: Two to three weeks (allow six)
Shipping Charges: $4.00 per order base charge; additional 50¢ per video for 4th class U.S. mail or UPS ground service. Additional mail services (UPS blue, FedEx, First Class U.S., etc.) available at higher rates per tape.
Add appropriate state sales tax.
Additional Info: 35,000-title catalogue (mostly talkies with a large selection of silents) available for $10.95. Allow three to four weeks for shipping.

NOSTALGIA FAMILY VIDEO

P.O. Box 606
Baker City, OR 97814
Phone: (800) 784-3362, orders only, 9–5 PT, M–F
Phone: (503) 523-9034, info line
Fax: (503) 523-7115
Payment Methods: Visa, Master-Card, personal check, money order. No COD's.
Average Delivery Time: Two weeks (allow five).
Shipping Charges: $3.50 for first title; $1.00 for each additional title on same order.
Return Policy: Defective videos exchanged for new cassette *of same title only* if returned within ten days.
Additional Info: For every three videos you purchase at full price, you get a fourth video of your choice free.

PARAMOUNT HOME VIDEO RELEASES

All Paramount Home Video Releases come in individually designed packaging, and feature a digitally recorded Wurlitzer organ score by Gaylord Carter.

PETER KAVEL

1123 Ohio Avenue
Alamogordo, NM 88310
Phone: (505) 437-6739
Payment Methods: Money orders or cashier's checks. Personal checks must allow time to clear the bank.
Average Delivery Time: two weeks.
Shipping Charges: $2.50 for the first tape; 60¢ for each additional tape on same order.
Additional Info: This video source specializes in a number of rare public domain titles, with a large selection of silents. Mr. Kavel carries quite a few titles from the silent era which cannot be found anywhere else.

REPUBLIC PICTURES HOME VIDEO

This company does not sell to the public. You must special order most of their titles through Critic's Choice Video or through Major Video Concepts if they are not in stock at your local video retailer. Each title comes in an individually designed package, with piano or organ score. Most of their videos are taken from the Paul Killiam restoration prints. Most selections also available on laser disc at a higher price.

SMITHSONIAN VIDEO COLLECTION

P.O. Box 23345
Washington, D.C. 20077-5365
Phone: (800) 669-1559

Payment Methods: Personal check, money order, Visa, MasterCard, American Express.

Average Delivery Time: Three to four weeks

Shipping Charges: Orders up to $21.99 — $3.50; $22.00 to $32.99 — $4.25; $33.00 to $42.99 — $5.00; $43.00 to $59.99 — $5.75; $60.00 or more — $6.50.

Return Policy: Satisfaction guaranteed, with option of refund, replacement, or exchange.

Additional Info: Smithsonian Video features their "Library of Congress" collection of silents, priced at $34.95 each, or $188.69 for the entire six-video collection.

VIDEO YESTERYEAR

Box C
Sandy Hook, CT 06482
Phone: (800) 243-0987 (9–5 ET, M–F)
Fax: (203) 797-0819

This company was among the first to offer silent titles on videocassette. For their silent titles, they hired Rosa Rio, an organist who actually worked as an accompanist during the silent era, to compose and perform original organ scores for each title. They were also the first to develop and use the "Accuspeed" process by which silent movies can be transferred to video at variable projection speeds, rather than at 24 frames per second.

Payment Methods: Visa, MasterCard, Carte Blanch, Diner's Club, personal check, money order. No COD's.

Average Delivery Time: Three to four weeks (allow six)

Shipping Charges: $3.95 per order flat rate. FedEx 2-day express available for an additional $6.00

Add appropriate state sales tax.

Additional Info: Offers VHS, Beta, and 8 mm formats; specify which you want. Free catalogue sent with purchase, $3.50 without. Catalogue serves as an excellent reference guide, with complete, detailed descriptions for each title.

WILL ROGERS MEMORIAL

Box 157
Claremore, Oklahoma 74018-0157
Phone: (800) 828-9643

This company has available most of the rare, existing Will Rogers silents, as well as talkies. Many Rogers silent titles are available from the Will Rogers Memorial which cannot be obtained anywhere else.

*   *   *   *

For the latest information available on new silent film video releases and silent film preservation, the author recommends subscribing to *Classic Images* magazine. For subscription information, write to: *Classic Images*, P.O. Box 809, Muscatine, IA 52761.

Bibliography

Amberg, George (compilation editor). *The New York Times Film Reviews: A One Volume Selection, 1913–1970.* New York: Arno Press, 1971.

Barry, Iris, and Eileen Bowser. *D.W. Griffith: American Film Master.* New York: Museum of Modern Art, 1965.

Blum Daniel. *A Pictorial History of the Silent Screen.* New York: Grosset and Dunlap, 1953.

Bodeen, DeWitt. *More from Hollywood: The Careers of Fifteen Great American Stars.* New York: A.S. Barnes, 1977.

Bohn, Thomas W., and Richard Stromgren. *Light and Shadows: A History of Motion Pictures.* Sherman Oaks, Calif.: Alfred Publishing, 1978.

Brooks, Louise. *Lulu in Hollywood.* New York: Alfred A. Knopf, 1982.

Brownlow, Kevin. *Napoleon: Abel Gance's Classic Film.* New York: Alfred A. Knopf, 1983.

_____. *The Parade's Gone By.* Los Angeles: University of California Press, 1968.

_____, and John Kobal. *Hollywood: The Pioneers.* New York: Alfred A. Knopf, 1979.

Card, James. *Seductive Cinema: The Art of Silent Film.* New York: Alfred A. Knopf, 1994.

Chaplin, Charlie. *My Autobiography.* New York: Simon and Schuster, 1964.

Critic's Choice Video Catalogues, 1993–94.

Discount Video Tapes Video Catalogues and supplements.

Drew, William M. *D.W. Griffith's Intolerance: Its Genesis and Vision.* Jefferson, N.C.: McFarland, 1986.

_____. *Speaking of Silents: First Ladies of the Screen.* Vestal, NY: The Vestal Press, 1989.

Eggert, William D., ed. *Quiet Times* (monthly periodical). Silent Film Society of Atlanta, 1992–1994.

Everson, William K. *American Silent Film.* New York: Oxford University Press, 1978.

Eyman, Scott. *Mary Pickford: America's Sweetheart.* New York: D.I. Fine, 1990.

Foothill Video Catalogue, 1994.

Franklin, Joseph. *Classics of the Silent Screen.* Secaucus, N.J.: Citadel Press, 1959.

Giroux, Robert. *A Deed of Death: The Story Behind the Unsolved Murder of Hollywood Director William Desmond Taylor.* New York: Alfred A. Knopf, 1990.

Gish, Lillian. *Dorothy and Lillian Gish.* New York: Charles Scribner's Sons, 1973.

_____ (with Ann Pinchot). *The Movies, Mr. Griffith, and Me.* Englewood Cliffs, N.J.: Prentice-Hall, 1969.

Grapevine Video Catalogues, 1993-94.

Griffith, Richard, and Arthur Mayer. *The Movies.* New York: Simon and Schuster, 1970.

Karr, Kathleen, ed. *The American Film Heritage: Impressions from the American Film Institute Archives.* Washington, D.C.: Acropolis Books, 1972.

Katz, Ephraim. *The Film Encyclopedia.* New York: Harper-Perennial, 1994.

Kilpatrick, Sidney. *A Cast of Killers.* New York: E.P. Dutton, 1986.

Kino on Video 1995 Catalogue.

Lamparski, Richard. *Whatever Became of... Eighth Series.* New York: Crown, 1982.

_____. *Whatever Became of... Ninth Series.* New York: Crown, 1985.

Loos, Anita. *Cast of Thousands.* New York: Grosset and Dunlap, 1977.

Marrero, Robert. *Dracula: The Vampire Legend — 70 Years on Film.* Key West, Fla.: Fantasma Books, 1992.

Mast, Gerald. *A Short History of the Movies.* New York: Macmillan, 1986.

Medved, Harry, and Michael Medved. *The Hollywood Hall of Shame: The Most Expensive Flops in History.* New York: Perigee Books, 1984.

Morris, Michael. *Madam Valentino: The Many Lives of Natacha Rambova.* New York: Abbeville Press, 1991.

Movies Unlimited Catalogues, 1994–1995.

Norris, Frank. *McTeague: A Story of San Francisco.* New York: Doubleday and McClure, 1899.

Nostalgia Family Video 1994 Classic Movie Catalogue.

Peary, Danny. *Alternate Oscars.* New York: Delta (Bantam, Doubleday, Dell), 1993.

_____, ed. *Close-Ups.* New York: Workman, 1978.

Ramsaye, Terry. *A Million and One Nights: A History of the Motion Picture Through 1925.* New York: Simon and Schuster, 1926.

Schulman, Irving. *Valentino.* New York: Simon and Schuster, 1967.

Slide, Anthony. *Early American Cinema.* New York: A.S. Barnes, 1970.

_____. *Nitrate Won't Wait: A History of Film Preservation in the United States.* Jefferson, N.C.: McFarland, 1992.

_____. *Silent Portraits: Stars of the Silent Screen in Historic Photographs.* Vestal, N.Y.: The Vestal Press, 1989.

Taylor, Deems. *A Pictorial History of the Movies.* New York: Simon and Schuster, 1943.

Truitt, Evelyn Mack. *Who Was Who on Screen.* New York: R.R. Bowker, 1983.

Video Yesteryear Catalogue #14, 1995.

Index

Bold print indicates the main entry on
titles or companies with multiple listings.